THE ART OF MACHINE LEARNING

T0093813

THE ART OF MACHINE LEARNING

A Hands-On Guide to Machine Learning with R

by Norman Matloff

no starch press®

San Francisco

Printed in the United States of America

27 26 25 24 23   1 2 3 4 5

ISBN-13: 978-1-7185-0210-9 (print)
ISBN-13: 978-1-7185-0211-6 (ebook)

 Published by No Starch Press®, Inc.
245 8th Street, San Francisco, CA 94103
phone: +1.415.863.9900
www.nostarch.com; info@nostarch.com

Publisher: William Pollock
Managing Editor: Jill Franklin
Production Manager: Sabrina Plomitallo-González
Production Editor: Jennifer Kepler
Developmental Editor: Jill Franklin
Cover Illustrator: Gina Redman
Interior Design: Octopod Studios
Technical Reviewer: Ira Sharenow
Copyeditor: George Hale
Proofreader: Jamie Lauer
Indexer: BIM Creatives, LLC

Library of Congress Control Number: 2023002283

For customer service inquiries, please contact info@nostarch.com. For information on distribution, bulk sales, corporate sales, or translations: sales@nostarch.com. For permission to translate this work: rights@nostarch.com. To report counterfeit copies or piracy: counterfeit@nostarch.com.

[S]

About the Author

Dr. Norm Matloff is a professor of computer science at the University of California, Davis, and was formerly a professor of statistics at that university.

Dr. Matloff was born in Los Angeles and grew up in East Los Angeles and the San Gabriel Valley. He has a PhD in pure mathematics from the University of California, Los Angeles. His current research interests are in machine learning, fair AI, parallel processing, statistical computing, and statistical methodology for handling missing data.

Dr. Matloff is a former appointed member of IFIP Working Group 11.3, an international committee concerned with database software security, established under the United Nations. He was a founding member of the UC Davis Department of Statistics and participated in the formation of the Department of Computer Science as well. He is a recipient of the campus-wide Distinguished Teaching Award and Distinguished Public Service Award at UC Davis.

He has served as editor in chief of the *R Journal* and on the editorial board of the *Journal of Statistical Software*. He is the author of several published textbooks. His R-based book, *Statistical Regression and Classification: From Linear Models to Machine Learning*, won the Ziegel Prize in 2017.

About the Technical Reviewer

Ira Sharenow is a senior data analyst based in the San Francisco Bay Area. He has consulted for numerous businesses, with R, SQL, Microsoft Excel, and Tableau being his main tools. Sharenow was the technical editor for Norman Matloff's previous book, *Statistical Regression and Classification: From Linear Models to Machine Learning*. In his spare time, he enjoys biking on Bay Area trails. His website is *https://irasharenow.com*.

BRIEF CONTENTS

CONTENTS IN DETAIL

PART I
PROLOGUE, AND NEIGHBORHOOD-BASED METHODS

1
REGRESSION MODELS   3

4
DEALING WITH LARGE NUMBERS OF FEATURES   61

PART II
TREE-BASED METHODS

5
A STEP BEYOND K-NN: DECISION TREES   81

9
CUTTING THINGS DOWN TO SIZE: REGULARIZATION   151

PART IV
METHODS BASED ON SEPARATING LINES AND PLANES

PART V
APPLICATIONS

12
IMAGE CLASSIFICATION 199

13
HANDLING TIME SERIES AND TEXT DATA 211

ACKNOWLEDGMENTS

Over my many years in the business, a number of people have been influential in my thinking on machine learning (ML) and statistical issues. I'll just mention a few.

First, I learn as much from my research students as they learn from me. I cite, in particular, those who have recently done ML work with me or have otherwise interacted with me on ML: Vishal Chakraborty, Yu-Shih Chen, Xi Cheng, Melissa Goh, Rongkui Han, Lan Jiang, Tiffany Jiang, Collin Kennedy, Kenneth Lee, Pooja Rajkumar, Ariel Shin, Robert Tucker, Bochao Xin, Wenxi Zhang, and especially Zhiyuan (Daniel) Guo, Noah Perry, Robin Yancey, and Wenxuan (Allan) Zhao. It has also been quite stimulating to collaborate on ML issues with Bohdan Khomtchouk (University of Chicago), Professor Richard Levenson (UC Davis School of Medicine), and Pete Mohanty (Google).

I owe many thanks to Achim Zeileis, one of the authors of the partykit package of R routines that form excellent implementations of data partitioning methods. He has been quite helpful in guiding me through the nuances of the package. Nello Cristianini kindly read an initially flawed draft of the SVM chapter of my earlier book, *Statistical Regression and Classification: From Linear Models to Machine Learning*, thus improving my present chapter on the topic as well.

Writing a technical book is a form of teaching. In that regard, I owe much to the late Ray Redheffer, for whom I was a teaching assistant way back in grad school. He excelled at getting students in large calculus classes to also do some advanced topics, even some simple proofs. The message was clear to me: even when teaching at an elementary level, one should expect students to *understand* what they are doing rather than merely memorize formulas and mimic common solution patterns. With a very applied field with major consequences, it is even more important that authors of ML books strive for their readers to *understand* what they are doing rather than simply learn library function call forms.

I'll also cite the late Chuck Stone. He was my fellow native of Los Angeles, my informal statistical mentor in grad school, and my close friend over the several decades he lived in the Bay Area. He was one of the four original developers of the CART method and did pioneering work in the theory of k-nearest neighbor methodology. He was quite highly opinionated and blunt—but that is exactly the kind of person who makes one think, question, and defend one's assumptions, whether they be on statistics, climate change, or the economy.

Ira Sharenow, the internal reviewer for both this book and *Statistical Regression and Classification*, once again did a first-rate job, as did No Starch Press's Jill Franklin.

I am really indebted to Bill Pollock, publisher of No Starch Press, for producing this book and two previous ones. Also thanks to John Kimmel, editor of my three books at CRC Press, who recently retired after a distinguished career. I owe much to Bill and John for their longtime encouragement and guidance. Thanks to their help, hopefully I've figured out this book-writing business by now.

INTRODUCTION

Machine learning! With such a science fiction-ish name, one might expect it to be technology that is strictly reserved for highly erudite specialists. Not true.

Actually, machine learning (ML) can easily be explained in commonsense terms, and anyone with a good grasp of charts, graphs, and the slope of a line should be able to both understand and productively *use* ML. Of course, as the saying goes, "The devil is in the details," and one must work one's way through those details. But ML is not rocket science, in spite of it being such a powerful tool.

0.1   What Is ML?

ML is all about prediction. Does a patient have a certain disease? Will a customer switch from her current cell phone service to another? What is actually being said in this rather garbled audio recording? Is that bright spot observed by a satellite a forest fire or just a reflection?

We predict an *outcome* from one or more *features*. In the disease diagnosis example, the outcome is having the disease or not, and the features may be blood tests, family history, and so on.

All ML methods involve a simple idea: similarity. In the cell phone service example, how do we predict the outcome for a certain customer? We look at past customers and select the ones who are most similar in features (size of bill, lateness record, yearly income, and so on) to our current customer. If most of those similar customers bolted, we predict the same for the current one. Of course, we are not guaranteed that outcome, but it is our best guess.

0.2   The Role of Math in ML Theory and Practice

Many ML methods are based on elegant mathematical theory, with support vector machines (SVMs) being a notable example. However, knowledge of this theory has very little use in terms of being able to apply SVM well in actual applications.

To be sure, a good *intuitive* understanding of how ML methods work is essential to effective use of ML in practice. This book strives to develop in the reader a keen understanding of the intuition, *without using advanced mathematics*. Indeed, there are very few equations in this book.

0.3   Why Another ML Book?

There are many great ML books out there, of course, but none really *empower* the reader to use ML effectively in real-world problems. In many cases, the problem is that the books are too theoretical, but I am equally concerned that the applied books tend to be "cookbooks" (too "recipe-oriented") that treat the subject in a Step 1, Step 2, Step 3 manner. Their focus is on the syntax and semantics of ML software, with the result that while the reader may know the software well, the reader is not positioned to *use* ML well.

I wrote this book because:

- There is a need for a book that *uses* the R language but is not *about* R. This is a book on ML that happens to use R for examples and not a book about the use of R in ML.

- There is a need for an ML book that recognizes that *ML is an art, not a science.* (Hence the title of this book.)

- There is a need for an ML book that avoids advanced math but addresses the point that, in order to use ML effectively, *one does need to understand the concepts well–the why and how of ML methods.* Most "applied" ML books do too little in explaining these things.

All three of these bullets go back to the "anti-cookbook" theme. My goal is, then, this:

I would like those who use ML to not only know the definition of random forests but also be ready to cogently explain how the various hyperparameters in random forests may affect overfitting. MLers also should be able to give a clear account of the problems of "p-hacking" in feature engineering.

We will *empower* the reader with strong, *practical*, real-world knowledge of ML methods—their strengths and weaknesses, what makes them work and fail, what to watch out for. We will do so without much formal math and will definitely take a hands-on approach, using prominent software packages on real datasets. But we will do so in a savvy manner. We will be "informed consumers."

0.4   Recurring Special Sections

There are special recurring themes and sections throughout this book:

Bias vs. Variance

Numerous passages explain in concrete terms—no superstition!—how these two central notions play out for each specific ML method.

Pitfalls

Numerous sections with the "Pitfall" title warn the reader of potential problems and show how to avoid them.

0.5   Background Needed

What kind of background will the reader need to use this book profitably?

- No prior exposure to ML or statistics is assumed.

- As to math in general, the book is mostly devoid of formal equations. As long as the reader is comfortable with basic graphs, such as histograms and scatterplots, and simple algebra notions, such as the slope of a line, that is quite sufficient.

- The book does assume some prior background in R coding, such as familiarity with vectors, factors, data frames, and functions. The R command line (> prompt, Console in RStudio) is used throughout. Readers without a background in R, or those wishing to have a review, may find my fasteR tutorial useful: *https://github.com/matloff/fasteR*.

- Make sure R and the qeML package are installed on your computer. For the package, the preferred installation source is GitHub, as it will always have the most up-to-date version of the package. You'll need the devtools package; if you don't already have it, type:

```
install.packages('devtools')
```

Then, to install qeML, type:

```
install_github('https://github.com/matloff/qeML')
```

The qeML package will also be on the CRAN R code repository but updated less frequently.

0.6 The qe*-Series Software

Most of the software used here will come from popular R packages:

- e1071
- gbm
- glmnet
- keras
- randomForest

Readers can use these packages directly if they wish. But in order to keep things simple and convenient for readers, we usually will be using wrappers for the functions in those packages, which are available in my package, qeML. This is a big help in two ways:

1. The wrappers provide a uniform interface.
2. That uniform interface is also *simple*.

For instance, consider day1, a bike rental dataset used at various points in this book. We wish to predict tot, total ridership. Here's how we would do that using random forests, an ML topic covered in this book:

```
qeRF(day1,'tot')
```

For support vector machines, another major topic, the call would be

```
qeSVM(day1,'tot')
```

and so on. Couldn't be simpler! No preparatory code, say, to define a model; just call one of the qe functions and go! The prefix qe- stands for "quick and easy." One can also specify method-specific parameters, which we will do, but still, it will be quite simple.

For very advanced usage, this book shows how to use those packages directly.

0.7 The Book's Grand Plan

Here is the path we'll take. The first three chapters introduce general concepts that recur throughout the book, as well as specific machine learning methods. The rough description of ML above—predict on the basis of similar cases—is most easily developed using an ML method known as *k-nearest neighbors (k-NN)*. Part I of the book will play two roles. First, it will cover k-NN in detail. Second, it will introduce the reader to general concepts that apply to all ML methods, such as choice of *hyperparameters*. In k-NN, the number of similar cases, usually denoted k, is the hyperparameter. For k-NN, what is the "Goldilocks" value of k—not too small and not too large? Again, choice of hyperparameters is key in most ML methods, and it will be introduced via k-NN.

Part II will then present a natural extension of k-NN, *tree-based methods*, specifically *random forests* and *gradient boosting*. These methods work in a flowchart-like manner, asking questions about features one at a time. In the disease diagnosis example given before, the first question might be, Is the patient over age 50? The next might be something like, Is the patient's body mass index below 20.2? In the end, this process partitions the patients into small groups in which the members are similar to each other, so it's like k-NN. But the groups do take different forms from k-NN, and tree methods often outperform k-NN in prediction accuracy and are considered a major ML tool.

Part III discusses methods based on linear relationships. Readers who have some background in linear regression analysis will recognize some of this, though again, no such background is assumed. This part closes with a discussion of the *LASSO* and *ridge regression*, which have the tantalizing property of deliberately shrinking down some classical linear regression estimates.

Part IV involves methods based on separating lines and planes. Consider again the cell phone service example. Say we plot the data for the old customers who left the service using the color blue in our graph. Then on the same graph, we plot those who remained loyal in red. Can we find a straight line that separates most of the blue points from most of the red points? If so, we will predict the action of the new customer by checking which side of the line his case falls on. This description not only fits *SVM* but also fits, in a sense, the most famous ML method, *neural networks*, which we cover as well.

Finally, Part V introduces several specific types of ML applications, such as *image classification*.

It's often said that no one ML method works best in all applications. True, but hopefully this book's structure will impart a good understanding of similarities and differences between the methods, appreciating where each fits in the grand scheme of things.

There is a website for the book at *http://heather.cs.ucdavis.edu/artofml*, which contains code, errata, new examples, and more.

0.8   One More Point

In reading this book, keep in mind that *the prose is just as important as the code*. Avoid the temptation to focus only on the code and graphs. A page that is all prose—no math, no graphs, and no code—may be one of the most important pages in the book. It is there that you will learn the all-important *why* of ML, such as why choice of hyperparameters is so vital. The prose is crucial to your goal of becoming adept at ML with the most insight and predictive power!

Keep in mind that those dazzling ML successes you've heard about come only after careful, lengthy tuning and thought on the analyst's part, requiring real insight. This book aims to develop that insight. Formal math is minimized here, but note that this means the math will give way to prose that describes many key issues.

So, let's get started. Happy ML-ing!

PART I

PROLOGUE, AND NEIGHBORHOOD-BASED METHODS

1

REGRESSION MODELS

In this chapter, we'll introduce *regression functions*. Such functions give the mean of one variable in terms of one or more others—for instance, the mean weight of children in terms of their age. All ML methods are *regression methods* in some form, meaning that they use the data we provide to estimate regression functions.

We'll present our first ML method, k-nearest neighbors (k-NN), and apply it to real data. We'll also weave in concepts that will recur throughout the book, such as dummy variables, overfitting, p-hacking, "dirty" data, and so on. We'll introduce many of these concepts only briefly for the time being in order to give you a bird's-eye view of what we'll return to in detail later: ML is intuitive and coherent but easier to master if taken in stages. Reader, please be prepared for frequent statements like "We'll cover one aspect for now, with further details later."

Before you begin, make sure you have R and the qeML and regtools packages, version 1.7 or newer for the latter, installed on your computer. (Run **packageVersion('regtools')** to check.) All code displays in this book assume that the user has already made the calls to load the packages:

```
library(regtools)
library(qeML)
```

So, let's look at our first example dataset.

1.1 Example: The Bike Sharing Dataset

Before we introduce k-NN, we'll need to have some data to work with. Let's start with this dataset from the UC Irvine Machine Learning Repository, which contains the Capital Bikeshare system's hourly and daily count of bike rentals between 2011 and 2012, with corresponding information on weather and other quantities. A more detailed description of the data is available at the UC Irvine Machine Learning Repository.[1]

The dataset is included as the day dataset in regtools by permission of the data curator. Note, though, that we will use a slightly modified version, day1 (also included in regtools), in which the numeric weather variables are given in their original scale rather than transformed to the interval [0,1].

Our main interest will be in predicting total ridership for a day.

SOME TERMINOLOGY

Say we wish to predict ridership from temperature and humidity. Standard ML parlance refers to the variables used for prediction—in this case, temperature and humidity—as *features*.

If the variable to be predicted is numeric, say, ridership, there is no standard ML term for it. We'll just refer to it as the *outcome* variable. But if the variable to be predicted is an R factor—that is, a categorical variable—it is called a *label*.

For instance, later in this book we will analyze a dataset on diseases of human vertebrae. There are three possible outcomes or categories: normal (NO), disk hernia (DH), or spondylolisthesis (SL). The column in our dataset showing the class of each patient, NO, DH, or SL, would be the labels column.

Our dataset, say, day1 here, is called the *training set*. We use it to make predictions in future cases, in which the features are known but the outcome variable is unknown. We are predicting the latter.

---

1. *https://archive.ics.uci.edu/ml/datasets/bike+sharing+dataset*

1.1.1 Loading the Data

The data comes in hourly and daily forms, with the latter being the one in the regtools package. Load the data:

```
> data(day1)
```

With any dataset, it's always a good idea to first take a look around. What variables are included in this data? What types are they, say, numeric or R factor? What are their typical values? One way to do this is to use R's head() function to view the top of the data:

```
> head(day1)
  instant      dteday season yr mnth holiday
1       1 2011-01-01      1  0    1       0
2       2 2011-01-02      1  0    1       0
3       3 2011-01-03      1  0    1       0
4       4 2011-01-04      1  0    1       0
5       5 2011-01-05      1  0    1       0
6       6 2011-01-06      1  0    1       0
  weekday workingday weathersit      temp
1       6          0          2 8.175849
2       0          0          2 9.083466
3       1          1          1 1.229108
4       2          1          1 1.400000
5       3          1          1 2.666979
6       4          1          1 1.604356
      atemp      hum windspeed casual registered
1  7.999250 0.805833 10.749882    331        654
2  7.346774 0.696087 16.652113    131        670
3 -3.499270 0.437273 16.636703    120       1229
4 -1.999948 0.590435 10.739832    108       1454
5 -0.868180 0.436957 12.522300     82       1518
6 -0.608206 0.518261  6.000868     88       1518
   tot
1  985
2  801
3 1349
4 1562
5 1600
6 1606
> nrow(day1)
[1] 731
```

We see there are 731 rows (that is, 731 different days), with data on the date, nature of the date (such as weekday), and weather conditions (such as the temperature, temp, and humidity, hum). The last three columns measure ridership from casual users, registered users, and the total.

You can find more information on the dataset with the ?day1 command.

1.1.2   A Look Ahead

We will get to actual analysis of this data shortly. For now, here is a preview. Say we wish to predict total ridership for tomorrow, based on specific weather conditions and so on. How will we do that with k-NN?

We will search through our data, looking for data points that match or nearly match those same weather conditions and other variables. We will then average the ridership values among those data points, and that will be our predicted ridership for this new day.

Too simple to be true? No, not really; the above description is accurate. Of course, the old saying "The devil is in the details" applies, but the process is indeed simple. But first, let's address some general issues.

1.2   Machine Learning and Prediction

ML is fundamentally about prediction. Before we get into the details of our first ML method, we should be sure we know what "prediction" means.

Consider the bike sharing dataset. Early in the morning, the manager of the bike sharing service might want to predict the total number of riders for the day. The manager can do so by analyzing the relations between the features—the various weather conditions, the work status of the day (weekday, holiday), and so on. Of course, predictions are not perfect, but if they are in the ballpark of what turns out to be the actual number, they can be quite helpful. For instance, they can help the manager decide how many bikes to make available, with pumped-up tires and so on. (An advanced version would be to predict the demand for bikes at each station so that bikes could be reallocated accordingly.)

1.2.1   Predicting Past, Present, and Future

The famous baseball player and malapropist Yogi Berra once said, "Prediction is hard, especially about the future." Amusing as this is, he had a point; in ML, prediction can refer not only to the future but also to the present or even the past. For example, a researcher may wish to estimate the mean wages workers made back in the 1700s. Or a physician may wish to make a diagnosis as to whether a patient has a particular disease, based on blood tests, symptoms, and so on, guessing their condition in the present, not the future. So when we in the ML field talk of "prediction," don't take the "pre-" too literally.

1.2.2   Statistics vs. Machine Learning in Prediction

A common misconception is that ML is concerned with prediction, while statisticians do *inference*—that is, confidence intervals and testing for quantities of interest—but prediction is definitely an integral part of the field of statistics.

There is sometimes a friendly rivalry between the statistics and ML communities, even down to a separate terminology for each (see Appendix B).

Indeed, statisticians sometimes use the term *statistical learning* to refer to the same methods known in the ML world as machine learning!

As a former statistics professor who has spent most of his career in a computer science department, I have a foot in both camps. I will present ML methods in computational terms, but with some insights informed by statistical principles.

HISTORICAL NOTE

Many of the methods treated in this book, which compose part of the backbone of ML, were originally developed in the statistics community. These include k-NN, decision trees or random forests, logistic regression, and L1/L2 shrinkage. These evolved from the linear models formulated way back in the 19th century, but which later statisticians felt were inadequate for some applications. The latter consideration sparked interest in methods that had less restrictive assumptions, leading to the invention first of k-NN and later of other techniques.

On the other hand, two other prominent ML methods, support vector machines (SVMs) and neural networks, have been developed almost entirely outside of statistics, notably in university computer science departments. (Another method, *boosting*, began in computer science but has had major contributions from both factions.) Their impetus was not statistical at all. Neural networks, as we often hear in the media, were studied originally as a means to understand the workings of the human brain. SVMs were viewed simply in computer science algorithmic terms—given a set of data points of two classes, how can we compute the best line or plane separating them?

1.3   Introducing the k-Nearest Neighbors Method

Our featured method in this chapter will be *k-nearest neighbors*, or *k-NN*. It's arguably the oldest ML method, going back to the early 1950s, but it is still widely used today, especially in applications in which the number of features is small (for reasons that will become clear later). It's also simple to explain and easy to implement—the perfect choice for this introductory chapter.

1.3.1   Predicting Bike Ridership with k-NN

Let's first look at using k-NN to predict bike ridership from a single feature: temperature. Say the day's temperature is forecast to be 28 degrees centigrade. How should we predict ridership for the day, using the 28 figure and our historical ridership dataset (our training set)? A person without a background in ML might suggest looking at all the days in our data, culling out those of temperature closest to 28 (there may be few or none with a temperature of exactly 28), and then finding the average ridership on those days. We would use that number as our predicted ridership for this day.

Actually, this intuition is correct! This, in fact, is the basis for many common ML methods, as we'll discuss further in Section 1.6 on the regression function. For now, just know that k-NN takes the form of simply averaging over the similar cases—that is, over the neighboring data points. The quantity k is the number of neighbors we use. We could, say, take the 5 historical days with temperatures closest to 28, average the numbers for those days, and use the result to predict ridership on a new 28-degree day.

Later in this chapter, we will learn to use the qe*-series implementation of k-NN, qeKNN(). For now, though, let's perform k-NN "manually," so as to get a better understanding of the method.

Okay, ready to go! In this section we will make our first predictions.

1.3.1.1 R Subsetting Review

Before presenting the code, let's review a few aspects of the R language. Recall that in R, the # symbol is for comments; that is, it is not part of the code itself but is for explanatory purposes. The comments in the code below and throughout the book are used as inline explanations of what the code is doing.

For the upcoming example, you'll also need to remember how subsetting works in R. Take this snippet, for instance:

```
> x <- c(5,12,13,8,88)
> x[c(2,4,5)]
[1] 12  8 88
```

The expression x[c(2,4,5)] extracts the 2nd, 4th, and 5th elements from the vector x. Also recall that here we refer to 2, 4, and 5 as *subscripts* or *indices*.

1.3.1.2 A First Prediction

Here, then, is our small, manually performed k-NN example:

```
> data(day1)
> tmps <- day1$temp
> dists <- abs(tmps - 28)  # distances of the temps to 28
> do5 <- order(dists)[1:5]  # which are the 5 closest?
> dists[do5]  # and how close are they?
[1] 0.005849 0.033349 0.045000 0.045000 0.084151
```

The distance between any two numbers is the absolute value of their difference: $|25 - 32| = 7$, so 25 is a distance 7 from 32. This is why we made the call to R's abs() (absolute value) function. R's order() function is like sort(), except that it shows us the indices of the sorted numbers. Here is an example:

```
> x <- c(12,5,8,88,13)
> order(x)
[1] 2 3 1 5 4
```

The values 2, 3, and so on are saying, "The first-smallest number in x was x[2], the second-smallest was x[3], and so on." The line

```
> do5 <- order(dists)[1:5]   # which are the 5 closest?
```

will place in do5 the indices of rows in day1 that have the 5-closest temperatures to 28. In this case, the temperatures are quite close to 28; the furthest is only 0.08 distant.

What were the ridership values on those days?

```
> day1$tot[do5]
[1] 7175 4780 4326 5687 3974
```

We then take the average of those values:

```
> mean(day1$tot[do5])
[1] 5188.4
```

We can now predict that on a day with a temperature of 28 degrees, about 5,200 riders will use the bike sharing service.

There are some issues left hanging, notably: Why take the 5 days nearest in temperature to 28? Is 5 too small a sample, or is it sufficient to make an accurate prediction? This is a central issue in ML, to which we'll return in Section 1.7.

1.4   Dummy Variables and Categorical Variables

To work with this dataset, and do ML in general, you'll need to be able to understand the several columns in the data that represent *dummy variables*. Dummy variables take on values 1 and 0 only, depending on whether they satisfy a particular condition. For instance, in the workingday column, 0 stands for "No" (the date in question is not a working day) and 1 stands for "Yes" (the date is a working day). The date 2011-01-05 has a 1 in the workingday column, meaning yes, this was a working day.

Dummy variables are sometimes more formally called *indicator variables* because they *indicate* whether a certain condition holds (code 1) or not (code 0). An alternative term popular in ML circles is *one-hot coding*.

Our bike sharing data also includes the categorical variables mnth and weekday. There is also a feature weathersit consisting of four categories (1 = clear, 2 = mist or cloudy, 3 = light snow or light rain, 4 = heavy rain or ice pellets or thunderstorm). That variable could be considered categorical as well.

One very common usage of dummy variables is coding of categorical data. In a marketing study, for instance, a factor of interest might be type of region of residence, say, Urban, Suburban, or Rural. Our original data might code these as 1, 2, or 3. However, those are just arbitrary codes, so, for example, there is no implication that Rural is 3 times as good as Urban. Yet ML algorithms may take it that way, which is not what we want.

The solution, used throughout this book and throughout the ML field, is to use dummy variables. We could have a dummy variable for Urban (1 = yes, 0 = no) and one for Suburban. Rural-ness would then be coded by having both Urban and Suburban set to 0, so we don't need a third dummy variable (having one might cause technical problems beyond the scope of this book). Of course, there is nothing special about using the first two values as dummies; we could have, say, one for Urban and one for Rural, without Suburban; the latter would then be indicated by 0 values in Urban and Rural.

In the current chapter, we focus on applications in which our outcome variable is numeric, such as total ridership in the bike sharing data. But in many applications, the outcome variable is categorical, such as our earlier example of predicting vertebral disease. In such settings, termed *classification applications*, the *Y* variable is categorical and must be converted to dummies.

Fortunately, most ML packages, including qeML, do conversions to dummies automatically, as we will see shortly.

1.5   Analysis with qeKNN()

Now that we have a better sense of what's going on under the hood, let's try using the qeKNN() function to perform some k-NN analysis. As noted in the introduction, this book uses the qe*-series wrapper functions. For k-NN, this means qeKNN(). The latter *wraps*, or provides a simple interface for, regtools's basic k-NN function, kNN(). In other words, qeKNN() calls kNN() but in a simpler, more convenient manner.

Before we start our analysis, we'll introduce some "X" and "Y" notation to help us keep track of what we're doing. Take notes—this will be important to remember for all subsequent chapters.

FEATURES X AND OUTCOMES Y

The following informal shorthand used to refer to features and outcomes is pretty standard in both the ML and statistics fields:

- Traditionally, one collectively refers to the features as *X* and the outcome to be predicted as *Y*.

- *X* is a set of columns in a data frame or matrix. If we are predicting ridership from temperature and humidity, *X* consists of those latter two columns in our data. *Y* here is the ridership column.

In 2-class classification applications, *Y* will typically be a dummy variable, a column of 1s and 0s. However, in multiclass classification applications, *Y* is a set of columns, one for each dummy variable. Equivalently, *Y* could be an R factor, stored in a single column.

One more bit of standard notation:

- The number of rows in *X*—that is, the number of data points—is typically denoted by *n*.
- The number of columns in *X*—that is, the number of features—is typically denoted by *p*.

This is just a convenient shorthand. It's easier, for instance, to say "X" rather than the more cumbersome "our feature set." Again, *X*, *Y*, *n*, and *p* will appear throughout this book (and elsewhere, as they are standard in the ML field), so be sure to commit them to memory.

1.5.1   Predicting Bike Ridership with qeKNN()

For the bike sharing example, we'll predict total ridership on any given day. Let's start out using as features just the dummy for working day and the numeric weather variables.

Let's extract those columns of the day1 data frame. As we saw in Section 1.1.1, they are in columns 8 and 10 through 13, with column 16 containing the outcome variable, the total ridership (tot). Thus we can obtain them via the following expression:

```
day1[,c(8,10:13,16)]
```

This extracts the desired columns.

NOTE   *Alternatively, you may prefer to use column names rather than numbers*

```
day1[c('workingday','temp','atemp','hum','windspeed','tot')]
```

in base R, or use the tidyverse or data.table, each of which works fine. Numeric data frame indexing is much easier to type, but use of column names may be clearer.

As pointed out in the introduction, this is a book about ML that happens to use R as its vehicle of instruction rather than a book about R in ML. The way that individual readers handle data manipulation in R is not the focus of this book, so feel free to use your own preferred way to achieve the same results.

So, we form the sub-data frame, and as usual, take a look.

```
> day1 <- day1[,c(8,10:13,16)]
> head(day1)
  workingday    temp    atemp      hum windspeed  tot
1          0 8.175849  7.999250 0.805833 10.749882  985
2          0 9.083466  7.346774 0.696087 16.652113  801
3          1 1.229108 -3.499270 0.437273 16.636703 1349
4          1 1.400000 -1.999948 0.590435 10.739832 1562
```

```
5            1 2.666979 -0.868180 0.436957 12.522300 1600
6            1 1.604356 -0.608206 0.518261  6.000868 1606
```

Now let's try a prediction. Say you are the manager this morning, and the day is a working day, with temperature 12.0, atemp 11.8, humidity 23 percent, and wind at 5 miles per hour. What is your prediction for the ridership?

All the qe*-series functions have a very simple call form:

```
qeSomeMLmethod(your_data_frame, Y_name, options_if_any)
```

The option used in this example will be k, the number of nearest neighbors, which we'll take to be 5. (If we do not specify k in the call, the default value is 25.)

```
> knnout <- qeKNN(day1,'tot',k=5)   # fit the k-NN model
holdout set has 73 cases
```

We are applying the k-NN method, taking our "Y" (or "outcome," as you'll recall) to be the variable tot in the data frame day1, with 5 neighbors. We'll discuss the holdout set shortly, but put that aside for now.

We saved the return value of qeKNN() in knnout. (Of course, you can use whatever name you wish.) It contains lots of information, but we won't consider it at this point. The function qeKNN() did the prep work, enabling us to use knnout to do future predictions.

So, how exactly is that done? The general form for the qe*-series functions is likewise extremely simple:

```
predict(output_from_qe_function, new_case)
```

Let's say, as manager of the bike sharing business, we know that today is a workday, and the temperature, atemp, humidity, and wind speed will be 12.8, 11.8, 0.23, and 5, respectively. Here is our prediction:

```
> today <- data.frame(workingday=1, temp=12.8, atemp=11.8, hum=0.23,
    windspeed=5)
> predict(knnout,today)   # predict new case
     [,1]
[1,] 6321
```

We fed knnout into the predict() function, along with our specified prediction point, today, yielding the predicted number of riders: about 6,300. Observe that the argument today was a data frame with the same column names as in the original dataset day1. This is needed, both here and in many R ML packages, in order to match up the names in the prediction point with the names of the training set.

NOTE   *If you run the above code yourself, you will likely get different output, due to randomness of the holdout set. There is a way to standardize the result so that different people obtain the same result; this will be explained in Section 1.12.3.*

Let's do another prediction, say, the same as above but with wind speed at 18:

```
> anotherday <- today
> anotherday$windspeed <- 18
> predict(knnout,anotherday)
     [,1]
[1,] 5000
```

People don't seem to want to ride as much in the wind.

The second argument, such as anotherday above, can be any data frame with the same column names. For instance, we could have asked for both predictions together:

```
> predict(knnout,rbind(today,anotherday))
     [,1] [,2]
[1,] 6321 5000
```

In Section 1.8, we will deepen our insight into k-NN by analyzing another dataset.

TECHNICAL NOTE: PREDICT() AND GENERIC FUNCTIONS

We saw that qeKNN() is paired with a predict() function. All functions in the qe*-series are similarly paired, which is a very common technique in R.

While all these functions appear to share the same predict(), each one actually has its own separate prediction function, such as predict.qeKNN() in the case of qeKNN(). The function predict() itself is called a *generic function* in R. It simply *dispatches* calls, meaning it relays the original call to a function specific to the type of analysis we are doing. Thus a call to predict() on an object created by qeKNN() will actually be relayed to predict.qeKNN(), and so on.

R has various generic functions, some of which you've probably already been using, perhaps without knowing it. Examples are print(), plot(), and summary(). We'll see an example of plot() in Section 9.6.

1.6   The Regression Function: The Basis of ML

To understand machine learning methods, you need to know *what* is being "learned." The answer is something called the *regression function*. Directly or indirectly (often the latter), it is the basis for ML methods. It gives the mean value of one variable, holding another variable fixed. Let's make this concrete.

Regression function is a general statistical and ML term, much broader than the concept of linear regression that some readers may have learned in a statistics course.

Recall our example above, where we took as our predicted value for a 28-degree day the mean ridership of days near that temperature. If we were to predict the ridership on a 15-degree day, we would use for our prediction the mean ridership of all days with a temperature of 15, or near 15, and so on. Denoting the regression function by $r()$, the quantities of interest are $r(28)$, $r(15)$, and so on.

We say $r()$ is the regression function of ridership on temperature. It is indeed a function; for every input (a temperature), we get an output (the associated mean ridership). And we use the function as our predictions; for instance, to predict ridership on a 15-degree day, we use an estimate of $r(15)$.

But it's an unknown function, not something familiar like sqrt(). So, we need to use our training data to infer values of the function. In ML parlance, we say that we "learn" this function, using our data, showing you where the L comes from in ML. (The M just means we use a computer or algorithm to do the learning.) For instance, in the above example, we *learn* $r(28)$ by averaging the ridership values over the days with a temperature close to 28. The word *learn* is thus reflected in *train*, in the term *training data*.

It is customary to use the "hat" notation for "estimate of." Thus we denote our estimate of $r()$ by $\hat{r}()$.

The regression function is also known as the *conditional mean*. In predicting ridership from temperature, $r(28)$ is the mean ridership, subject to the *condition* that temperature is 28. That's a subpopulation mean, which is quite different from the overall population mean ridership.

Let's summarize these important points:

- The regression function $r()$ gives the mean of our outcome variable as a function of our features.

- We estimate $r()$ from our training data. We call the estimate $\hat{r}()$.

- We use $\hat{r}$ as the basis of our predictions.

Any function has arguments. A regression function has as many arguments as we have features. Let's take humidity as a second feature, for instance. To predict ridership for a day with temperature 28 and humidity 0.51, we would use the mean ridership in our dataset among days in which temperature and humidity are approximately 28 and 0.51. In regression function notation, that's $r(28, 0.51)$. In the example on page 12, the value of interest was $r(1, 12.8, 11.8, 0.23, 5)$.

As previously noted, the regression function forms the basis, directly or indirectly, in all predictive ML methods. It will come up repeatedly throughout the book.

1.7 The Bias-Variance Trade-off

In the introduction, specifically in Section 0.8, we implored the reader:

> A page that is all prose—no math, no graphs, and no code—may be one of the most important pages in the book.

The pages in this current section are prime examples of this, as the *Bias-Variance Trade-off* is one of the most famous topics in the field. My Google query yielded 18,400,000 results! It is an absolutely central issue in ML, which we will treat in depth in Chapter 3. However, you should be aware of it from the beginning, so let's give an overview.

The issue is, for example, the choice between greater or smaller values of k. Larger values of k have smaller variance but larger bias, and smaller values of k have the opposite effect. Let's see how this works.

1.7.1 Analogy to Election Polls

First consider an analogy to election surveys. During an election campaign, voter polls will be taken to estimate the popularity of the various candidates. An analyst takes a random sample of the set of all telephone numbers and solicits opinions from those who pick up the phone.

Suppose we are interested in p, the proportion of the entire population that favors Candidate C. Since we just have a sample from that population, we can only estimate the value of p using the proportion $\widehat{p}$ who like Candidate C in our sample. Accordingly, the poll results are accompanied by a *margin of error*, to recognize that the reported proportion $\widehat{p}$ is only an estimate of p. (Those who have studied statistics may know that the margin of error is the radius of a 95 percent confidence interval.)

The margin of error gives an indication of the accuracy of our estimate. It measures sampling variability. A large value means that our estimate of p varies a lot from one sample to another; if the pollster were to call a new random sample of phone numbers, the value of our estimated p likely would be rather different, possibly quite different if the sample size is small. Of course, the pollster is not going to take a second sample, but the amount of sampling variability from one sample to the next tells us how reliable $\widehat{p}$ is an estimate of p. The margin of error reflects that sampling variability, and if it is large, then our sample size was too small.

The key issue, then, is sampling variability, which is called the *variance* of $\widehat{p}$. It can be computed in the polling example from the margin of error.

A bias issue may also arise. Suppose the pollster has a list of landline phones but not cell phones. Many people, especially younger ones, don't have a landline, so calling only those with landlines may bias our results.

1.7.2 Back to ML

Returning to ML, consider the bike sharing example in Section 1.5.1, where we wished to have the value of $r(1, 12.8, 11.8, 0.23, 5)$, which we wish to use as our predicted value. We will obtain an estimate, $\hat{r}(1, 12.8, 11.8, 0.23, 5)$, as the actual predicted value.

We treat the data on the number of riders per day as a sample from the (rather conceptual) population of all days, past, present, and future. Using the k-NN method (or any other ML method), we are only obtaining an estimate $\hat{r}$ of the true population regression function $r()$. Forming a prediction from just the closest $k = 5$ neighbors works from a very small sample. Imagine the pollster sampling only 5 voters! In another sample, the closest days to our point to be predicted would be different, with different ridership values. *In other words, this is a variance issue.*

On the other hand, using just $k = 5$, we found in Section 1.3.1.2 that the 5 neighbors were all quite close to the prediction point. Suppose we look at the nearest $k = 50$ neighbors. In that case, we risk using data points far from the prediction point, which are thus not very similar to it. *This would create a bias problem.*

In sum, larger values of k reduce variance but at the expense of increasing bias. We want to find a "Goldilocks" value for k—that is, one not too small and not too large.

However, note that computation time and the amount of memory the method requires are also important factors: if the best method takes too long to run or uses too much memory, we may end up choosing a different method.

1.8 Example: The mlb Dataset

To cement your understanding of qeKNN() and introduce another example that we can refer to throughout the rest of the book, let's try a similar operation on the mlb dataset. This dataset, provided courtesy of the UCLA Statistics Department, records the heights and weights of Major League Baseball players in inches and pounds, respectively. It's included in regtools.

Let's glance at the data first so we know what we're working with:

```
> data(mlb)
> head(mlb)
              Name Team         Position Height
1    Adam_Donachie  BAL          Catcher     74
2       Paul_Bako  BAL          Catcher     74
3 Ramon_Hernandez  BAL          Catcher     72
4    Kevin_Millar  BAL    First_Baseman     72
5     Chris_Gomez  BAL    First_Baseman     73
6   Brian_Roberts  BAL   Second_Baseman     69
  Weight   Age PosCategory
1    180 22.99     Catcher
2    215 34.69     Catcher
3    210 30.78     Catcher
4    210 35.43   Infielder
5    188 35.71   Infielder
6    176 29.39   Infielder
```

Let's predict the weight of a new player for whom it is only known that height and age are 72 and 24, respectively.

```
> w <- mlb[,c(4:6)]  # extract height, weight, and age
> z <- qeKNN(w,'Weight')  # fit k-NN model
holdout set has  101 rows
> predict(z,data.frame(Height=72,Age=24))
      [,1]
[1,] 182.56
```

Note again that we needed to specify the prediction point (72,24) in the same data frame form as `mlb`, the dataset on which we had fit the model.

1.9   k-NN and Categorical Features

In the previous baseball player example, both of the features, height and age, were numeric. But what if we were to add a third feature, `Position`, a categorical variable? Since k-NN is distance-based, the features need to be numeric in order to compute distances between data points. How can we use k-NN with non-numeric features?

The answer, of course, is that the categorical variables (that is, R factors) should be converted to dummy variables. We could do this here via the regtools function `factorToDummies()`. However, as the qe*-series functions do this conversion internally when needed, we need not convert `Position` to dummies on our own. The `qeKNN()` function will also make a note in its output for later use by `predict()`, to make the same conversions when predicting.

For example, suppose we want to calculate another new player's weight, using the categorical `Position` feature, in addition to height and age:

```
> knnout1 <- qeKNN(mlb[,3:6],'Weight',25)  # extract Position, Height, Age
> predict(knnout1,data.frame(Height=72,Age=24,Position='Catcher'))
      [,1]
[1,]  197
```

In our first prediction, not using `Position`, our predicted value was about 183 pounds. But if we know that the new player is a catcher, we see that, at least in this case, our predicted value increases to 197. This makes sense; catchers do tend to be heavyset so they can guard home plate.

The qe*-series functions identify categorical features by their status as R factors. In the example here, `Position` is indeed an R factor. As noted, the internals of `qeKNN()` and `predict.qeKNN()` will automatically do the conversion to dummies for us, which is a major convenience.

Typically, categorical features will already be expressed as factors in data frames. In some cases, a feature will be categorical but expressed in terms of numeric codes. If so, apply `as.factor()` to the feature to convert it to factor form.

1.10 Scaling

A theme encountered in many ML methods is that of *scaling* our data. In your future ML projects, it's good practice to keep scaling in mind. It's used in many ML methods and may produce better results even if a method doesn't require it.

Let's go back to the baseball player data. Consider two players, one of height 70 and age 24 and one of height 72 and age 30. Taking these two pairs of numbers in an algebra context, the distance between them is the distance between the points (70,24) and (72,30) in the plane:

$$\sqrt{(70-72)^2 + (24-30)^2} = 6.32$$

Distances like this would be computed in k-NN. But what if height were converted to, say, meters, and age to months? The heights would be divided by 39.37, while age would be multiplied by 12:

```
> sqrt((70/39.37-72/39.37)^2 + (12*24-12*30)^2)
[1] 72.00002
```

That creates a problem in that age would dominate the computation, with height playing only a small role. Since height obviously is a major factor in predicting weight, the change in units would probably reduce our prediction ability.

The solution is to do away with units like inches, meters, and so on, which is called *scaling*. To scale our data, we first subtract the mean, giving everything mean 0, called *centering*. Then we divide each feature by its standard deviation, *scaling*. This gives everything a standard deviation of 1. Now all the features are unitless and commensurate. (Usually, when doing scaling, we also do centering, and the combined process is simply called scaling.)

To make this more concrete, as a former or current student, you may recall one of your professors converting examination scores in this way: "To get an A, you needed to be 1.5 standard deviations above the mean." That professor was subtracting the mean exam score, then dividing by the standard deviation. The R function scale() performs this operation for us, but to illustrate, here is how we would do it on our own:

```
> ht <- mlb$Height
> ht <- (ht - mean(ht)) / sd(ht)
> mlb$Height <- ht
```

The qeKNN() function has an argument scaleX for this purpose. Its default value is TRUE, so scaling was done by default in our above k-NN examples. In each X column (recall this means feature column) of our data, qeKNN() will transform that column by calling scale(). (Actually, we can scale all the X variables with a single scale() call.)

Of course, we must remember to do the same scaling—dividing by the same standard deviations—in the X values of new cases that we predict, such as new days in our bike sharing example. The qe*-series functions make a note of this, which is then used by the paired predict() functions.

NOTE *Keep in mind that scale() won't work on a vector in which all values are identical, as the standard deviation would be 0. We can check for this by calling the regtools function constCols(), which will report all constant columns in our data frame.*

In the bike sharing data, day1 uses unscaled data, for instructional purposes. The "official" version of the data, day, does scale. It does so in a different manner, though: it is scaled such that the values of the variables lie in the interval [0,1]. One way to do that is to transform by:

$$x \rightarrow \frac{x - \min(x)}{\max(x) - \min(x)}$$

This has an advantage over scale() by producing *bounded variables*—that is, numbers bounded by 0 and 1. By contrast, scale() produces variables in the interval $(-\infty, \infty)$, and a variable with a small standard deviation will likely have very large scaled values, giving that variable undue influence in the analysis.

The regtools function mmscale() does the above mapping to [0,1]. Here is a small example:

```
> x <- data.frame(u=3:5,v=c(12,5,13))
> x
  u  v
1 3 12
2 4  5
3 5 13
> mmscale(x)
      [,1]  [,2]
[1,]  0.0 0.875
[2,]  0.5 0.000
[3,]  1.0 1.000
```

The u column had a mean of 4, with a minimum and maximum of 3 and 5, respectively. Therefore, the 4 in the second row was replaced by (4 – 3) / (5 – 3) = 1/2, for example. As you can see, all the resulting values are in [0,1] and are unitless—that is, no inches or months.

1.11 Choosing Hyperparameters

In the introduction, we mentioned that the number of nearest neighbors k is a *hyperparameter* or *tuning parameter*, a value chosen by the user that affects the predictive ability of the model. As noted in Section 1.7, k is a "Goldilocks" quantity that needs to be carefully set for best performance—not too small and not too large.

Finding the best k can be a challenge. Luckily, k-NN has only one hyperparameter, but as you will find later in the book, most ML methods have several; in some advanced methods outside the scope of the book, there may even be a dozen or more. Choosing the "right" combination of values for several hyperparameters is especially difficult, but even choosing a good value for a single hyperparameter is nontrivial.

We take our first look below at ways to tackle the challenging problem of picking hyperparameters and then go into more details in Chapter 3. Spend a little extra time on this section, since this issue will arise repeatedly in this book and throughout your ML career.

1.11.1   Predicting the Training Data

Almost all methods for choosing hyperparameters involve testing our model by predicting new cases. In the most basic form, we go back and predict our original training data. This sounds odd—we know the ridership values in the data, so why predict them? The idea is to try various values of k and see which one predicts our known data the best. That then would be the value of k that we use for predicting new X data in the future.

This is not ideal, and in practice a slight modification of this approach is used. We will use it too, but before presenting it, let's go through an illustration of what can go wrong. Let's predict the third data point in day1 using the smallest possible value of k: 1.

```
> kno <- qeKNN(day1,'tot',1)
> datapoint3X <- day1[3,-6]   # remote Y value
> predict(kno,datapoint3X)
     [,1]
[1,] 1349
> day1[3,6]
[1] 1349
```

We predicted exactly correctly! But wait a minute . . . that seems suspicious, and it is. The closest neighbor to data point 3 (the third row in our data) is itself! The distance from that point to itself is 0. Similarly, row 8 is the closest data point to row 8, row 56 is the closest data point to row 56, and so on. Of course we were 100 percent correct; we took the average of the 1-closest neighbor, thus just duplicating the Y value. The same analysis shows that even, say, $k = 5$ would give us overly optimistic prediction accuracy. One of the 5 neighbors would still be the original data point, thus biasing our prediction.

The takeaway is that when we evaluate the prediction accuracy of a given value of k, we should predict on a different dataset than the one to which we fit the k-NN method. But, you protest, we only have one dataset. How can we get another for properly assessing prediction accuracy? That's the topic of the following section on holdout sets.

1.12   Holdout Sets

Again, as noted in the previous section, to assess the predictive accuracy of our model, we need to try it out on "fresh" data, not the data it was fit on. But we don't have any new data, so what can be done? Key to solving this conundrum are the notions of *holdout sets* and *cross-validation* covered in this section. They are central to ML and will recur throughout the book.

In the 731 data points in day1, we could randomly cull out, say, 100 of them. These will serve as our *holdout set*, or *test set*. The remaining 631 will temporarily be our training set. We fit the model to this training set, then see how well it predicts on the holdout set, which serves as "fresh" data not biased by training. (In examples here, the holdout size is 73, as the default size is 10 percent of the dataset size.)

Technically, our accuracy in future predictions will be best if we fit our model on the entire dataset, in which case we set holdout=NULL. However, in preliminary exploration, it's important to have some idea as to how well our model works on new data. Thus it's best to have a holdout set during the exploration phase, then refit the model on the entire data once we've chosen hyperparameters and so on.

Before we select our holdout set, if we are to evaluate quality of prediction, we need a criterion for evaluating prediction accuracy.

1.12.1   Loss Functions

For a data point in the holdout set, we could take the absolute difference between the actual value and predicted value, then average those absolute differences over all holdout points to get the Mean Absolute Prediction Error (MAPE). This is an example of a *loss function*, which is simply a criterion for goodness of prediction. We could take MAPE as that criterion, with smaller values being better.

Another popular loss function is Mean Squared Prediction Error, or MSPE, where we average the squares of the prediction errors rather than their absolute values. MSPE is the more common of the two, but I prefer to use MAPE, as MSPE overly accentuates large errors. Say we are predicting weight in the MLB data. Consider two cases in which we are in error by 12 and 15 pounds. Those two numbers are fairly similar, but their squares, 144 and 225, are quite different.

For classification applications, the most commonly used loss function is simply the overall probability of misclassification. We predict each Y in the holdout set, tally the number of times we are wrong, and divide by the size of the holdout set.

1.12.2   Holdout Sets in the qe*-Series

The qe*-series functions will automatically perform the above process of finding the MAPE, or overall probability of misclassification, then report the result in the output component testAcc. These functions will sense whether our application is a classification problem according to whether we specify

Y (second argument in any qe*-series call) as an R factor. If so, then the mis-classification probability will be computed instead of MAPE.

We'll turn again to the bike sharing dataset for an example of finding qeKNN's automatically generated MAPE:

```
> knnout <- qeKNN(day1,'tot',5)
holdout set has  73 rows
> knnout$testAcc
[1] 1203.644
```

Using 5 nearest neighbors, we make an average prediction error of about 1,200 riders. That's not great, but better than the alternative, as follows.

Suppose we had no access to weather conditions and so on. How could we predict ridership? One natural idea would be to just use the overall mean:

```
> meanTot <- mean(day1$tot)
> meanTot
[1] 4504.349
```

In other words, every day, including the one at hand, we would predict about 4,500 riders. How well would we fare using this strategy?

```
> mean(abs(day1$tot - meanTot))
[1] 1581.793
```

If we were to always predict ridership using the overall mean riders per day, our average prediction error would be nearly 1,600. Using the weather variables and workingday as predictors does help bring MAPE down to 1,200.

Can we find a better value for *k* than 5? Let's try, say, 10 and 25:

```
> qeKNN(day1,'tot',10)$testAcc
holdout set has  73 rows
[1] 1127.333
> qeKNN(day1,'tot',25)$testAcc
holdout set has  73 rows
[1] 1131.108
```

Of the values we've tried, *k* = 10 seems to work best, though we must keep in mind the randomness of the holdout sets. Indeed, it is better to try several holdout sets for each candidate value of *k*, the topic of our next section.

1.12.3   Motivating Cross-Validation

When using qeKNN's automatically generated MAPEs, it is important to remember that the software is choosing the holdout set at random. The holdout set size is only 73, a somewhat small sample—imagine our election pollster above sampling only 73 voters. Thus there will be considerable *sampling variation* between MAPE in one holdout set and another. We can solve this problem through performing *cross-validation*—that is, averaging the values of MAPE over multiple holdout sets.

To demonstrate sampling variation, let's try running the same code a couple more times:

```
> qeKNN(day1,'tot',10)$testAcc
holdout set has  73 rows
[1] 1094.211
> qeKNN(day1,'tot',10)$testAcc
holdout set has  73 rows
[1] 1157.5
```

We can see that we cannot rely too much on that one MAPE value; the sample size of 73 is too small. There is a lot more to say on this issue, and as noted, we will resume this discussion in Chapter 3. Suffice it to say now that we should look at many holdout sets and then perform cross-validation by averaging the resulting testAcc values.

By the way, we can control R's random number generator by using the set.seed() function:

```
> set.seed(9999)
> qeKNN(day1,'tot',10)$testAcc
holdout set has  73 rows
[1] 1210.373
> qeKNN(day1,'tot',10)$testAcc
holdout set has  73 rows
[1] 1090.622
> set.seed(9999)  # try it again
> qeKNN(day1,'tot',10)$testAcc
holdout set has  73 rows
[1] 1210.373
> qeKNN(day1,'tot',10)$testAcc
holdout set has  73 rows
[1] 1090.622
```

We will often do this in the book. It sets a certain sequence of random numbers, in case the reader wishes to run the code and check the results. By using the same seed, 9999 here, the same training and holdout sets will be generated as what I had here. (I just chose 9999 as a favorite; there is nothing special about it.)

Clearly, we will obtain more accurate results by generating several holdout sets, thus averaging the resulting MAPE values. This is called *cross-validation*, which will be discussed in detail in Chapter 3.

1.12.4   Hyperparameters, Dataset Size, and Number of Features

Recall the discussion in Section 1.7.2 regarding a trade-off involving the choice of the number of nearest neighbors k:

- If we set $k = 5$, we will be averaging just 5 data points, which seems too few. This is a variance problem; averages of 5 Y values at a given X will vary a lot from one sample to another.

- On the other hand, setting $k = 50$, we would likely have some points in the neighborhood that are far away from the point to be predicted and thus unrepresentative.

  For example, in the bike data, say we are predicting ridership on a 20-degree day, which is rather comfortable. Points in our training set with an uncomfortable temperature like 40 are not very relevant to the prediction at hand and would tend to make our prediction too low. This is a bias problem.

So, we have a trade-off. We want to make k large to achieve low variance, but setting a large k incurs the risk of substantial bias. But ... what if our bike sharing dataset were to have, say, $n = 73000$ data points rather than 731? In that case, the 50th-nearest neighbor might actually be pretty close to the prediction point, solving our bias problem. Then we could afford to use a larger k so as to hold down variance. In other words:

All else being equal, the larger n is, the larger we can make k.

This still doesn't tell us what specific k to choose. We'll return to this issue in Chapters 3 and 4, but it is something to at least be aware of at this early stage.

The corresponding statement concerning the number of features p is:

All else being equal, the larger p is, the larger we must make k.

This is less intuitive than the previous statement involving n, but roughly this is the issue. Having more features means more variability in interpoint distances, thus increasing variance in predictions. To counter this, we need a larger k.

1.13   Pitfall: p-Hacking and Hyperparameter Selection

In non-ML settings, *p-hacking* refers to the following pitfall in analyses of large studies. Say one is studying genetic impacts on some outcome, with very large numbers of genes involved. Even if no gene has a real impact, due to sampling variation, one of them will likely appear to have a "significant" impact just by accident. Though we won't go into detail on how to solve this just yet, you should be aware of it from the beginning.

p-hacking also has major implications for the setting of hyperparameters in ML. Let's say we have four tuning parameters in an ML method, and we try 10 values of each. That's $10^4 = 10000$ possible combinations. Even if all of them are equally effective, the odds are that one of them will accidentally have a much better MAPE value. What seems to be the "best" setting for the hyperparameters may be illusory.

The `regtools` function `fineTuning()` takes steps to counter the possibility of p-hacking in searches for the best tuning parameter combination. We'll cover more on this in Chapter 7.

1.14 Pitfall: Long-Term Time Trends

Before we move on to the next chapter, let's cover three major pitfalls you may encounter while working with the methods introduced here that may influence the quality of your predictions: dirty data, missing data, and long-term trends in the data. We will deal with the last pitfall first.

In the few experiments we did with the MLB data, we found that the best MAPE value might be around 1,100. This seems rather large, but recall we are not using all of our data. Look again at the bike dataset in Section 1.1.1. There are several variables involving timing of the observation: date, season, year, and month. To investigate whether the timing data can improve our MAPE value, let's graph ridership against time. (The data is in chronological order.)

```
> plot(day1$tot,type='l')  # plotting type is 'l', lines between points
```

The result is in Figure 1-1. Clearly, there is both a seasonal trend (the dips are about a year apart) and an overall upward trend. The bike sharing service seems to have gotten much more popular over time. Statistical techniques that analyze data over the course of time are known as *time series methods*. They arise a lot in ML in various contexts. We'll investigate this in Chapter 13, but let's give it a try here without new tools.

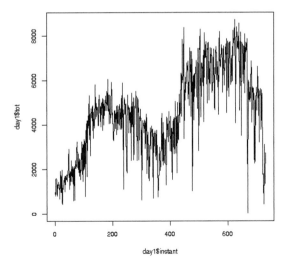

Figure 1-1: Time trends, bike data

Column 1 in the bike sharing data, instant, is the day number, with the first day of the dataset having value 1, the second day with value 2, and so on, through the last day, 731.

Let's add instant to our feature set. Recall our earlier selection of columns in Section 1.5.1:

```
> day1[,c(8,10:13,16)]
```

The features we decided to explore at that time were in columns 8, 10 through 13, and 16. Now we want to also use instant, which is in column 1:

```
> data(day1)
> day2 <- day1[,c(1,8,10:13,16)]
> kno <- qeKNN(day2,'tot',k=5)   # rerun k-NN on the new data
holdout set has  73 rows
> kno$testAcc
[1] 662.9836
```

Ah, much better! Our MAPE is down to about 663.

When using k-NN and the other methods covered in this book, keep in mind that conditions in the phenomena under study may vary through time, possibly becoming a major factor. In some cases, the time variable may not even be explicit but implied in the ordering of the records. Failure to explore this may result in a substantial deterioration in the quality of prediction, so keep an eye out for places where you may run into this pitfall.

1.15 Pitfall: Dirty Data

Beyond accounting for long-term time trends, you may also encounter problems caused by dirty data. For an example of this, look at the entry in the bike sharing data for January 1, 2011.

```
> head(day1)
  instant     dteday season yr mnth holiday
1       1 2011-01-01      1  0    1       0
```

As you can see in the holiday column, the dataset claims this is not a holiday. But of course January 1 is a federal holiday in the United States. Also, although the documentation for the dataset states there are 4 values for the categorical variable weathersit, there actually are just values 1, 2, and 3:

```
> table(day1$weathersit)

  1   2   3
463 247  21
```

Errors in data are quite common and, of course, an obstacle to good analysis. For instance, consider the New York City taxi data that will be discussed in depth in Chapter 5, which contains pickup and dropoff locations, trip times, and so on. One of the dropoff locations, if one believes the numbers, is in Antarctica! (You can take a look at *https://data.cityofnewyork.us/ Transportation/2018-Yellow-Taxi-Trip-Data/t29m-gskq.*)

Whenever working with a new dataset, the analyst should do quite a bit of exploring—for example, with `hist()` and `table()`, as we've seen here. You should also be wary of *multivariate outliers*, meaning data points that are not extreme in any one of their components but, when viewed collectively, are unusual. For instance, suppose a person is recorded as having height 74 inches (29.1 cm) and age 6. Neither that height nor that age would be cause for concern individually (assume we have people of all ages in our data), but in combination it seems quite suspicious. In this case, k-NN is a useful tool! A data point like the 74-inch six-year-old described above would be unusually distant from the other points and might be exposed that way.

Alas, there is no formulaic way to detect anomalous data points. This mirrors the nature of ML in general, as we've emphasized. There is no magic "recipe." This is an advanced topic in statistics and beyond the scope of this book.

1.16   Pitfall: Missing Data

In R, the value NA means the data is not available—that is, missing. Datasets commonly include NAs, maybe many. How should we deal with this?

There are entire books devoted to the study of missing value analysis. We cannot cover the topic in any depth here, but we will briefly discuss one common method, *listwise deletion*, to at least introduce the issues at stake.

Say our data consists of people, and we have variables Age, Gender, Years of Education, and so on. If, for a particular person, Age is missing but the other variables are intact, this method would simply skip over that case. But there are two problems with this:

- If we have a large number of features, odds are that many cases will have at least one NA. This would mean throwing out a lot of precious data.

- Skipping over cases with NAs may induce a bias. In survey data, for instance, the people who decline to respond to a certain question may be different from those who do respond to it, and this may affect the accuracy of our predictions.

Note that when we find missing values are coded numerically rather than as NAs, we should change such values to NAs.

As with dirty data, developing one's personal approach to handling missing values comes with experience. Learn some tools and gradually develop your approach, which will largely be different for each person. The CRAN Task View series includes one on missing data.

1.17 Direct Access to the regtools k-NN Code

As mentioned in the introduction, most of the code in this book uses popular R packages that are specific to each different ML method. We use the qe*-series of wrappers to interface those packages as a uniform, simple convenience, but of course one can also choose direct access.

One reason for doing so is that the functions in those standard R packages contain many advanced options not available via the wrappers. In the particular case of qeKNN(), but *not* for the other qe*-series functions, direct access may also be faster if one is doing just a single prediction.

In most applications, such specialized usage will not be necessary, but our book will show how to use the functions directly if the reader is interested. Note that we will not be able to demonstrate how to use those advanced options, as they are numerous and frequently involve advanced concepts. Instead, we will simply show how to use one of our existing examples with a direct call.

Here are the particulars for our k-NN code. The qeKNN() function wraps regtools::kNN(), which has arguments as follows:

```
> library(regtools)
> args(kNN)
function (x, y, newx = x, kmax, scaleX = TRUE, PCAcomps = 0,
    expandVars = NULL, expandVals = NULL, smoothingFtn = mean,
    allK = FALSE, leave1out = FALSE, classif = FALSE, startAt1 = TRUE,
    saveNhbrs = FALSE, savedNhbrs = NULL)
```

Here x and y are our X and Y, newx is the X at which we wish to predict, and kmax is k.

Let's retrace our steps from Section 1.8:

```
> x <- mlb[,c(4,6)]  # height, age
> y <- mlb[,5]  # weight
> newx <- c(72,24)  # ht, age of new player to be predicted re weight
> kmax <- 25  # k
> knnout <- kNN(x,y,newx,kmax)
> knnout$regests  # predicted value
[1] 183.76
```

Note that the model fitting and prediction are combined into one step, though the latter can be postponed if desired.

The prediction here is slightly different from the earlier one, as the latter had a holdout set. If we suppress formation of a holdout set, we obtain the same result:

```
> kno <- qeKNN(mlb[,4:6],'Weight',k=25,holdout=NULL)
> predict(kno,data.frame(Height=72,Age=24))
        [,1]
[1,] 183.76
```

More information on kNN() is available by typing **?kNN** (not ?knn).

1.18 Conclusions

We are off to a good start! You should now have a good idea of both the k-NN method and several general ML concepts: the regression function, how k-NN estimates it, the general concept of the Bias-Variance Trade-off, how hyperparameters affect it, and how to use holdout sets to find a good point on that trade-off spectrum.

You are already armed with enough tools to experiment with some data analysis of your own. Please do!

The next chapter will introduce the issues in classification applications.

2

CLASSIFICATION MODELS

The last chapter briefly introduced *classification applications*, in which we predict dummy or categorical variables. These differ from the *numeric applications* we've analyzed, such as predicting the number of bike riders, which is a numeric entity. For instance, in a marketing application, we might wish to predict whether a customer will purchase a certain product. In that case, we'd represent the "Y" outcome with a dummy variable, using 1 for buying the item and 0 for not buying it. There are two *classes* here: Buy and Not Buy.

We discussed an example of categorical Y in the "Some Terminology" box in Section 1.1. In that example, a physician has divided patients into three classes—that is, three categories—depending on their spinal condition: normal (NO), disk hernia (DH), and spondylolisthesis (SL). Here Y is the class, or category, for the given patient. Thus Y is a categorical variable with three categories. If Y is coded as an R *factor*, which is usually the case, then the factor will have three levels. On the other hand, we might code Y as a vector of dummy variables, with one for each class.

We will analyze this vertebrae data in detail in Section 2.3.1, stating where to obtain it and so on. But let's do a sneak preview to illustrate the previously described notions of class, or category.

```
> vert <- read.table('column_3C.dat',header=FALSE,stringsAsFactors=TRUE)
> head(vert)
     V1    V2    V3    V4     V5    V6 V7
1 63.03 22.55 39.61 40.48  98.67 -0.25 DH
2 39.06 10.06 25.02 29.00 114.41  4.56 DH
3 68.83 22.22 50.09 46.61 105.99 -3.53 DH
4 69.30 24.65 44.31 44.64 101.87 11.21 DH
5 49.71  9.65 28.32 40.06 108.17  7.92 DH
6 40.25 13.92 25.12 26.33 130.33  2.23 DH
> table(vert$V7)

 DH  NO  SL
 60 100 150
> class(vert$V7)
[1] "factor"
> levels(vert$V7)
[1] "DH" "NO" "SL"
```

The vertebral condition is in the last column. We see that in this dataset, there were 60 patients of class DH and so on.

This chapter goes into more detail regarding classification applications, beginning with a brief discussion of a conceptual issue, the notion of a *regression function*, and then getting right to the data analysis. We'll bring in some new datasets, again analyzing them using qeKNN() but showing some special issues that arise in classification contexts.

2.1   Classification Is a Special Case of Regression

Classification applications are quite common in ML. In fact, they probably form the majority of ML applications. How does the regression function $r(t)$ (see Section 1.6) play out in such contexts?

Recall that the regression function relates mean Y to X. If we are predicting weight from height and age, then $r(71, 25)$ means the mean weight of all people of height 71 inches and age 25. But how does this work if Y is a dummy variable?

In classification settings, the regression function, a conditional mean, becomes a conditional probability. To see why, consider a classification application in which the outcome Y is represented by a dummy variable coded 1 or 0, such as the marketing example at the start of this chapter. After collecting our k-nearest neighbors, we average their 1s and 0s. Say, for example, that $k = 8$, and the outcomes for those 8 neighbors are 0,1,1,0,0,0,1,0. The average is then $(0 + 1 + 1 + 0 + 0 + 0 + 1 + 0) / 8 = 3/8 = 0.375$. Since this means that $3/8$ of the outcomes were 1s, you can think of the average of 0-or-1 outcomes as the *probability* of a 1.

In the marketing example, the regression function is the probability that a customer will buy a certain product, conditioned on the customer's feature values, such as age, gender, income, and so on. We then guess either Buy or Not Buy according to whichever class has the larger probability. Since there are just two classes here, that's equivalent to saying we guess Buy if and only if its class probability is greater than 0.5. (This strategy minimizes the overall probability of misclassification. However, other criteria are possible, which is a point we will return to later.)

The same is true in multiclass settings. Consider the medical application above. For a new patient whose vertebral status is to be predicted, ML would give the physician three probabilities—one for each class. As above, these probabilities come from averaging 1s and 0s in dummy variables, with one dummy for each class. The preliminary diagnosis would be the spinal class with the highest estimated probability.

In summary:

The function $r()$ defined for use in predicting numeric quantities applies to classification settings as well. In those settings, mean values reduce to probabilities, and we use those to predict class.

This view is nice as a unifying concept.

NOTE *The reader may wonder why we use three dummy variables to classify patients' spinal conditions. As noted in Section 1.4, just two should suffice here; however, certain other methods covered later on require more than two. For consistency, we'll always take the approach of using as many dummies as classes. Note that this convention is for* Y; *categorical features in* X *will still usually have one fewer dummy than values that the feature can take on.*

Therefore, classification problems are really special cases of regression, which is a point we'll often return to in this book. However, the field uses some confusing terminology, which one must be aware of.

Previously, we distinguished between, on the one hand, *numerical* applications, say, predicting the *number* of bike riders, and, on the other hand, *classification* applications, such as the earlier marketing and medical examples where we are predicting a *class*.

However, it is customary in the ML field to call numeric applications *regression problems*. This, of course, is a source of confusion, since both numeric and classification applications involve the regression function! Sigh ... As long as you are aware of this, it's not a big issue, but in this book we will use the term *numeric-Y applications* for clarity.

2.2 Example: The Telco Churn Dataset

For our first example of a classification model, we'll take the Telco Customer Churn dataset. In marketing circles, the term *churn* refers to customers moving from one purveyor of a service to another. A service will then hope to identify customers who are likely "flight risks," or those with a substantial probability of leaving. So, we have two classes: Churn or No Churn (that is, Leave or Stay).

You can download and learn more about the dataset at *https://www .kaggle.com/blastchar/telco-customer-churn.* Let's load it and take a look:

```
> telco <- read.csv('WA_Fn-UseC_-Telco-Customer-Churn.csv',header=TRUE)
> head(telco)
  customerID gender SeniorCitizen Partner Dependents tenure
1 7590-VHVEG Female             0     Yes         No      1
2 5575-GNVDE   Male             0      No         No     34
3 3668-QPYBK   Male             0      No         No      2
4 7795-CFOCW   Male             0      No         No     45
5 9237-HQITU Female             0      No         No      2
6 9305-CDSKC Female             0      No         No      8
  PhoneService    MultipleLines InternetService
1           No No phone service             DSL
2          Yes               No             DSL
3          Yes               No             DSL
4           No No phone service             DSL
5          Yes               No     Fiber optic
6          Yes              Yes     Fiber optic
...
> names(telco)
 [1] "customerID"       "gender"
 [3] "SeniorCitizen"    "Partner"
 [5] "Dependents"       "tenure"
 [7] "PhoneService"     "MultipleLines"
 [9] "InternetService"  "OnlineSecurity"
[11] "OnlineBackup"     "DeviceProtection"
[13] "TechSupport"      "StreamingTV"
[15] "StreamingMovies"  "Contract"
[17] "PaperlessBilling" "PaymentMethod"
[19] "MonthlyCharges"   "TotalCharges"
[21] "Churn"
```

That last column is the response; Yes in the Churn column means yes, the customer bolted.

Let's move on to data preparation, such as checking for NA values. This is a rather complex dataset, necessitating extra prep—a bonus for learners of data science like readers of this book!

2.2.1   Pitfall: Factor Data Read as Non-factor

Many features in the telco dataset are R factors (that is, nonnumeric quantities such as gender and InternetService). Most R ML packages, including the qe*-series functions, allow factors. But wait ... they're not factors after all. By default, read.csv() treats nonnumeric items as character strings:

```
> class(telco$Churn)
[1] "character"
```

Since our software expects R factors, we need to tell R to treat nonnumeric items as factors. (Actually, depending on your version of R, and your default settings, this may actually be your default value. If you are not sure, go ahead and set this in your call.)

```
> telco <- read.csv('WA_Fn-UseC_-Telco-Customer-Churn.csv',header=TRUE,
    stringsAsFactors=TRUE)
> class(telco$Churn)
[1] "factor"
```

Failure to do this will result in character or numeric values, causing problems when we run the ML functions.

2.2.2 Pitfall: Retaining Useless Features

In some datasets, some columns have no predictive value and should be removed. The customerID feature is of no predictive value (though it might be if we had multiple data points for each customer), so we'll delete the first column:

```
> tc <- telco[,-1]
```

Retaining useless features can lead to overfitting.

2.2.3 Dealing with NA Values

As noted in Section 1.16, many datasets contain NA values for missing (not available) data. Let's see if this is the case here:

```
> sum(is.na(tc))
[1] 11
```

There are indeed 11 NA values present.

We'll use listwise deletion here as a first-level analysis (see Section 1.16), but if we were to pursue the matter further, we may look more closely at the NA pattern. R actually has a complete.cases() function, which returns TRUE for the rows that are intact. Let's delete the other cases:

```
> ccIdxs <- which(complete.cases(tc))
> tc <- tc[ccIdxs,]
```

If we don't need to know which particular cases are excluded, we could simply run:

```
> tc <- na.exclude(tc)
```

How many cases are left?

```
> nrow(tc)
[1] 7032
```

It's generally a good idea to check this.

Among other things, the number of remaining rows affects the size of the value we choose for the number of near neighbors k (see Section 1.12.4).

2.2.4   Applying the k-Nearest Neighbors Method

Let's see how to call the qeKNN() function in classification problems, say, by setting k to 75:

```
> set.seed(9999)
> knnout <- qeKNN(tc,'Churn',75,yesYVal='Yes')
```

As an example of prediction, say we have a new case to predict, such as a hypothetical customer like the one in row 8 of the data but who is male and a senior citizen. To set this up, we'll copy row 8 of tc and make the stated changes in the gender and SeniorCitizen columns:

```
> newCase <- tc[8,]
> newCase$gender <- 'Male'
> newCase$SeniorCitizen <- 1
```

Note, too, that since this revised row will be our "X," we need to remove the "Y" portion—that is, remove the Churn column. We saw earlier that Churn is column 21, but remember, we removed column 1, so it's now in column 20.

```
> newCase <- newCase[,-20]
```

Alternatively, we could have used the subset() function in base R,

```
> newCase <- subset(newCase,select=-Churn)
```

the data.table package, or the tidyverse. As noted on page 11, it is up to readers to choose whichever R constructs they feel most comfortable with; our focus in this book is on ML, with R playing only a supporting role.

Now we make the prediction for the new case:

```
> predict(knnout,newCase)
[,1]
[1,] 0.3066667
```

The class of interest to us is Churn, so we check the probability of Churn for this case, which is 0.32. Since it's under 0.5, we guess No Churn.

Calls to qeKNN() for classification problems are essentially the same as for numeric-outcome applications. The form of the output is slightly different.

But ... how does qeKNN() know that this is a classification application rather than a numeric-Y problem? Our specified Y variable, Churn, is an R factor, signaling to qeKNN() that we are running a classification application.

Let's check the classification accuracy.

```
> knnout$testAcc
[1] 0.2247511
```

We have a misclassification rate of about 22 percent, which is not too bad. Once again, however, I must emphasize that those numbers are subject to sampling variation, which we will discuss further in Chapter 3.

2.2.5   Pitfall: Overfitting Due to Features with Many Categories

Suppose we had not removed the customerID column in our original data, telco. How many distinct IDs are there?

```
> length(levels(telco$customerID))
[1] 7043
```

The number of IDs is also the number of rows, as there's one record per customer.

Recall that qeKNN(), like functions in many R packages, internally converts factors to dummy variables. If we had not removed this column, there would have been 7,042 columns in the internal version of tc just stemming from this ID column! Not only would the result be unwieldy, but the presence of all these columns would dilute the power of k-NN.

This latter phenomenon is known as *overfitting*. Using too many features will actually reduce accuracy in predicting future cases. Chapter 3 covers this in greater detail, but for now, one might loosely think of the data as being "shared" by too many features, with not much data available to each one. Note that overfitting is a concern both in classification and numeric-Y applications.

There also may be computational issues if we were to include the ID. Having 7,000 customer IDs would mean 7,000 dummy variables. That means the internal data matrix has over 7000×7000 entries—about 50 million. And at 8 bytes each, that means something like 0.4GB of RAM. We've got to remove this column.

Even with ML packages that directly accept factor data, one must keep an eye on what the package is doing—and what we are feeding into it. It's good practice to watch for R factors with a large number of levels. They may appear useful, and may in fact be so. But they can also lead to overfitting and computational or memory problems.

2.3 Example: Vertebrae Data

Consider another UCI dataset, Vertebral Column Dataset,[1] which is on diseases of the vertebrae. It is described by the curator as a dataset that contains "values for six biomechanical features used to classify orthopaedic patients into 3 classes (normal, disk hernia, or spondilolysthesis [sic])." They abbreviate the three classes as NO, DH, and SL.

This example is similar to the last one, but with three classes instead of two. Recall that in a two-class problem, we predict on the basis of whether the probability of the class of interest is greater than 0.5. In the telco example, that class was Churn, so we predict either Churn or No Churn, depending on whether the Churn probability is greater than 0.5. That probability turned out to be 0.32, so we predicted No Churn. But with three or more classes, none of the probabilities might be above 0.5; we simply choose the class with the largest probability.

2.3.1 Analysis

Let's read in the data and, as usual, take a look around.

```
> vert <- read.table('column_3C.dat',header=FALSE,stringsAsFactors=TRUE)
> head(vert)
      V1    V2    V3    V4     V5    V6 V7
1 63.03 22.55 39.61 40.48  98.67 -0.25 DH
2 39.06 10.06 25.02 29.00 114.41  4.56 DH
3 68.83 22.22 50.09 46.61 105.99 -3.53 DH
4 69.30 24.65 44.31 44.64 101.87 11.21 DH
5 49.71  9.65 28.32 40.06 108.17  7.92 DH
6 40.25 13.92 25.12 26.33 130.33  2.23 DH
> nrow(vert)
[1] 310
```

The patient status is column V7. We see, by the way, that the curator of the dataset decided to group the rows by patient class. That's why the qe*-series functions randomly choose the holdout sets.

Let's fit the model. The question of how to choose k is still open, but we need to take into account the size of our dataset. We only have 310 cases here, in contrast to the $n = 7032$ we had in the customer churn example. Recall from Section 1.12.4 that the larger our number of data points n is, the larger we can set the number of nearest neighbors k, so with this small dataset, let's try a small value here, say, $k = 5$.

```
> set.seed(9999)
> kout <- qeKNN(vert,'V7',5)
```

---

1. *http://archive.ics.uci.edu/ml/datasets/vertebral+column*

As an example of prediction, consider a patient similar to the first one in our data but with V2 being 25 rather than 22.55. What would our predicted class be?

```
> z <- vert[1,-7]  # exclude Y
> z$V2 <- 25
> predict(kout,z)
$predClasses
[1] "dfr.DH"

$probs
      dfr.DH dfr.NO dfr.SL
[1,]    0.6    0.2    0.2
```

We'd predict the DH class, with an estimated probability of 0.6. Now let's find the overall accuracy of our predictions using this model.

```
> kout$testAcc
[1] 0.1935484
```

We would have an error rate of about 19 percent. Note, though, that due to the small sample size (310), our predictions would, in this case, be quite susceptible to sampling variation.

2.4   Pitfall: Error Rate Improves Only Slightly Using the Features

When working with any ML method, on any dataset, it's important to check whether your predictions have a better chance of success than those based on random chance, without using the features. Recall our analysis along those lines in Section 1.12.2. Let's see an example in the classification realm.

Consider the telco dataset in Section 2.2. We found that in using 19 features to predict whether a customer will be loyal or not, we would err about 22 percent of the time. Is 22 percent good?

To answer that, consider what happens if we don't have any feature to predict from. Then we would be forced to predict on the basis of what most customers do. What percentage of them bolt?

```
> mean(telco$Churn == 'Yes')
[1] 0.2653699
```

This says about 27 percent of the customers leave. We will often do computations of this form, so let's review how it works. The expression

```
telco$Churn == 'Yes'
```

evaluates to a bunch of TRUEs and FALSEs. But in R, as in most computer languages, TRUE and FALSE are taken to be 1 and 0, respectively. So, we are taking the mean of a bunch of 1s and 0s, giving us the proportion of 1s. That's the proportion of Yes entries.

So, without customer information, we would simply predict everyone to stay—and we would be wrong 27 percent of the time. In other words, using customer information reduces our error rate from 27 to 22 percent—helpful, yes, but not dramatically so. Of course, we might do better with other values of k, and the reader is urged to try some, but it does put our analysis in perspective.

As you can see, a seemingly "good" error rate may be little or no better than random chance. Always remember to check the unconditional class probabilities—that is, the ones computed without X.

Let's consider the example in Section 2.3 in this regard. We achieved an error rate of about 26 percent. If we didn't use the features, guessing instead the most prevalent class overall, would our error rate increase?

To that end, let's see what proportion each class has, ignoring our six features. We can answer this question easily.

```
> table(vert$V7) / nrow(vert)
      DH        NO        SL
0.1935484 0.3225806 0.4838710
```

The call to table() gives us the category counts, so dividing by the total number of counts gives us the proportions.

If we did not use the features, we'd always guess the SL class, as it is the most common. We would then be wrong a proportion of 1 − 0.4838710 = 0.516129 of the time, which is much worse than the 26 percent error rate we attained using the features. Using the features greatly enhances our predictive ability in this case.

Actually, the qe*-series functions in regtools compute the featureless error rate for us. In the vertebrae example above:

```
> kout$baseAcc
[1] 0.5089606
```

Note that the result is a little different from the earlier figure of 0.516129. This is because the latter was computed on the full dataset, while this one was computed with holdout: the mean came from the training set while the Y values were from the holdout set.

As seen here, in classification settings, baseAcc will show the overall misclassification rate if one does not use the features. Of course, the same comparison—error rates using the features and not—is of interest in numeric-Y settings. Therefore, if we were to ignore the features, our guess for a new Y would be the overall mean value of Y in the training set, which is analogous to our using the conditional mean if we do use the features. Without the features, the analog of MAPE is then the mean absolute difference between the overall mean Y and the actual Y in the test set. This is reported in baseAcc.

As an example, consider again the bike ridership data from Chapter 1.

```
> data(day1)
> day1 <- day1[,c(8,10:13,16)]  # extract the desired features
> set.seed(9999)
> knnout <- qeKNN(day1,'tot',k=5)  # fit the k-NN model
holdout set has  73 rows
> knnout$testAcc
[1] 1203.644
> knnout$baseAcc
[1] 1784.578
```

Here, using our chosen set of 5 predictors, MAPE was about 1,204, versus 1,785 using no predictors.

2.5   The Confusion Matrix

In multiclass problems, the overall error rate is only the start of the story. We might also calculate the (unfortunately named) *confusion matrix*, which computes per-class error rates. Let's see how this plays out in the vertebrae data.

The qe*-series functions include the confusion matrix in the return value.

```
> kout$confusion
      pred
actual DH NO SL
    DH  6  2  0
    NO  2  6  2
    SL  1  1 11
```

Of the 6 + 2 + 0 = 8 data points with actual class DH, 6 were correctly classified as DH, but 2 were misclassified as NO, though none were wrongly predicted as SL.

This type of analysis enables a more finely detailed assessment of our predictive power. It's quite frequently used by MLers to identify potential areas of weakness of one's model.

2.6   Clearing the Confusion: Unbalanced Data

Here, we will discuss issues regarding *unbalanced data*, a common situation in classification problems that is much discussed in ML circles.

Recall that in our customer churn example earlier in this chapter, about 73 percent of the customers were "loyal," while 27 percent moved to another telco. With the 7,032 cases in our data, those figures translate to 5,141 loyal cases and 1,901 cases of churn. The loyal cases outnumber the churn ones by a ratio of more than 2.5 to 1. Often, this ratio can be 100 to 1 or even more. Such a situation is termed *unbalanced*. (In this section, our discussion will mainly cover the two-class case, but multiclass cases are similar.)

Many analysts recommend that if one's dataset has unbalanced class sizes, one should modify the data to create equal class counts. Their reasoning is that application of ML methods to unbalanced data will result in almost all predictions being that we guess the class of a new data point to be the dominant class—for instance, we always guess No Churn rather than Churn in the telco data. That is not very informative!

Illustrations of the problem and offered remedies appear in numerous parts of the ML literature, ranging from web tutorials[2] to major CRAN packages, such as caret, parsnp, and mlr3. In spite of warnings by statisticians,[3] all of these sources recommend that you artificially equalize the class counts in your data, say, by discarding "excess" data from the dominant class.

While it is true that unbalanced data will result in always, or almost always, predicting the dominant class, remedying by artificially equalizing the class sizes is unwarranted and, in many cases, harmful. Clearly, discarding data is generally not a good idea; it will always weaken one's analysis. Moreover, depending on the goals of the given application, it may actually be desirable to always guess the dominant class.

2.6.1 Example: The Kaggle Appointments Dataset

To illustrate how best to deal with unbalanced data, let's look at a dataset from Kaggle,[4] a firm with the curious business model of operating data science competitions. The goal is to use this dataset to predict whether a patient will fail to keep a doctor's appointment; if the medical office can flag the patients at risk of not showing up, staff can make extra efforts to avoid the economic losses resulting from no-shows.

Read in the data:

```
> ma <- read.csv('KaggleV2-May-2016.csv',header=TRUE,
    stringsAsFactors=TRUE)
> names(ma)
 [1] "PatientId"       "AppointmentID"  "Gender"          "ScheduledDay"
 [5] "AppointmentDay"  "Age"            "Neighbourhood"   "Scholarship"
 [9] "Hypertension"    "Diabetes"       "Alcoholism"      "Handicap"
[13] "SMS_received"    "No.show"
> nrow(ma)
[1] 110527
```

Should we remove the patient ID, as we did in the telco data, to avoid overfitting? We see that on average, each patient appears less than twice in the data, meaning there is not much data per patient:

```
> length(unique(ma$PatientId))
[1] 62299
```

2. https://www.datacamp.com/tutorial/diving-deep-imbalanced-data
3. https://www.fharrell.com/post/classification/
4. https://www.kaggle.com/joniarroba/noshowappointments

So, yes, we probably should not include this feature. Using the same reasoning, it makes sense to remove the appointment ID, neighborhood, appointment day, and scheduled day variables:

```
> ma <- ma[,-c(1,2,4,5,7)]
> names(ma)
[1] "Gender"      "Age"          "Scholarship"  "Hypertension" "Diabetes"
[6] "Alcoholism"  "Handicap"     "SMS_received" "No.show"
```

About 20 percent of cases are no-shows (counterintuitively, Yes here means "Yes, the patient didn't show up"):

```
> table(ma$No.show)
   No    Yes
88208 22319
```

Yes, it is indeed unbalanced data.

Recall that the concern is that our predicted *Y*s will also be unbalanced—that is, most or all will predict the patient to show up. Let's check this by inspecting the output of running qeKNN(). Here is the call:

```
> kout <- qeKNN(ma,'No.show',25)
```

There is a lot of information in most qe*-series function return values. Here are the components of the qeKNN() function output:

```
> names(kout)
 [1] "whichClosest"  "regests"     "scaleX"         "classif"
 [5] "xminmax"       "mhdists"     "x"              "y"
 [9] "noPreds"       "leave1out"   "startAt1adjust" "classNames"
[13] "factorsInfo"   "trainRow1"   "holdoutPreds"   "testAcc"
[17] "baseAcc"       "confusion"   "holdIdxs"
```

That holdoutPreds component is actually the return value of regtools::kNN(), discussed in Section 1.17. (The R notation p::e means the entity e in the package p.) Let's see what is in there:

```
> names(kout$holdoutPreds)
[1] "predClasses" "probs"
```

Checking the documentation, we find that predClasses is the vector of predicted *Y*s in the holdout set, which is just what we need. Let's tabulate them:

```
> predY <- kout$holdoutPreds$predClasses
> table(predY)
predY
 No Yes
990  10
```

First, how do we deal with *two* dollar signs ($) in this expression?

---

kout$holdoutPreds$predClasses

Remember, the notation u$v means component v within the object u. So, uvw means the component *w* within the object u$v! So yes, we have an R list within an R list here, which is common in the R world.

At any rate, we see that with our model here, we predict in the vast majority of cases that the patient will show up (again, Yes means a no-show), confirming the concern many people have about unbalanced data.

In fact, the predictions are even more unbalanced than the data itself; we saw about 20 percent of the Ys in the overall dataset were no-shows, while here that is true for only 1.3 percent of the predicted holdout Ys. Actually, this is to be expected: remember, if the model finds the probability of breaking the appointment to be greater than 0.5, the prediction will be that they don't show up, even if they actually did.

This is exactly the problem cited by the sources mentioned earlier who recommend artificially balancing the data. They recommend altering the data in a manner that makes all classes represented equally in the data. They suggest one of the following remedies (or variants) to equalize the class sizes:

Downsample
Replace the No cases in our data with 22,319 randomly chosen elements from the original 88,208. We then will have 22,319 Yes records and 22,139 No records, thus achieving balance.

Upsample
Replace the Yes cases with 88,208 randomly selected elements from the original 22,319 (with replacement). We then will have 88,208 Yes records and 88,208 No records, thus achieving balance.

One would apply one's chosen ML method, say, k-NN, to the modified data, and then predict new cases to be no-shows according to whether the estimated conditional probability is larger than 0.5 or not.

2.6.2   A Better Approach to Unbalanced Data

Again, downsampling is undesirable; data is precious and shouldn't be discarded. The other approach to balancing, upsampling, doesn't make sense either—why would adding fully duplicate data help?

In addition, balancing assumes equal adverse impact from false negatives and false positives, which is unlikely in applications like the appointments data. One could set up formal utility values here for the relative costs of false negatives and false positives. But in many applications, we need more flexibility than what a fully mechanical algorithm gives us. For instance, consider credit card fraud. As noted in global accounting network PricewaterhouseCoopers's publication *Fraud: A Guide to Its Prevention,*

Detection and Investigation, "Every fraud incident is different, and reactive responses will vary depending on the facts that are unique to each case."[5]

The easier and better solution is to simply have our ML algorithm flag the cases in which there is a substantial probability of fraud, say, above some specified threshold, then take it "by hand" from there. Once the algorithm has selected a set of possible instances of fraud, the (human) auditor will take into account that estimated probability—now worrying not only that it is larger than the threshold but also *how much larger*—as well as such factors as the amount of the charge, special characteristics not measured in the available features, and so on.

The auditor may not give priority, for instance, to a case in which the probability is above the threshold but in which the monetary value of the transaction is small. On the other hand, the auditor may give this transaction a closer look, even if the monetary value is small, if the probability is much higher than the threshold value.

Thus, the practical solution to the unbalanced-data "problem" is not to artificially resample the data but instead to identify individual cases of interest in the context of the application. This then means cases of sufficiently high probability to be of concern, again in the context of the given application.

Recall that the `probs` component of a `qe*`-series call in a classification application gives the estimated probabilities of the various classes—exactly what we need. For instance, in the missed-appointments dataset, we can check `probs` to find the probability a patient will be a no-show.

Note that `probs` has one row for each case to be predicted. Since the missed-appointments data has two classes, there will be two columns. We saw previously that the Yes class (that is, missed appointments) is listed second. Let's take a look.

```
> preds <- predict(kout,ma[,-9])  # exclude "Y", column 9
> table(preds$probs)
     0   0.04   0.08   0.12   0.16    0.2   0.24   0.28
   604   6283   9959  16465  17713  18427  12641   8943
  0.32   0.36    0.4   0.44   0.48   0.52   0.56    0.6
  7081   5293   3306   2123   1038    298    154    121
  0.64   0.68   0.72
    27     25     26
```

There are quite a few patients who, despite being more likely than not to keep the appointment, still have a substantial risk of no-show. For instance, 18,427 people have a 0.2 estimated probability of failing to keep their

---

5. *https://www.pwc.com.au/consulting/assets/risk-controls/fraud-control-jul08.pdf*

appointment. An additional 28,435 patients have more than a 25 percent chance of not showing up:

```
> sum(preds$probs > 0.75)
[1] 80451
```

The reasonable approach would be to decide on a threshold for no-show probability, then determine which patients fail to meet that threshold. With a threshold of 0.75, for instance, any patient whose probability of keeping the appointment is greater than that level might be given special attention. We would make extra phone calls to them, explain penalties for missed appointments, and so on.

If those calls prove too burdensome, we can increase the threshold. Or, if the calls turn out to be highly effective, we can reduce it. Either way, the point is that the power is now in the hands of the end user of the data, where it ought to be. Artificially balancing the data denies the user that power.

2.7   Receiver Operating Characteristic and Area Under Curve

We have seen MAPE used as a measure of predictive power in numeric-Y problems, while overall misclassification error (OME) is used in classification applications. Both are very popular, but in the classification case, there are other common measures, two of which we will discuss now.

2.7.1   Details of ROC and AUC

Many analysts use the *Area Under Curve (AUC)* value as an overall measure of predictive power in classification problems. The curve under consideration is the *Receiver Operating Characteristic (ROC)* curve.

To understand ROC, recall Section 2.6.2, where we spoke of a threshold for class prediction. If the estimated class probability is on one side of the threshold, we predict Class 1, and on the other side, we predict Class 0. Threshold values can be anywhere from 0 to 1; we choose our value based on our goals in the particular application.

The ROC curve then explores various scenarios. How well would we predict if, say, we take the threshold to be 0.4? What about 0.7? And so on? The question "How well would we predict?" is addressed by two numbers: the *true positive rate (TPR)* and the *false positive rate (FPR)*.

TPR, also known as the *sensitivity*, is the probability that we guess Class 1, given that the class actually is Class 1. FPR, the *specificity*, is the probability that we guess Class 1, given that the true class is Class 0. Note that the threshold value determines FPR and TPR. The ROC curve then plots TPR against FPR as the threshold varies.

The AUC is then the total area under the ROC curve. It takes on values between 0 and 1. The higher the curve, the better, as it implies that for any fixed FPR, TPR is high. Thus, the closer AUC is to 1.0, the better the predictive ability.

2.7.2 The qeROC() Function

The qeROC() function wraps roc() in the pROC package. It performs ROC analysis on the output of a qe*- function, say, qeKNN(), using the call form:

```
qeROC(dataIn, qeOut, yName, yLevelName)
```

Here, dataIn is the dataset on which the qe*- function had been called, qeOut is the output of that function, yName is the name of *Y* in dataIn, and yLevelName is the *Y* level (in the R factor sense) of interest. Note that the latter allows for the multiclass case.

As noted, qeROC() calls pPROC::roc(). The return value of the former consists of the return value of the latter. It may be useful to assign the return value to a variable for further use (see below), but if this is not done, the ROC curve is plotted and the AUC value is printed out.

Note that qeROC() operates on the holdout set. This is important for the same reasons that the testAcc output of the qe*-series functions use the holdout set (see Section 1.12).

2.7.3 Example: Telco Churn Data

Let's see what the ROC curve has to say about the Telco Churn data, continuing our earlier k-NN analysis.

```
> w <- qeROC(tc,knnout,'No')
...
> w$auc
Area under the curve: 0.8165
```

The plot is shown in Figure 2-1. Let's see how to interpret it.

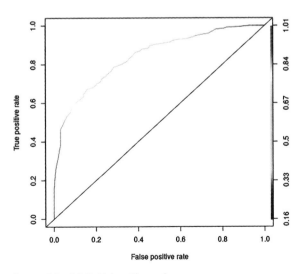

Figure 2-1: ROC, Telco Churn data

The 45-degree line is drawn to represent pure guessing, with our rate of prediction of a positive class being the same, regardless of whether we have a true positive or not. Again, the further the ROC curve is above this line, the better.

2.7.4   Example: Vertebrae Data

The qeROC() function can also be used in multiclass settings:

```
> qeROC(vert,kout,'V7','DH')
Area under the curve: 0.9181
> qeROC(vert,kout,'V7','NO')
Area under the curve: 0.7985
> qeROC(vert,kout,'V7','SL')
Area under the curve: 0.8706
```

Since this is a small dataset, we opted for larger holdout (under the 10 percent default, the holdout would only have 31 cases). But even then, one must keep in mind that those AUC values are subject to considerable sample variation. Thus we must be cautious in concluding that we are less accurate in predicting the 'NO' cases.

Anyway, what do these numbers mean in this multiclass context? Actually, they are the same ones one would get by running three individual ROC analyses (on the same holdout set); qeROC() is just a convenience function in this case, alleviating the user of the need to run roc() three times. And since no new computation is done (the class probabilities are scaled to sum to 1.0), this also saves the user computation time if the dataset is large.

2.7.5   Pitfall: Overreliance on AUC

AUC can be a useful number to complement OME, and many analysts regard it as an integral part of their ML toolkits. However, one should use it cautiously.

Mathematically, AUC is the average value of ROC over all possible threshold values. But recall, each threshold value corresponds implicitly to a relative utility. In a credit card fraud dataset, for instance, we may believe it is far worse to decide a transaction is legitimate when it is actually fraudulent, compared to vice versa. The problem, then, is that there are some threshold values that we would never even consider using for a particular application. Yet they are averaged into the AUC value, thus rendering the latter less meaningful.

2.8 Conclusions

We now have a solid foundation in the two basic types of ML problems: numeric-Y and classification. Along the way, we've picked up some miscellaneous skills, such as removing useless features and dealing with NA values.

It's now time to take a serious look at how to choose the value of k and, more generally, hyperparameters in all ML methods, which is a topic that we have been glossing over so far. We will look at this in detail in the next two chapters.

3

BIAS, VARIANCE, OVERFITTING, AND CROSS-VALIDATION

We now look in detail at a vital topic touched on in Sections 1.7, 1.12.4, and 2.2.5—overfitting. In this chapter, we'll explain what bias and variance really mean in ML contexts and how they affect overfitting. We'll then cover a popular approach to avoiding overfitting known as *cross-validation*.

The problem of overfitting exemplifies the point made in the title of this book: ML is an art, not a science. There is no formulaic solution to various problems, especially overfitting. Professor Yaser Abu-Mostafa of Caltech, a prominent ML figure, once summed it up: "The ability to avoid overfitting is what separates professionals from amateurs in ML."[1] And my Google query on "overfitting" yielded 6,560,000 results!

Don't be intimidated. The professor is correct, but avoiding overfitting is not difficult, provided one has a good understanding of bias and variance. One uses this understanding and gains skill through experience.

---

1. *https://www.youtube.com/watch?v=EQWr3GGCdzw*

3.1 Overfitting and Underfitting

So, what is all the fuss about overfitting? We've given a hint here and there in earlier chapters. Now let's go into the topic in depth.

Recall our discussion in Section 1.7 of the Bias-Variance Trade-off involved in choosing hyperparameter values, specifically the value k in k-NN. Once again, let's take the bike sharing data (Section 1.1) as our motivating example. As before, say we wish to predict ridership, such as for a day in which the temperature is 28 degrees. We will look at the days in our data with temperatures nearest to 28. Our predicted value will be the average ridership among those days.

Say we take $k = 5$. Even those outside the technology world might intuitively feel that a value of 5 for k is "too small a sample." There is too much variability in ridership from one set of 5 days to another, even if their temperatures are near 28. If we had a sample from a different set of 731 days than the one we have, we'd have a different set of 5 closest days to 28, with a different average ridership. With $k = 50$, a lot of high and low ridership values would largely cancel out during the averaging process, but not so with just $k = 5$. This argues for choosing a larger value than 5 for k. This is a *variance* issue: choosing too small a value for k brings us too much sampling variability.

On the other hand, if we use, say, the $k = 25$ days with temperatures closest to 28, we risk getting some days whose temperatures are rather far from 28. Say, for instance, the 25th-closest day had a temperature of 35. People do not want to ride bikes in such hot weather. If we include too many hot days in our prediction for the 28-degree day, we will have a tendency to underpredict the true ridership. In such a situation, $k = 25$ may be too large. That's a *bias* issue: choosing too large a value of k may induce a systemic tendency to underpredict or overpredict.

NOTE *We'll repeatedly mention variance and bias in this chapter and in later ones. It's important to keep in mind what quantity's variance and bias is under discussion: predicted values. Say we are predicting ridership for a 28-degree day. The larger the value of* k *we use, the lesser the variability in our predicted value, but the greater the bias of that value.*

Variance and bias are at odds with each other. For a given dataset, we can reduce one only at the expense of the other. This trade-off is central to choosing the values of hyperparameters, as well as choosing which features to use. Using too small a k—trying to reduce bias below what is possible on this data—is called *overfitting*. Using too large a k—an overly conservative one—is called *underfitting*. We hope to choose our hyperparameter values in the "sweet spot," neither overfitting nor underfitting.

3.1.1 Intuition Regarding the Number of Features and Overfitting

A similar statement holds for features: using too large a value for p (that is, the number of features) results in overfitting, while using too small a value gives us underfitting. Here is the intuition behind this.

Recall mlb, the dataset on Major League Baseball players (in Section 1.8). We might predict weight from height and age. But what if we were to omit height from our feature set? That would induce a bias. Roughly speaking, we'd be tacitly assuming everyone is of middling height, which would result in our tending to overpredict the weight of shorter players while underpredicting that of the taller ones.

On the other hand, it turns out that the more predictors we use (in general, not just for this data), the higher the variance of our predicted values. To see this, say we are conducting a marketing study, predicting purchases of winter parkas, and wish to account for geography of customers. There are about 42,000 ZIP codes (US postal codes). Say we use ZIP code as one of our features in predicting purchases. We would then have 42,000 dummy variables and would have other features such as age, gender, and income, or $p > 42000$. If our data consists of, say, 100,000 customers, we would have on average only 2 or 3 data points per ZIP code. Again, even nontechies would point out that this is far too small a sample, causing variance to rise. In other words, having too large a value of p increases variance. Once again, we see a tension between variance and bias.

3.1.2 Relation to Overall Dataset Size

But there's more. In choosing a "good" value of k or p, we need to take into consideration n, the number of data points we have. Recall that in the bike sharing example, we had $n = 731$ (that is, only 731 days' worth of data). Is that large enough to make good predictions? Why should that number matter? Actually, it relates directly to the Bias-Variance Trade-off. Here's why.

In our bike sharing example above, we worried that with $k = 25$ nearest neighbors, we might have some days among those 25 whose temperatures are rather far from 28. But if we had, say, 2,000 days instead of 731, the 25th-closest might still be pretty close to 28. In other words:

> The larger n is, the larger we can make k while still avoiding overly large bias.

Similarly, consider the ZIP code issue mentioned above. With 100,000 customers, we would have on average only 2 or 3 data points per ZIP code. But what if our dataset consisted of 50 million customers? Then it may be useful to include the dummies for ZIP codes, as we may have a sufficient number of customers from most ZIP codes. Remember, p denotes the number of features, and this counts each dummy variable separately. Thus, inclusion of ZIP codes in our feature set would increase p by about 42,000.

In other words:

The larger n is, the larger the value we can use for p—that is, the more features we can use while still avoiding overly large variance.

3.1.3 Well Then, What Are the Best Values of k and p?

Mind you, this still doesn't tell us how to set a good "Goldilocks" value of k—not too small and not too large. The same holds for choosing p (that is, choosing the number of features to use); in fact, it's an even more challenging problem, as it is a question of not only *how many* features to use but also *which ones*.

As we have stated so many times:

This is a fact of life in machine learning. For most issues, there are no neat, magic-formula answers. Again, ML is an art, not a science. However, holdout methods are used in practice, and they generally work pretty well, especially as the analyst gains experience.

We'll present holdout methods in full detail later in this chapter.

Also, a rough rule of thumb, suggested by some mathematical theory, is to follow this limitation:

$$k < \sqrt{n} \qquad (3.1)$$

That is, the number of nearest neighbors should be less than the square root of the number of data points.

What about choosing p? As noted, a feature set is not "large" or "small" on its own. Instead, its size p must be viewed relative to the number of data points n. Overfitting can arise by using too many features for a given dataset size. In classical statistics, a rough—though in my experience, conservative—rule of thumb has been to follow another "square root of n" limitation:

$$p < \sqrt{n} \qquad (3.2)$$

That is, the number of features should be less than the square root of the number of data points. Under this criterion, if our data frame has, say, 1,000 rows, it can support about 30 features. This is not a bad rough guide and is supported by theoretical results for parametric models.

However, in modern statistics and ML, it is now common to have—or at least start with—a value of p much larger than n. We will see this with certain methods used later in the book. We'll stick with $p < \sqrt{n}$ as a reasonable starting point. If our data satisfies that rule, we can feel safe. But if p is larger, we should not automatically consider it to be overly large.

3.2 Cross-Validation

The most common approach to choosing the value of hyperparameters or choosing feature sets is to minimize MAPE (numeric-Y case) or the overall misclassification error (OME, classification case). For k-NN and a numeric-Y setting, we may find MAPE for each of a range of candidate values of k and then choose the one producing minimal MAPE.

In deciding what value of k to use, we need to assess the predictive ability of various values of that hyperparameter. But in doing so, we need to make sure we are using a "fresh" dataset to predict. This motivates splitting the data into two sets: a training set and a holdout, or test, set.

However, holdout sets are chosen randomly. This induces additional randomness, on top of the sampling variation we already have. We saw an example of this in Section 1.12.3. So, in choosing k in k-NN, for instance, one holdout set may indicate $k = 5$ as best, while another would favor $k = 12$. To be thorough, we should not rely on a single holdout set. This leads to the method of *K-fold cross-validation*, where we generate many holdout sets, averaging MAPE, OME, or other criterion over all those sets. Note that k, the number of neighbors, is different from K, the number of *folds*, or possible holdout sets.

3.2.1 K-Fold Cross-Validation

To see how K-fold cross-validation works, consider the "leaving one out" method, in which we set a holdout set size of 1. Say we wish to evaluate the predictive ability of $k = 5$. For each of our n data points, we would take the holdout set to be that point and take the remaining $n - 1$ points as our training set; we then predict the holdout point. This gives us n predictions, and we calculate MAPE as the average absolute prediction error among those n predictions. In other words, we would proceed as in the following pseudocode for data frame d:

```
set sumMape = 0
for i = 1,2,...,n
    set training set = d[-i,]
    set test set = d[i,]
    apply k-NN to training set, with k = 5
    predict the test set
    sumMape = sumMape + abs(predicted Y - actual Y)
MAPE = sumMape / n
```

We'd call this *n*-fold cross-validation. Alternatively, we could take our holdout sets to have size 2, say, by partitioning the set $1,2,\ldots,n$ into non-overlapping adjacent pairs. Now there are $n/2$ possible holdout sets (folds). For each fold, we apply k-NN to the remaining data and then predict the data in that fold. MAPE is then the average over the $n/2$ folds.

One might expect that $K = n$ is best, since then MAPE will be based on the most trials. On the other hand, each trial will be based on predicting just 1 data point, which is presumably less accurate. There also may be computational and theoretical issues that we won't go into here. How should we then choose K?

Note that K is not a hyperparameter, as it is not a trait of k-NN. It is simply a matter of how to estimate MAPE reliably. But yes, it's one more thing to think about. Many analysts recommend using a value of 5 or 10.

Another approach is as follows, say, for holdout sets of size 2. We simply choose many random holdout sets, as many as we have time for, as in the following pseudocode:

```
set sumMape = 0
for m = 1,2,...,r
    set test set = a random pair of data points (not necessarily adjacent)
    set training set = the remaining n-2 points
    apply k-NN to training set, with a candidate k
    predict the test set
    sumMape = sumMape + mean(abs(predicted Ys - actual Ys))
MAPE = sumMape / r
```

Here, r is the number of holdout sets. The larger value we choose for r, the more accurate MAPE will be. It just depends on how much computation time we wish to expend. (The plurals, such as predicted Ys, allude to the fact that any holdout set has two Y values to predict.)

3.2.2 Using the replicMeans() Function

We can use the regtools function replicMeans() to implement K-means cross-validation. The function name is short for "replicate an action and then take the mean of the results."

For instance, say we have some data frame d in which we are predicting a column y. Consider the effect of the following call:

```
cmd <- "qeKNN(d,'y')$testAcc"
crossvalOutput <- replicMeans(10,cmd)
```

This says to run cmd 10 times and return the mean of the result. Since the command is to run qeKNN(), 10 runs will use 10 different holdout sets, yielding 10 different values of testAcc. The end result will be that the function returns the average of those 10 values, which is exactly what we want.

3.2.3 Example: Programmer and Engineer Data

Here we will introduce a new dataset, pef, to be used at several points in the book, and illustrate cross-validation on this data.

The pef dataset is included in the regtools package, which in turn is included in qeML. It is drawn from the 2000 US census, showing data on programmers and engineers. Here is a glimpse:

```
> data(pef)
> head(pef)
        age       educ occ sex wageinc wkswrkd
1 50.30082 zzzOther 102   2   75000      52
2 41.10139 zzzOther 101   1   12300      20
3 24.67374 zzzOther 102   2   15400      52
4 50.19951 zzzOther 100   1       0      52
5 51.18112 zzzOther 100   2     160       1
6 57.70413 zzzOther 100   1       0       0
> dim(pef)
[1] 20090    6
```

So, data on a bit more than 20,000 workers is stored here.

The education variable here needs some explanation. The census has codes for education of various levels, down to even none at all. But for this dataset, there won't be many (if any) workers with, say, just a sixth-grade education. For that reason, the educ column here has been simplified to just three levels: master's (code 14), PhD (16), and "other" (coded as zzzOther by the software, regtools::toSubFactor()). Most of the "other" workers have a bachelor's degree, but even those with less have been lumped into this level.

Why do this? The qe*-series functions convert any feature that is an R factor to dummy variables, and for some such functions, the output is displayed in terms of the dummies. So, consolidation as above compactifies output. Even running head() would give very wide output if all education levels were included and dummy variables were displayed.

Second, simplification of this nature may, in general, be needed to avoid overfitting—remember, each dummy variable counts separately in the feature count p—even though in this dataset we are well within the "$p < \sqrt{n}$" rule of thumb.

For detailed information on this dataset, such as the various occupation codes, type ?pef at the R prompt.

3.2.3.1 Improved Estimation of MAPE

Suppose we wish to predict wageinc, wage income, in this pef dataset. Let's take a first cut at it:

```
> z <- qeKNN(pef,'wageinc',k=10)
holdout set has  1000 rows
> z$testAcc
[1] 25296.21
```

On average, our predictions are off by about \$25,300. This is a rather large number, but as emphasized in Section 2.4, we must always gauge prediction accuracy of a feature set compared to predicting *without* the features:

```
> z$baseAcc
[1] 32081.36
```

So, just predicting everyone to have the overall mean income would give us a much larger MAPE.

At any rate, our point here concerns not this particular dataset but the general accuracy of MAPE if the latter is based on just a single holdout set. We really need to look at multiple holdout sets using cross-validation. Let's do that using `replicMeans()`.

```
> cmd <- "qeKNN(pef,'wageinc')$testAcc"
> replicMeans(10,cmd)
holdout set has  1000 rows
holdout set has  1000 rows
holdout set has  1000 rows
holdout set has  1000 rows
holdout set has  1000 rows
holdout set has  1000 rows
holdout set has  1000 rows
holdout set has  1000 rows
holdout set has  1000 rows
holdout set has  1000 rows
[1] 25633.51
attr(,"stderr")
[1] 412.1483
```

So, the indicated `qeKNN()` call was run 10 times, yielding 10 holdout sets, having an average value of about \$25,633 for accuracy on the test set. This is somewhat larger than the \$25,296 figure we had obtained earlier based on just one holdout set. Thus, we should treat this new figure as more reliable.

That \$412 number is the *standard error*. Multiplying it by 1.96 gives us the margin of error. If we feel that is too large, we can call `replicMeans()` with, say, 100 replications (that is, 100 holdout sets).

We could then try other values of k, running `replicMeans()` for each one as above and then finally choosing the value that gives the best MAPE or OME. If we have more than a few such values, it would be easier to use the `qeML` function `qeFT()`, which will be presented in Chapter 7.

3.2.4 Triple Cross-Validation

Suppose we split our data into training and test sets, and then fit many different combinations of hyperparameters, choosing the combination that does best on the test set. Again we run into the problem of potential p-hacking, meaning that the accuracy rates reported in the test set may be overly optimistic.

One common solution is to partition the data into three subsets rather than two, with the intermediate one being termed the *validation set*. We fit the various combinations of hyperparameters to the training set and evaluate them on the validation set. After choosing the best combination, we then evaluate (only) that combination on the test set to obtain an accuracy estimate untainted by p-hacking.

3.3 Conclusions

In summary, the main concepts in this brief but vital chapter are:

- In choosing a hyperparameter such as k-NN's k, and in choosing a feature set, variance and bias are at odds with each other. For a fixed dataset, a small k or large p increases variance while reducing bias, and vice versa.

- With a larger n, we can afford to take a larger value of k or p.

- Unfortunately, there is no hard-and-fast formula for the "Goldilocks" values of k and p. But there are some very rough rules of thumb, and careful use of holdout sets and cross-validation will serve us pretty well. As one gains experience, one also becomes more skilled at this.

Again, use of holdout sets is the main remedy, including using multiple holdout sets if there is concern about accuracy of MAPE or OME on a single set.

4

DEALING WITH LARGE NUMBERS OF FEATURES

In the previous chapter, we talked about *overfitting*—that is, using too many features in a given setting. Having a large number of features may also cause issues with long computation times. This chapter is all about reducing the size of our feature set—in other words, *dimension reduction*.

Note that it's not just a need to use *fewer* features; we also need to decide *which* features, or even which *combinations* of features, to use. We'll cover principal component analysis (PCA), one of the best-known techniques for dealing with large values of p, which is based on forming new features by combining old ones and then using just a few of the new ones as our feature set.

4.1 Pitfall: Computational Issues in Large Datasets

Again, overfitting is a major issue in ML. As noted in the last chapter, plugging the term into Google gave me 6,560,000 results! And, in addition to predictive-accuracy problems of overfitting, we also need to worry about computation. The larger the number of features, the longer our computation will take.

In some cases, computation times can be extremely challenging. For example, one write-up of AlexNet, a neural network for image classification, reported that the network takes *five or six days* to train on two extremely powerful computers.[1]

Moreover, the energy usage in the computation can be staggering.[2] Training a large natural language processing model can use energy whose production results in emission of over 78,000 pounds of CO_2 into the atmosphere. By comparison, the average automobile will emit about 126,000 pounds of CO_2 in its lifetime.

Most readers of this book will not encounter exceptionally large applications like the above. But computation can be a significant problem even on merely "large-ish" datasets, such as some considered in this chapter. Your code's run time—for a single function call—may not be measured in days, but it certainly could run into minutes or, in some cases, even hours.

In addition, a large dataset may use too much memory. A dataset with a million rows and 1,000 columns has a billion elements. At 8 bytes each, that's 8GB of RAM. The amount of memory the algorithm uses may be several multiples of that.

Discussions of dimension reduction seldom mention excessive data loss due to NA values, but it can be a major factor. If there is even one NA value in a given row of our data, most ML software libraries will discard the entire row. The more columns we have, the more likely it is that any given row will have at least one NA value, and thus the more likely the row will be discarded. In other words:

> If our data is prone to NA values, the larger p is, the smaller our effective value of n.

Thus we have yet another incentive to drop some features. This will result in an increase in the number of complete cases included in our analysis, resulting in better prediction ability.

As usual, it's a trade-off: if we remove too many features, some may have substantial predictive ability. So, we hope to discard a few less-important ones.

4.2   Introduction to Dimension Reduction

In this chapter, and in this book generally, our primary tool for attacking the problems posed by big data will be to reduce p, the number of features in our dataset. This is known as *dimension reduction*. While we could take the approach of simply removing features we believe won't be very helpful, there are other, more systematic methods that can be applied.

---

1. *https://medium.com/@smallfishbigsea/a-walk-through-of-alexnet-6cbd137a5637*
2. *https://arxiv.org/pdf/1906.02243.pdf*

Dimension reduction has two goals, which are both equally important:

1. Avoid overfitting. If we don't have $p < \sqrt{n}$ (see Section 3.1.3), we should consider possibly reducing p.

2. Reduce computation. With larger datasets, k-NN and most of the methods in this book will have challenging computational requirements, and one obvious solution is to reduce p.

4.2.1 Example: The Million Song Dataset

Say you've run into a recording of an old song without a label specifying its name and you wish to identify it. The Million Song Dataset allows us to predict a song's release year from 90 audio characteristics, so let's try it out, since knowing the year might help you find the song's title. You can download the data from the UC Irvine Machine Learning Repository.[3] (Actually there are only about 0.5 million songs in this version.)

A dataset of this size may involve a substantial computational burden. Let's investigate that, finding the time to do just a single prediction.

Read in the data from the downloaded file and assign the result to yr.

```
> yr <- read.csv('YearPredictionMSD.txt',header=FALSE)
```

Note that in spite of the *.txt* suffix in the filename, it is actually a CSV file, so we used read.csv().

Also, the above file read was slow. The reader may consider using fread() from the data.table package on large files like this. Here the call would be:

```
> library(data.table)
> yr <- fread('YearPredictionMSD.txt')
> yr <- as.data.frame(yr)
```

Since kNN() requires data frame or R matrix input (Appendix C), we needed that last line to convert from a data.table to a data frame.

Let's take a look:

```
> yr <- read.csv('YearPredictionMSD.txt',header=FALSE)
> yr[1,]
      V1       V2       V3      V4       V5        V6        V7        V8
1 2001 49.94357 21.47114 73.0775 8.74861 -17.40628 -13.09905 -25.01202
         V9      V10      V11     V12      V13      V14      V15      V16
1 -12.23257 7.83089 -2.46783 3.32136 -2.31521 10.20556 611.1091 951.0896
        V17      V18      V19      V20      V21      V22      V23      V24
1 698.1143 408.9848 383.7091 326.5151 238.1133 251.4241 187.1735 100.4265
       V25      V26       V27      V28      V29       V30       V31     V32
1 179.195 -8.41558 -317.8704 95.86266 48.10259 -95.66303 -18.06215 1.96984
        V33      V34     V35     V36      V37       V38       V39       V40
1 34.42438 11.7267 1.3679 7.79444 -0.36994 -133.6785 -83.26165 -37.29765
```

---

3. *https://archive.ics.uci.edu/ml/datasets/yearpredictionmSD*

	V41	V42	V43	V44	V45	V46	V47	V48
1	73.04667	-37.36684	-3.13853	-24.21531	-13.23066	15.93809	-18.60478	82.15479

	V49	V50	V51	V52	V53	V54	V55	V56
1	240.5798	-10.29407	31.58431	-25.38187	-3.90772	13.29258	41.5506	-7.26272

	V57	V58	V59	V60	V61	V62	V63	V64
1	-21.00863	105.5085	64.29856	26.08481	-44.5911	-8.30657	7.93706	-10.7366

	V65	V66	V67	V68	V69	V70	V71	V72
1	-95.44766	-82.03307	-35.59194	4.69525	70.95626	28.09139	6.02015	-37.13767

	V73	V74	V75	V76	V77	V78	V79	V80
1	-41.1245	-8.40816	7.19877	-8.60176	-5.90857	-12.32437	14.68734	-54.32125

	V81	V82	V83	V84	V85	V86	V87	V88
1	40.14786	13.0162	-54.40548	58.99367	15.37344	1.11144	-23.08793	68.40795

	V89	V90	V91
1	-1.82223	-27.46348	2.26327

We see there are over 515,000 rows (that is, 515,000 songs) and 91 columns. That first column is the year of release, followed by 90 columns of arcane audio measurements. That means column 1 is our outcome variable and the remaining 90 columns are (potential) features.

4.2.2 The Need for Dimension Reduction

We have 90 features here. With over 500,000 data points, the rough rule of thumb $p < \sqrt{n}$ from Section 3.1.3 says we probably could use all 90 features without overfitting. But k-NN requires a lot of computation, so dimension is still an important issue.

As an example of the computational burden, let's see how long it takes to predict one data point, say, the first row of our data. As explained in Section 1.17, to predict just one data point, it is faster to call kNN() directly rather than calling its wrapper, qeKNN(). The latter operates on a large scale, which we don't need in this instance, and which will compute many quantities not needed here. (It computes the estimated regression function at every point of the training set. This is effective only if we plan to do a lot of predictions in the future.)

Recall that the arguments of kNN() are the X data, the Y data, the data point to be predicted, and k. Here, then, is the code:

```
> system.time(kNN(yr[,-1],yr[,1],yr[1,-1],25))
   user  system elapsed
 30.866   8.330  39.201
```

That's over 39 seconds just to predict one data point. If we predict a substantial portion of the entire original dataset, say, with holdout = 100000, that means we incur that 39-second wait 100,000 times, which would be prohibitive.

Thus we may want to cut down the size of our feature set, whether out of computational concerns, as was the case here, or in other cases because of a need to avoid overfitting.

Feature selection is yet another aspect of ML that has no perfect solution but for which some pretty good approaches have been developed. Before we get into the main approach this chapter deals with, PCA, let's look at a few other techniques to get a better sense of the challenges we face when selecting features.

4.3 Methods for Dimension Reduction

Now that we see the need for dimension reduction, how can we achieve it? We'll cover a few approaches here: consolidation and embedding, *all-possible subsets*, and PCA. These are generally applicable, and we will present some techniques for some specific ML methods later in the book.

4.3.1 Consolidation and Embedding

Economists talk of *proxy* variables. We may wish to have data on some variable U but, lacking it, use instead a variable V for which we do have data and that captures much of the essence of U. V is said to be a "proxy" for U. Related techniques in ML are *consolidation* and *embedding*.

In the context of dimension reduction, proxies can have a different use. Say we do have data on U, but this variable is categorical with a huge number of categories (that is, a huge number of levels in the R factor implementation of the variable). That would mean having a huge number of dummy variables, or high dimension. One way to reduce dimension in such settings would be to combine levels, yielding a new categorical variable V with fewer dummies. Or even better, we may be able to use a numerical V, thus no dummies, just that one variable.

Again consider the ZIP code example of Section 3.1.1, where the hypothetical goal was to estimate parka sales. If there were 42,000 ZIP codes, then in terms of dummy variables, we would have 42,000 dummies. We might cut that down by, say, choosing to use only the first digit of the ZIP code. That would mean, for instance, combining levels 90000, 90001, ..., 99999 in a single level, 9. (Not all of those ZIP codes actually exist, but the principle is the same.) The ZIP codes for UC Davis and UCLA, 95616 and 90024, respectively, would now both reduce to simply 9.

Obviously, this would result in loss of information; it would induce some bias into the Bias-Variance Trade-off. But we would still get fairly good geographic detail—for instance, the 9s are all on the West Coast—for the purpose of, say, predicting parka purchases. That way, we'd have a lot of data points for each of the 10 (abbreviated) ZIP codes 0 through 9, thus reducing variance.

This would reduce 42,000 dummies to 9. Better yet, we might choose to use an *embedding*. We could fetch the average daily winter temperature per ZIP code from government data sites (remember, we're selling parkas), and use that temperature instead of ZIP code as our feature. Now we would have only 1 feature, not 42,000, and not even 9.

4.3.2 The All Possible Subsets Method

One might think, "To choose a good feature set, why not look at all possible subsets of features? We would find MAPE or OME for each one and then use the subset that minimizes that quantity." This is called the *All Possible Subsets Method*.

In the song dataset, for instance, in predicting holdout data, we would proceed as follows: for each subset of our 90 columns, we could predict our holdout set, then use the set of columns with the best prediction record. There are two big problems here:

1. We'd need tons of computation time. The 2-feature sets alone would number over 4,000. The number of feature sets of all sizes is 2^{90}, one of those absurd figures like "number of atoms in the universe" that one often sees in the press.

2. We'd risk serious p-hacking issues. The chance of some pair of columns accidentally looking very accurate in predicting release year is probably very high.

4.3.3 Principal Components Analysis

But this method isn't infeasible after all if we change our features by using one of the most popular approaches to dimension reduction: PCA. In the song data, for instance, instead of having to investigate an impossible 2^{90} number of subsets, we need look only at 90. Here is how it works.

To apply PCA to the Million Song Dataset, we will replace our 90 features with 90 new ones, to be constructed as 90 combinations of the originals. In our data frame, we'd replace the 90 original feature columns with these 90 new features, known as *principal components (PCs)*.

Sounds like no gain, right? We are hoping to *reduce* the number of features, whereas in the above scenario we simply swapped one set of 90 features for another set of that size. But as will be seen below, we will accomplish that goal by using the All Possible Subsets Method on these new features, though in a certain ordering.

Our first subset to check will be PC1; then the pair PC1 and PC2; then the triple PC1, PC2, PC3; and so on. That means only 90 subsets in all, and typically we stop well short of 90 anyway.

You'll see that it will be a lot easier to choose subsets among these new features than among the original 90.

4.3.3.1 PC Properties

The PCs have two special properties. First, they are uncorrelated; roughly speaking, the value of one has no effect on the others. In that sense, we might think of them as not duplicating each other. Why is that important? If, after reducing our number of predictors, some of them were to partially duplicate each other, it would seem that we should reduce the number even further. Thus having uncorrelated features means unduplicated features, and we feel like we've achieved a minimal, nonduplicative set.

Second, the PCs are arranged in order of decreasing variance. Since a feature with small variance is essentially constant, it probably won't be a useful feature. Accordingly, we might retain just the PCs that are of substantial variance. Since the variances are ordered, that means retaining, say, the m PCs having the largest variances. Note that m then becomes another hyperparameter.

Each PC is a *linear combination* of our original features—that is, a PC is a sum of constants times the features. If, for instance, the latter were Height, Weight, and Age, a PC might be 0.12 Height + 0.59 Weight − 0.02 Age. Recall from algebra that these numbers, 0.12, 0.59, and −0.02, are called *coefficients*.

In ML, one's focus is prediction rather than description. For instance, in the bike rental data, someone may be interested in investigating *how* the features affect ridership, say, how many extra riders we might have on holidays. That would be a description application, which is not usually a concern in ML. So, those coefficients, such as 0.12, 0.59, and −0.02, are not very relevant for us. Instead, the point is that we are creating new features as combinations of the original ones, and we may not examine the coefficients themselves.

With these new features, we have many fewer candidate sets to choose from: the first PC, the first two PCs, the first three PCs, and so on. We are choosing from just 90 candidate feature sets rather than the unimaginable 2^{90} we would have if we looked at all possible subsets. We can choose among those subsets using cross-validation or another method introduced below. Remember, smaller sets save computation time (for k-NN now and other methods later) and help avoid overfitting and p-hacking.

4.3.3.2 PCA in the Million Song Dataset

Base-R includes several functions to do PCA, including the one we'll use here, prcomp(). CRAN also has packages that implement especially fast PCA algorithms, such as RSpectra, which are very useful for large datasets.

We'll mainly use qePCA(), a regtools function that wraps prcomp(), but you should get at least some exposure to the latter function itself, as follows. Here is the call:

```
> pcout <- prcomp(yr[,-1])
```

Remember, PCA is for the X data, not Y, so we skipped the year field here, which is in column 1.

As an example, let's say we've decided to use the first 20 PCs. We do this by retaining the first 20 columns of the rotation component of the output, which contains the coefficients of the PCs (such as the 0.59 and so on above). Let's first understand this component:

```
> rt <- pcout$rotation
> dim(rt)
[1] 90 90
> rt[1:10,1:10]
```

	PC1	PC2	PC3	PC4	PC5
V2	-1.492918e-03	-0.0001759914	0.0006706243	-0.0005624011	-0.0027970362
V3	-6.293541e-03	0.0064782264	0.0027845347	-0.0051094877	-0.0239474483
V4	-4.794322e-03	-0.0034153809	-0.0066157025	-0.0044176142	0.0071294386
V5	2.143497e-03	0.0041913051	0.0022151336	-0.0016482743	-0.0087460406
V6	3.013464e-03	0.0013071748	-0.0013400543	0.0032640501	0.0028682836
V7	1.892908e-03	0.0052421454	0.0031921120	-0.0003470488	0.0028807861
V8	-1.518245e-04	-0.0001992038	-0.0004968169	0.0010151582	-0.0061954012
V9	3.160014e-04	0.0009142221	-0.0001189277	-0.0008729237	0.0014144888
V10	-7.203671e-04	-0.0001721222	0.0003838908	-0.0012362764	-0.0009607571
V11	3.348651e-05	0.0011663312	0.0003964205	-0.0008766769	-0.0002092245

	PC6	PC7	PC8	PC9	PC10
V2	3.227906e-04	-0.0012293820	0.0009259120	-0.0009496448	0.0007397941
V3	-1.247137e-02	-0.0185123792	0.0122138115	-0.0186672476	0.0099506738
V4	-9.063568e-03	0.0160957668	0.0123209033	-0.0018904928	-0.0039866354
V5	2.708827e-03	-0.0085000743	-0.0070522158	0.0008992783	0.0003743787
V6	-7.412826e-03	-0.0003856357	0.0003811818	-0.0002785585	0.0022809304
V7	9.840927e-05	-0.0009025075	-0.0006593167	0.0032070603	0.0024775608
V8	3.425829e-03	-0.0038602270	-0.0040122340	0.0005974108	0.0009542331
V9	-1.280174e-03	0.0032705198	0.0059051252	-0.0025076692	-0.0049897536
V10	-4.725944e-05	-0.0035063179	-0.0002710257	-0.0016148579	0.0007367726
V11	-1.940717e-03	-0.0015004583	0.0036280402	-0.0025576335	-0.0025080611

So, rt has 90 rows and 90 columns, with numerical entries. We see that the names of the rows and columns are V2, V3, ..., and PC1, PC2, ..., respectively. The row names come from our feature names (the first is *Y*, not a feature):

```
> names(yr)
 [1] "V1"  "V2"  "V3"  "V4"  "V5"  "V6"  "V7"  "V8"  "V9"  "V10" "V11" "V12"
[13] "V13" "V14" "V15" "V16" "V17" "V18" "V19" "V20" "V21" "V22" "V23" "V24"
...
[85] "V85" "V86" "V87" "V88" "V89" "V90" "V91"
```

The column names are for the PCs. We have 90 features, thus 90 PCs, named PC1, PC2, and so on.

In this example, we have said that we want to use only the first 20 PCs for dimension reduction. Thus we will discard columns PC21 through PC90 in rt:

```
> pcout$rotation <- rt[,1:20]
```

So, we're now using only those first 20 PCs. Now we convert our original data accordingly:

```
> pcX <- predict(pcout,yr[,-1])
```

This is our new *X* data. We'll look at how to use it shortly, but first, what happened in that predict() call? The function is not actually predicting anything here. It simply converts the original features to new ones. Let's take a closer look at that.

First, recall that, in R, predict() is a *generic* function (see Section 1.5.1). The prcomp() function returns an object of class 'prcomp' (check this by typing class(pcout) for the data above). So, the call to predict() here gets relayed to predict.prcomp(), which the R people wrote for the purpose here—to do conversion from old features to new ones.

So, our call predict(pcout,yr[,-1]) tells R, "Please convert the features in yr[,-1] to PC features, based on what's in pcout." Since we previously had altered pcout$rotation to use just 20 PCs, now calling predict() on pcout will generate a new 20-column data frame to use instead of our original 90-column one:

```
> dim(pcX)
[1] 515345     20
```

We have the same number of rows as in the old *X*—as we should since it's still the song data (albeit transformed), with 515,345 songs. But now we have 20 columns instead of 90, representing the fact that we now have only 20 features. Note, by the way, that none of these new columns was a column in yr; each new column is a certain mixture of the original ones.

Now, how would we do k-NN prediction using PCA? Imagine that we have a new case whose 90 audio measures are the same as the eighth song in our dataset, except that there is a value 32.6 in the first column. Let's store that in w.

```
> w <- yr[8,-1]
> w[1] <- 32.6
```

Since we changed our *X* data in our training set to PCA form, we'll do the same for w:

```
> newW <- predict(pcout,w)
> newW
          PC1       PC2       PC3      PC4      PC5       PC6       PC7      PC8
8 -1129.298 -168.8051 -368.4595 567.6397 -424.265 -291.5593 -168.7774 17.12907
          PC9      PC10      PC11     PC12     PC13     PC14     PC15      PC16
8  243.8396 -134.2792 -35.67449 191.6426 37.70002 50.17716 -66.3604 -72.97002
         PC17      PC18     PC19     PC20
8  -131.9982 -223.3206 -50.0114 52.04066
```

We would then call qeKNN() on our new data.

To do so directly, though, would be tedious, and we'll usually use the labor-saving qePCA() function instead. But let's put prediction aside for the moment while we discuss the issue of choosing the number of PCs to use.

4.3.4 But Now We Have Two Hyperparameters

Before now, to attain the most accurate predictions, we only needed to try a range of values for the number of nearest neighbors k, but in this case, we'll have to test a range of values for both k and the number of PCs m. It's nothing new, of course, since we always needed to decide which features to use; overfitting can arise from having both too small a value of k and too many features. Now, by converting to PCA, we at least have formalized the latter in a hyperparameter m. So, we've actually made life a little easier.

Say we try each of 10 k values paired with each of 10 m values and find the holdout MAPE for each pair. We would then choose to use the pair with the smallest MAPE. But that's 10 × 10 = 100 pairs to try, say, with K-fold cross-validation applied to each pair (that is, running many holdout sets for each pair).

Recall there are two major problems with this. First, each pair will take substantial computation time, making for a very long total run time, and second, we should be concerned about potential p-hacking (see Section 1.13): one of those 100 pairs may seem to predict song release year especially accurately, simply by coincidence.

As an alternative, we might try to choose m directly. A common intuitive approach is to look at the variances of the PCs (squares of standard deviations). A variable with small variance is essentially constant and thus presumably of little or no use in predicting Y. So, the idea is to discard PCs having small variance. Let's take a look:

```
> pcout$sdev^2
 [1] 4.471212e+06 1.376757e+06 8.730969e+05 4.709903e+05
 [5] 2.951400e+05 2.163123e+05 1.701326e+05 1.553153e+05
 [9] 1.477271e+05 1.206304e+05 1.099533e+05 9.319449e+04
...
```

That e notation means powers of 10. The first one, for instance, means 4.471212×10^6.

We see the variances rapidly decrease. The twelfth one is about 90,000, which is tiny relative to the first, at over 4 million. We might therefore decide to take $m = 12$. Once we've done that, we are back to the case of choosing just one hyperparameter, k.

There is still no magic formula for choosing the number of PCs m, but the point is that once we decide on a value of m, we can now choose k separately. We may, for instance, choose m in this intuitive manner and then use cross-validation to get k. This may be easier than finding the best (k, m) pair simultaneously.

It is common for analysts to look at those variances as a cumulative proportion of the total. Here R's cumsum() (cumulative sums) function will come in handy. This is how that function works:

```
> u <- c(12,5,13)
> cumsum(u)   # 12+5 = 17, 12+5+13 = 30
[1] 12 17 30
```

```
> cumsum(u) / length(u)   # convert to proportions
[1]  4.000000  5.666667 10.000000
```

Let's apply that to the PC variances:

```
> pcsds <- pcout$sdev^2
> cumsum(pcsds) / sum(pcsds)
 [1] 0.4691291 0.6135814 0.7051886 0.7546059 0.7855726 0.8082685 0.8261192
 [8] 0.8424152 0.8579151 0.8705719 0.8821084 0.8918866 0.9003893 0.9075907
[15] 0.9146712 0.9212546 0.9269892 0.9324882 0.9376652 0.9416823 0.9455962
[22] 0.9493949 0.9530321 0.9564536 0.9597000 0.9627476 0.9653836 0.9678344
[29] 0.9700491 0.9720936 0.9739898 0.9756223 0.9771978 0.9785780 0.9799187
[36] 0.9811843 0.9824226 0.9836061 0.9847728 0.9858420 0.9868994 0.9879009
[43] 0.9888200 0.9896491 0.9904612 0.9912403 0.9919651 0.9926362 0.9932901
[50] 0.9938841 0.9944387 0.9949139 0.9953413 0.9957644 0.9961658 0.9965495
[57] 0.9968947 0.9971970 0.9974792 0.9977482 0.9979897 0.9982232 0.9984284
[64] 0.9985960 0.9987592 0.9989146 0.9990633 0.9992035 0.9993261 0.9994199
[71] 0.9995115 0.9995965 0.9996681 0.9997329 0.9997858 0.9998289 0.9998700
[78] 0.9999061 0.9999277 0.9999483 0.9999608 0.9999708 0.9999792 0.9999856
[85] 0.9999907 0.9999948 0.9999974 0.9999987 0.9999996 1.0000000
```

So, if, for example, we were to take $m = 12$, our chosen PCs would make up about 89 percent of total variance in this data. Or we might think that's too much dimension reduction and opt for, say, a 95 percent cutoff, thus using $m = 23$ PCs.

NOTE   *Note the phrasing "might," "if, for example," and "say" here. As we've seen before, for many things in ML, there are no mechanical, formulaic "recipes" for one's course of action. Once again, keep in mind that ML is an art, not a science. And one becomes skilled in that art with experience, not by recipes.*

4.3.5   Using the qePCA() Wrapper

Our goal, then, is to first use PCA for dimension reduction and then do our k-NN prediction with the first m PCs as features. To do this, the following rather elaborate set of actions would need to be performed. Fortunately, there is a function to automate these steps, but as usual, we need to understand those steps first before turning to the convenience function.

Say the X and Y portions of our training data are stored in trnX and trnY, respectively.

1. We call prcomp(trnX) to calculate the PC coefficients. Let's name this result pcout, as above.

2. We limit the number of columns in pcout$rotation to reflect the desired number of PCs.

3. We call predict(pcout,trnX) to convert our X data to PC form, say, pcX. Now our new training set consists of pcX and trnY.

4. We now apply qeKNN() on pcX and trnY. Say we name the result knnout.

5. Subsequently, when new *X* data comes in, say, `newX`, we would first call `predict(pcout,newX)` to convert to PC form. Say we name the results `pcNewx`.

6. For our *Y* prediction, we then call `predict(knnout,pcNewX)` to obtain our predicted *Y*.

By the way, did you notice that we are using `predict()` in two different ways here, one to convert to PC form and another to do k-NN prediction? Here we see the R concept of generic functions in action. In that first context, R relays the `predict()` call to `predict.prcomp()`, while in the second, the relay is to `predict.qeKNN()`.

There are a lot of steps in the procedure above, but it does have a pattern, which implies that we should automate it with code. That is the purpose of the wrapper function `qePCA()`.

With `qePCA()`, one specifies the data and *Y* column name, as in other qe*-series functions, and also specifies the following: the desired ML method (say, k-NN), the usual hyperparameters for that method (*k*), and the desired proportion of total variance for the PCs.

For instance, the call

```
z <- qePCA(yr,'V1','qeKNN',opts=list(k=25),0.85)
```

states that we want to predict the year (`V1`) in the song data using k-NN and $k = 25$. It also says we want as many PCs as will give us 85 percent of the total variance of the features.

So, how well do we predict using $k = 25$ and 85 percent total variance?

```
> z$testAcc
[1] 7.373
```

In guessing which year a song was released, we will, on average, be off by about 7 years.

To later predict a new case—say, `w`, the example song we used in Section 4.3.3.2—we would make the call:

```
> w <- yr[8,-1]
> w[1] <- 32.6
> predict(z,w)
        [,1]
[1,] 1994.96
```

So, we'd guess that such a song was released around the year 1995.

All of this is far simpler than the above multistep process; `qePCA()` saves us a lot of work!

4.3.6   PCs and the Bias-Variance Trade-off

Now that we know how to use PCA for dimension reduction and subsequent prediction, let's return to the issue of how to choose the number of nearest neighbors k and number of PCs m. Note that choosing m is equivalent to choosing the variance proportion in the last argument in qePCA().

As usual, we have a bias-variance issue, for both k and m. We've discussed the trade-off in terms of k before; what about m?

Actually, the situation for m is not new either. Recall what we said in Section 3.1.1 regarding the mlb dataset:

> We might predict weight from height and age. But what if we were to omit height from our feature set? That would induce a bias. Roughly speaking, we'd be tacitly assuming everyone is of middling height, which would result in our tending to overpredict the weight of shorter players while underpredicting that of the taller ones.

In other words, omitting a feature induces a bias. Or, equivalently, adding features reduces bias. Since the PCs *are* features, we see that the more PCs we use, the smaller the bias. But that same section goes on to point out that the more features we have, the higher the variance in our predictions, which is not good. Note, too, that using more PCs results in longer computation time.

To illustrate this, let's devise a little experiment to investigate the effect of varying m, the number of PCs.

Since our song dataset is rather large, let's consider a random subset and see how well we do with proportions of total variance at various levels. We'll use a subset of, say, 25,000, and check computation time and prediction accuracy:

```
set.seed <- 9999
yr1 <- yr[sample(1:nrow(yr),25000),]  # extract 25,000 random rows
res <- matrix(nrow=9,ncol=4)
for (i in 1:9) {  # loop to do proportions 0.05, 0.15,..., 0.95
    pcaProp <- 0.05 + i*0.10
    st <- system.time(z <- qePCA(yr1,'V1','qeKNN',opts=list(k=25),pcaProp))
    res[i,1] <- pcaProp
    res[i,2] <- st[3]  # the actual elapsed run time
    res[i,3] <- z$qeOut$testAcc
    res[i,4] <- z$numPCs  # m
}
```

The results are shown in Table 4-1. The first column shows the proportion of total variance, leading to a number of PCs m shown in the fourth column. In viewing the latter, remember that the full number of possible PCs is 90. The second column shows run time. It increases with m, of course; a larger m means k-NN must do more computation.

The most important column in this investigation is the third, the MAPE values. We see that for a large increase in computation time, we attain only a moderate reduction in MAPE. Moreover, the best MAPE uses only 11 of the 90 PCs.

However, always keep in mind that these MAPE values are subject to sampling variation. They come from holdout sets, and as you know, holdout sets are randomly chosen. For each variance proportion level, we should look at several holdout sets, not just one, using cross-validation. We could do this by applying `replicMeans()` to the `qePCA()` call, though it would be time-consuming.

That means we cannot be sure that $m = 11$ is best. At the least, though, we see that the data indicates that we should probably use a lot fewer than 90 PCs. Also, in addition to the famous Bias-Variance Trade-off, there is the trade-off involving the analyst's time. We may feel that setting $m = 11$ is good enough.

Table 4-1: Behavior for Different Values of m

pcaProp	Time (s.)	MAPE	# of PCs
0.15	1.137	8.40020	2
0.25	1.230	7.83712	3
0.35	2.051	8.12444	6
0.45	7.222	7.46536	11
0.55	17.812	7.88648	16
0.65	35.269	7.66808	24
0.75	51.041	7.55740	33
0.85	72.916	7.85736	46
0.95	94.761	7.72288	66

Furthermore, remember as discussed in Section 3.1.2, the larger n is, the larger we can afford to make p. In the above analysis, we had $n = 25000$ and $p = m$ and settled on $m = 11$. But for the full dataset, $n = 500000$, presumably we should use more than 11 PCs.

Thus, we may be tempted to run the above code on the full dataset. Yet even for $n = 25000$, the run time was about half an hour; it would be many hours for the full dataset of more than 500,000 records. So, we may just settle for $m = 11$ and possibly do a more refined analysis later if time permits.

4.4 The Curse of Dimensionality

The *Curse of Dimensionality (CoD)* says that ML gets harder and harder as the number of features grows. For instance, mathematical theory shows that in high dimensions, every point is approximately the same distance to every other point. Let's briefly discuss the intuition underlying this bizarre situation. Clearly, it has implications for k-NN, which relies on distances, and indeed for some, if not all, other ML methods as well.

To get a rough idea of the CoD, consider data consisting of students' grades in mathematics, literature, history, geography, and so on. The distance between the data vectors of Students A and B would be the square root of

$$(\text{math grade}_A - \text{math grade}_B)^2 + (\text{lit grade}_A - \text{lit grade}_B)^2 +$$
$$(\text{history grade}_A - \text{history grade}_B)^2 + (\text{geo grade}_A - \text{geo grade}_B)^2$$

That expression is a sum, and one can show that sums with a large number of terms (only four here, but we could have many more) have small standard deviations relative to their means. A quantity with small standard deviation is nearly constant, so in high dimensions—that is, in settings with large p (a large number of features)—distances are nearly constant.

This is why k-NN fares poorly in high dimensions. This issue is not limited to k-NN; much of the ML toolbox has similar problems. The computation of linear/logistic regression (see Chapter 8) involves a sum of p terms, and similar computations arise in support vector machines and neural networks.

In fact, lots of problems arise in high dimensions. Some analysts lump them all together into the CoD. Whatever one counts as CoD, clearly, higher dimensions are a challenge—all the more reason to perform dimension reduction.

4.5 Other Methods of Dimension Reduction

Dimension reduction is one of the most actively researched and debated issues in ML and statistics. While this chapter focused on PCA, a common approach to the problem, there are a number of other approaches.

4.5.1 Feature Ordering by Conditional Independence

One approach that I find useful (and contributed slightly to its development) is *Feature Ordering by Conditional Independence (FOCI)*. It is based on solid mathematical principles (too complex to explain here) and works quite well, I've found.

The qeML package includes a FOCI wrapper, qeFOCI. Here is the call in its basic form:

```
qeFOCI(data,yName)
```

Since the computational requirement can be large for this method, there are also parallelized options, such as the following:

```
qeFOCI(data,yName,parPlat='locThreads')
```

This will split the computation into chunks, with each of your computer's cores working on one chunk.

Let's try FOCI on the census data from Section 3.2.3:

```
> qeFOCI(pef,'wageinc')
$selectedVar
    index   names
 1:    10 wkswrkd
 2:     1     age
 3:     6 occ.102
 4:     2 educ.14
 5:     3 educ.16
 6:     5 occ.101
 7:     4 occ.100
 8:     9   sex.1
 9:     8 occ.140
10:     7 occ.106


$stepT
 [1] 0.1909457 0.2373486 0.2501502 0.2736589 0.2838555 0.2879643 0.2946782
 [8] 0.2978845 0.2985381 0.3004416

attr(,"class")
[1] "foci"
```

Note that qeFOCI() converts R factors to dummy variables. So, we see assessment of, for instance, each of the occupations. The one coded 102 seems to have good predictive power, while occupation 106 perhaps less so.

The stepT component of the output gives a type of correlation; the more predictors we add, the greater the predictive collective power of the variables. If we wish to be more conservative, we might cut off our choice when this correlation seems to level off, say, after 6 or 7 variables in this case.

How about the song data? To ease the computational burden, I took a 10 percent subsample of the data and ran with 2 cores. Yet even then, it ran for more than 20 minutes:

```
> yr1 <- yr[sample(1:nrow(yr),50000),]
> system.time(z <- qeFOCI(yr1,'V1',numCores=2,parPlat='locThreads'))
[[1]]
 [1]  1 14  2  3  9 10  5  4 21  6 17 13 22

[[2]]
 [1]  1 14  3  2 50 16 40 23 21

   user  system elapsed
 79.873  10.489 1253.839
> z
$selectedVar
```

```
      index names
1:       1    V2
2:      14   V15
3:       3    V4
4:       2    V3
5:      50   V51

$stepT
 [1] 0.0496876 0.1006503 0.1306439 0.1547381 0.1695977 0.1687346 0.0000000
 [8] 0.0000000 0.0000000 0.0000000 0.0000000 0.0000000 0.0000000 0.0000000
...
```

There were 2 cores used, and each applied FOCI to its chunk of data. The first core chose variables 1, 14, 2, and so on, while the second chose some of the same variables but also different ones; for instance, the second core chose variable 50, but the first did not. We designed the parallel version of the algorithm to take the union of the two sets of variables, so variable 50 does appear in the final list. Only the top 7 were chosen, though, as the correlation did not increase past that point.

4.5.2   Uniform Manifold Approximation and Projection

The Uniform Manifold Approximation and Projection (UMAP) method is similar in usage pattern to PCA in that we find new variables as functions of the original ones and then retain only the top few in terms of predictive ability. The difference, though, is that with UMAP, the new variables are complex nonlinear functions of the old ones.

The qeML package has a wrapper for UMAP, qeUMAP(). As noted, it is used in a similar manner to qePCA(). We will not pursue this further here in the book, but the reader is urged to give it a try.

4.6 Going Further Computationally

For very large datasets, I highly recommend the data.table package. The bigmemory package can help with memory limitations, though it is for specialists who understand computers at the operating system level. Also, for those who know SQL databases, there are several packages that interface to such data, such as RSQLite and dplyr.

4.7 Conclusions

In this chapter, we've developed an understanding of how computation issues interact with the Bias-Variance Trade-off when we work with large-scale data. We may, for instance, wish to restrict our number of features well before reaching the point at which adding more variables is statistically unprofitable. Our featured remedy here has been PCA, though we have briefly cited others.

PART II

TREE-BASED METHODS

Here we cover *tree methods*, which are extensions of the neighborhood concept. As we move into these and other sophisticated models, we'll bring in a more sophisticated tool for hyperparameter selection, the qeML function qeFT().

Chapter 5 introduces decision trees, one of the earliest ML methods, which is still very popular today. This leads to two even more popular methods, random forests and gradient boosting, which are covered in Chapter 6.

5

A STEP BEYOND K-NN: DECISION TREES

In k-NN, we looked at the neighborhood of the data point to be predicted. Here again we will look at neighborhoods, but in a more sophisticated way. This approach will be easy to implement and explain, lends itself to nice pictures, and has more available hyperparameters with which to fine-tune it.

Here we will introduce *decision trees (DTs)*, one of the mainstays in the ML field. Besides being used directly, DTs are also the basis for *random forests* and *gradient boosting*, which we will cover in later chapters.

5.1 Basics of Decision Trees

Though some ideas had been proposed earlier, the DT approach became widely used due to the work of statisticians Leo Breiman, Jerry Friedman, Richard Olshen, and Chuck Stone. They called their method *classification and regression trees (CART)* and described it in their book *Classification and Regression Trees* (Wadsworth, 1984).

A DT method basically sets up the prediction process as a flow chart, hence the name *decision tree*. For instance, look at Figure 5-1 in Section 5.2.1. There we are predicting ozone level from features such as temperature and wind speed. In predicting a new case, we start at the top of the tree and follow some path to the bottom, making decisions along the way as to whether to turn left or right. At the bottom of the tree, we make our prediction.

We produce a tree using our training set data. The top of the tree (the *root node*) contains all of that data. We then split the data into two parts according to whether some feature is smaller or larger than a given value. This creates two new nodes, below and to the left or right of the root node. Then we split each of *those* parts into two further parts and so on. Thus an alternative name for the process is *recursive partitioning*.

At each step, we have the option of stopping—that is, making no further splits along that particular path or branch within the tree. In that case, the non-split node is called a *leaf* or *terminal node* of the tree. Any given branch of the tree will end at some leaf node.

In the end, to predict a new case, we start at the root of the tree and work our way down to a leaf. Our predicted Y value then depends on the type of application. In numeric-Y cases, our predicted Y is then the average of all the Y values in that node. For classification applications, our predicted Y value is the class that is most numerous in the given leaf node. Or equivalently, express Y as dummy variables and take the average of each dummy. This gives us the probabilities of the various classes, and we set the predicted class to be the one of largest probability.

It is in this sense that DTs are analogous to k-NN. A leaf node serves as analogous to the neighborhood concept of k-NN.

Various schemes have been devised to decide (a) *whether* to split a given node in the tree, and (b) if so, *how* to do the split. More on this shortly.

5.2   The qeDT() Function

R's CRAN repository has several DT packages, but two I like especially are partykit and its earlier version, party. (These names are a pun on the term *recursive partitioning*.) Our qe*-series function qeDT() wraps party::ctree(). To illustrate, let's run an example from the package.

The dataset here, airquality, is built into R and looks like this:

```
> head(airquality)
  Ozone Solar.R Wind Temp Month Day
1    41     190  7.4   67     5   1
2    36     118  8.0   72     5   2
3    12     149 12.6   74     5   3
4    18     313 11.5   62     5   4
5    NA      NA 14.3   56     5   5
6    28      NA 14.9   66     5   6
7    23     299  8.6   65     5   7
```

Our goal is to predict ozone level from the other features:

```
> airq <- subset(airquality, !is.na(Ozone))  # remove rows with Y NAs
> dim(airq)
[1] 116   6
> dtout <- qeDT(airq,'Ozone',holdout=NULL)
```

Since this is such a small dataset, we decided against having a holdout set.

We predict new data points as usual (after all, the qe*-series is supposed to give a uniform interface to the various functions they wrap). Say we have a new day to predict, with values the same as in airq[1,] but with wind at 8.8 miles per hour. What value would we predict for the ozone level?

```
> w <- airq[1,-1]
> w[2] <- 8.8
> w
  Solar.R Wind Temp Month Day
1     190  8.8   67     5   1
> predict(dtout,w)
        Ozone
[1,] 18.47917
```

We would predict ozone at about 18.5 parts per million.

As you know, qe*-series functions are wrappers, and their return objects usually include a component containing the return object from the wrapped function. This is the case here for qeDT():

```
> names(dtout)
[1] "ctout"    "classif"   "trainRow1"
```

Here ctout is the object returned by ctree() when the latter is invoked from qeDT(). By the way, ctout is of class 'party'.

We are using default hyperparameters here and might get better predictions with a better set of them. More on this in Section 5.6, but let's focus now on how the tree process works by plotting the flow chart.

5.2.1 Looking at the Plot

Most DT packages allow you to plot the tree, which sometimes can provide useful insights for the analyst. In our setting here, though, we will use the plot to gain a better understanding of how the DT process works.

The call is simple:

```
> plot(dtout)
```

As mentioned before, plot() is an R *generic function* (that is, a placeholder). The above call is dispatched to plot.qeDT(dtout). And since the latter has been written to call plot() on the ctout component, in the end, that plot() call above will eventually be dispatched to plot.party().

Figure 5-1 shows the plot. As we are just getting an overview now, don't try to grasp the entire picture in a single glance.

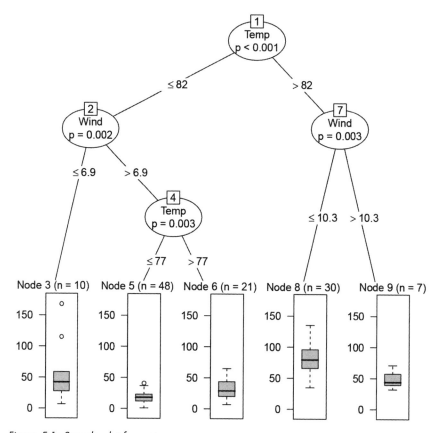

Figure 5-1: Sample plot from ctree

A DT indeed takes the form of a flow chart. For a day with given levels of Solar.R, Wind, and so on, what value should we predict for Ozone? The graph shows our prediction procedure.

Now let's see what happens when we predict a new point, say, w from above. We start at the root, Node 1, and look at Temp. Since the value of the latter for w is 67, which is smaller than 82 degrees, we go left, to Node 2. There we ask whether Wind is less than or equal to 6.9 miles per hour. It's 8.8, so we go right, to Node 4, where we are told to compare Temp to 77. Again, the value in w is 67, so we go left, to Node 5.

We saw earlier that our predicted value was 18.47917. How did the tree produce this from Node 5?

Our predicted value will be the mean *Y* value for all training set data points in Node 5. There is information in dtout as to which data points are in that node. Specifically, the termNodeMembers component of qeDT() output is an R list, with one element for each tree node. To gain an understanding of the workings of that function, let's check Node 5 "by hand":

```
> dtout$termNodeMembers[['5']]
 [1]   1   2   3   4   5   6   7   8  10  11  12
[12]  13  14  15  16  17  18  19  20  21  22  23
[23]  26  31  32  33  34  35  45  74  76  79  80
[34]  96  97  99 101 102 104 105 106 108 109 111
[45] 112 114 115 116
```

We see that 48 data points of airq ended up in Node 5, specifically the points airq[1,], airq[2,], and so on. DT then computes the mean Y for these points:

```
> node5indices <- dtout$termNodeMembers[['5']]
> mean(airq$Ozone[node5indices])
[1] 18.47917
```

This matches the value we obtained from predict().

5.3   Example: New York City Taxi Data

Let's try all this on a larger dataset. Fortunately for us data analysts, the New York City Taxi and Limousine Commmission makes available voluminous data on taxi trips in the city.[1] A small portion of that data is available as yell10k in the regtools package.

That dataset consists of 10,000 random records from the January 2019 dataset. It retains only 7 of the original 18 features, and some date conversion has been done.

It would be nice if taxi operators had an app to predict travel time, which many passengers may wish to know. This will be our goal here.

Here's the data:

```
> data(yell10k)
> head(yell10k)
        passenger_count trip_distance PULocationID DOLocationID PUweekday
2969561               1          1.37          236           43         1
7301968               2          0.71          238          238         4
3556729               1          2.80          100          263         3
7309631               2          2.62          161          249         4
3893911               1          1.20          236          163         5
4108506               5          2.40          161          164         5
        tripTime
2969561      598
7301968      224
3556729      761
7309631      888
3893911      648
4108506      977
```

---

1. *https://www.nyc.gov/site/tlc/about/tlc-trip-record-data.page*

Here PU and DO mean "pickup" and "dropoff." Trip distance is in miles, and trip time is in seconds.

On the other hand, trip distance is not enough; the pickup and dropoff locations are important, as some parts of the city may be slower to navigate than others. The original data also had time of day, which is important but not used here for simplicity.

5.3.1 Pitfall: Too Many Combinations of Factor Levels

Now, note the location IDs:

```
> length(unique(yell10k$PULocationID))
[1] 143
> length(unique(yell10k$DOLocationID))
[1] 205
> 143*205
[1] 29315
```

There are potentially 29,315 pickup and dropoff combinations! Since we have only $n = 10000$ data points, we risk serious overfitting problems. And at the very least, having so many potential tree nodes will affect run time on the training set.

Furthermore, when I tried this with the partykit package rather than party, I encountered an error message: "Too many levels." The documentation recommends using party in such cases, but even then we would likely run into trouble with larger datasets of this type.

This suggests possible use of consolidation or embedding (see Section 4.3.1). We may, for instance, wish to form groups of contiguous locations. Or we could try an embedding—that is, replacing location IDs by latitude and longitude. But let's see what happens without taking such measures.

5.3.2 Tree-Based Analysis

As noted, this dataset may present challenges, especially regarding possible overfitting issues. Let's give it a try:

```
> dtout <- qeDT(yell10k,'tripTime')
holdout set has  1000 rows
> dtout$testAccAA
[1] 211.7106
> dtout$baseAcc
[1] 433.8724
```

Not bad; we cut MAPE in half by using the features here. Again, we might do considerably better with nondefault hyperparameter combinations, as well as by adding some of the features in the original dataset that are not in yell10k.

The dataset, even in the scaled-down form we are using here, is far too complex for plotting its tree. We can still display it in printed form:

```
> dtout

    Conditional inference tree with 40 terminal nodes

Response:  tripTime
Inputs:  passenger_count, trip_distance, PULocationID, DOLocationID, PUweekday
Number of observations:  9000

1) trip_distance <= 3.08; criterion = 1, statistic = 5713.065
  2) trip_distance <= 1.39; criterion = 1, statistic = 3517.53
    3) trip_distance <= 0.79; criterion = 1, statistic = 1216.608
      4) trip_distance <= 0.49; criterion = 1, statistic = 404.09
        5) trip_distance <= 0.16; criterion = 1, statistic = 138.913
          6)*  weights = 107
        5) trip_distance > 0.16
          7) trip_distance <= 0.27; criterion = 0.998, statistic = 83.348
            8)*  weights = 51
          7) trip_distance > 0.27
            9) DOLocationID == {13, 68, 75, 87, 100, 107, 125, 137, 142, 148,
                161, 162, 209, 230, 233, 234, 237, 264}; criterion = 0.982,
                statistic = 83.545
              10)*  weights = 138
...
```

Though the display is quite complex even in printed form, forcing only a partial listing here, and though it contains some quantities we have not yet described, one may still glean some interesting information. First we see that there were 40 terminal nodes, as opposed to 5 in our previous example, reflecting the greater complexity of this dataset. (There are 79 nodes in the entire tree, as can be seen by typing dtout$nNodes.)

Second, we see in part how that reduction was accomplished: DT was able to form its own groups of pickup and dropoff locations, such as in Node 9:

```
        9) DOLocationID == {13, 68, 75, 87, 100, 107, 125, 137, 142, 148,
            161, 162, 209, 230, 233, 234, 237, 264}; criterion = 0.982,
            statistic = 83.545
          10)*  weights = 138
```

We go left if DOLocationID is one of 13, 68, and so on, and otherwise go right. This addresses our concerns in Section 5.3.1. The DT grouped the locations for us! No wonder DTs are so popular!

If we type an expression when we are in R interactive mode, R prints that expression. Here we typed dtout, so it's equivalent to typing print(dtout). But print() is yet another R generic function, and we will thus have a similar chain of calls as for plot() above, ending with print.party(dtout$ctout).

One thing worth checking in DT analysis is the numbers of data points in the various leaf nodes. Say some node has rather few data points. That's analogous to having too few points in a k-NN neighborhood. Just as we can try different values of k in the latter case, here we may wish to tweak some DT hyperparameters.

We'll look at hyperparameters in Section 5.6, but for now, let's see how to check for leaf nodes with rather few data points:

```
> dtout$termNodeCounts
  6   8  10  12  13  16  17  19  20  24  25  27  28  31  32  34  36  37  42  43
107  51 138  71 148 262 245 190 423 492 216  18 361 370 309 266 304  17 496 101
 44  47  48  49  52  54  55  57  58  63  64  66  67  69  71  72  74  76  78  79
317 110 395 286 127 145 287 552 177 266 240  95 245 211 378 105 165 233  10  71
```

There are a few small nodes, notably Node 78 with only 10 data points. This is a possible reason to tweak the hyperparameters.

5.4 Example: Forest Cover Data

Another UCI dataset, Covertype, aims to "[predict] forest cover type from cartographic variables only."[2] The idea is that one might use remote sensing to determine what kinds of grasses there are in difficult-to-access regions. There are 581,012 data points, with 54 features, such as elevation, hillside shade at noon, and distance to the nearest surface water. There are seven different cover types, which are stored in column 55.

This example is useful for a number of reasons. Here we'll see DT in action in a classification problem, with multiple classes, and of a size larger than what we've seen so far. And besides, what could be better in a chapter on trees than data on forests!

Input the data, say, with data.table::fread() for speed:

```
> library(data.table)
> cvr <- fread('covtype.data.gz')
> cvr[1,]
     V1 V2 V3  V4 V5  V6  V7  V8  V9  V10 V11 V12
1: 2596 51  3 258  0 510 221 232 148 6279   1   0
   V13 V14 V15 V16 V17 V18 V19 V20 V21 V22 V23
1:   0   0   0   0   0   0   0   0   0   0   0
   V24 V25 V26 V27 V28 V29 V30 V31 V32 V33 V34
1:   0   0   0   0   0   0   0   0   0   0   0
```

---

2. *https://archive.ics.uci.edu/ml/datasets/covertype*

	V35	V36	V37	V38	V39	V40	V41	V42	V43	V44	V45
1:	0	0	0	0	0	0	0	0	1	0	0

	V46	V47	V48	V49	V50	V51	V52	V53	V54	V55
1:	0	0	0	0	0	0	0	0	0	5

The class, in column V55, was read in as an integer, whereas qe*-series functions need Y to be R factors in classification problems. We could have used fread()'s colClasses argument, but let's just fix it directly:

```
> cvr$V55 <- as.factor(cvr$V55)
```

There are seven classes, but some are much more common than others:

```
> table(cvr$V55)
```

1	2	3	4	5	6	7
211840	283301	35754	2747	9493	17367	20510

Cover types 1 and 2 are the most numerous.

Since both n and p are large, let's run on a random subset of 50,000 records to more conveniently illustrate the ideas. This approach is also common in data analysis: do a preliminary analysis on a subset of the data, again for convenience, but then do a more thorough analysis on the full data.

```
> cvr50k <- cvr[sample(1:nrow(cvr),50000),]
> dto <- qeDT(cvr50k,'V55')
holdout set has   1000 rows
> dto$testAcc
[1] 0.249
> dto$baseAcc
[1] 0.5125714
```

Again, we are doing much better with the features (25 percent error rate) than without them (51 percent).

We might also look at the confusion matrix:

```
> dto$confusion
      pred
actual   1   2   3   4   5   6   7
     1 241 103   0   0   0   0   3
     2  65 402   3   0   3   8   1
     3   0   4  54   0   1  12   0
     4   0   0   3   3   0   0   0
     5   1  10   0   0   8   1   0
     6   0   3  18   0   0  20   0
     7  10   0   0   0   0   0  23
```

Class 1 is often mispredicted as Class 2, and vice versa.

With the larger sample size n and number of features p here, a really large tree might be generated. In fact, it is much larger than in our previous examples:

```
> dto$nNodes
[1] 1065
> dto$nTermNodes
[1] 533
```

The tree has 1,000 nodes, and about half of those are terminal nodes!

5.5   Decision Tree Hyperparameters: How to Split?

DT packages differ from one another in terms of the details of their node-splitting actions. In most cases, the process is quite complex and thus beyond the scope of this book. The splitting process in party is no exception, but we need to have at least a rough overview of the process. We will focus on a major splitting criterion in party known as the *p-value*.

Look again at Figure 5-1. The oval contents show that the feature used to split is Wind, with a p-value of 0.002 and with a split point of 6.9. But originally, as the tree was being built, that oval was empty, with no lines emanating out of the bottom. How, then, was this node built to what we see in the figure?

Node 2 inherited data points from the left branch out of Node 1. Then the following algorithm was run:

```
pv = null vector
for feature f in Solar.R, Wind, Temp, Month, Day do:
   for split_point in the values of f do:
      compute a p-value pval
      append pval to pv
```

We do the following on the output of the above pseudocode:

- If the smallest p-value is below a user-specified criterion, split the node using whichever feature and split point yielded the smallest p-value (in this case, Wind and 6.9).

- If, on the other hand, the smallest p-value was not smaller than the user-specified criterion, do not split the node.

We see, for instance, that for Node 2 and the potential (and later, actual) splitting feature Wind, there are many candidates for a potential split point:

```
> sort(airq$Wind)
  [1]  2.3  2.8  3.4  4.0  4.1  4.6  4.6  4.6  5.1  5.1  5.1  5.7  5.7  6.3  6.3
 [16]  6.3  6.3  6.3  6.3  6.9  6.9  6.9  6.9  6.9  6.9  6.9  6.9  7.4  7.4  7.4
 [31]  7.4  7.4  7.4  7.4  7.4  7.4  7.4  8.0  8.0  8.0  8.0  8.0  8.0  8.0  8.6
 [46]  8.6  8.6  9.2  9.2  9.2  9.2  9.2  9.2  9.7  9.7  9.7  9.7  9.7  9.7  9.7
 [61]  9.7  9.7 10.3 10.3 10.3 10.3 10.3 10.3 10.3 10.3 10.3 10.9 10.9 10.9
 [76] 10.9 10.9 10.9 11.5 11.5 11.5 11.5 11.5 11.5 11.5 11.5 11.5 11.5 12.0 12.0
 [91] 12.0 12.0 12.6 12.6 13.2 13.8 13.8 13.8 13.8 14.3 14.3 14.3 14.3 14.9 14.9
[106] 14.9 14.9 14.9 15.5 15.5 15.5 16.6 16.6 18.4 20.1 20.7
```

Any of the values $2.8, 3.4, \ldots, 20.1$ could be used. The algorithm takes each one into consideration.

Intuitively, we would like the split to produce two approximately balanced subsets, say, with a split at 9.7. But a more urgent requirement is that the two subsets differ a lot in their mean values of Y. If mean Y is fairly similar in the two candidate subsets, the node is deemed homogeneous and not split—at least for that feature.

Well, then, what constitutes differing by "a lot"? This is decided by a formal statistical significance test. This book does not assume a background in statistics, and, for our purposes here, we just state that a test is summarized by a number known as a p-value.

Testing has come under much criticism in recent years, and for good reason, in my opinion (see the file *NoPVals.md* in `regtools`). However, for the node-splitting purpose here, the p-value threshold is just another hyperparameter, named `alpha` in `qeDT()`. This default value is 0.05.

If the p-value is less than `alpha` for some candidate feature and candidate split point pair, then the node is deemed worth splitting. The feature and split point chosen are the pair with the smallest p-value. We see in Figure 5-1 that the minimum p-value happened to be 0.002, which was associated with the `Wind` feature and a split point of 6.9. Since $0.002 < 0.05$, the node was split accordingly.

If no split point meets the above criterion, the node is not split. That happened in Node 3, so it became a terminal node.

5.6 Hyperparameters in the qeDT() Function

As noted, DTs may be viewed as an extension of the k-NN idea. Each leaf node forms a kind of neighborhood whose data points have similar values of certain features. Recall from Chapter 3 that small neighborhoods lead to larger variance in a predicted Y value—just too small a sample to work from—while large neighborhoods may have bias problems (that is, points in the same neighborhood may be quite different from each other and thus not representative).

In a DT context, then, we should look at the leaf nodes to consider the Bias-Variance Trade-off. If there are too many small terminal nodes, we risk a variance problem, while too many large terminal nodes may mean a bias issue.

Here is where hyperparameters come into play. They control the tree configuration in various ways, and we can use cross-validation to choose the tree configuration with the best predictive ability.

The general call form is:

```
> args(qeDT)
function (data, yName, alpha = 0.05, minsplit = 20, minbucket = 7,
    maxdepth = 0, mtry = 0, holdout = floor(min(1000, 0.1 * nrow(data))))
```

The data, yName, and holdout arguments are common to all the qe*-series functions. The remainder, alpha, minsplit, minbucket, maxdepth, and mtry, all deal with splitting criteria. Here are their roles:

alpha   As explained above.

minsplit   Here we can specify the minimum size for any node. The default of 20 means that we will not allow any node splitting to result in a node with fewer than 20 data points.

minbucket   Like minsplit, but specifically for terminal nodes.

maxdepth   Maximum number of levels or rows of the tree. In Figure 5-1, we have 4 levels, with the root in Level 1 and the leaf nodes in Level 4.

mtry   If this is nonzero, it is the number of features to try at each node; see below.

If mtry is nonzero, our splitting algorithm changes a bit:

```
pv = null vector
randomly choose mtry features among Solar.R, Wind, Temp, Month, Day
for f in chosen feature set do
    for split_point in the values of f do:
        compute a p-value pval
        append pval to pv
```

This adds some randomness to the tree construction process, a step toward the ML method of *random forests*. We will see in the next chapter why this may be useful, but for the strict DT method, it is usually not used.

Consider each of the above hyperparameters in terms of the Bias-Variance Trade-off. Say we wish to make the leaf nodes smaller. All else being equal, we could accomplish this by making alpha larger, minsplit smaller, minbucket smaller, maxdepth larger, and mtry larger (or 0).

For instance, with a larger alpha, more p-values will be below this high threshold, so it is more likely that a node will split. As we go further down a tree, fewer data points remain, so if we encourage splits, when we reach a node that can't be split, it won't have many points left in it.

These hyperparameters don't work independently of each other, so setting too many of them probably becomes redundant.

5.7 Conclusions

Decision trees play a fundamental role in ML, and we will see them again in our material on bagging and boosting. As with any ML algorithm, we must deal with various hyperparameters, another topic to be viewed in depth later in the book.

6

TWEAKING THE TREES

AdaBoost is the best off-the-shelf classifier in the world.
–CART co-inventor Leo Breiman, 1996

XGBoost is the algorithm of choice for many winning teams of machine learning competitions.
–Wikipedia entry, 2022

 Here we talk about two general techniques in ML, *bagging* and *boosting*, and apply them to form extensions of decision tree analysis. The extensions, *random forests* and *tree-based gradient boosting*, are widely used—in fact, even more so than individual tree methods.

6.1 Bias vs. Variance, Bagging, and Boosting

For want of a nail the shoe was lost;
for want of a shoe the horse was lost;
and for want of a horse the man was lost.
 —Old proverb

We must always bear in mind that we are dealing with sample data. Sometimes the "population" being sampled is largely conceptual; for example, in the taxi data in Section 5.3, we are considering the data a sample from the ridership in all days, past, present, and future. But in any case, there is sampling variation.

In the bike rental data, say, what if the data collection period had continued one more day? Even this slight change might affect the exact split at the top of the tree, Node 1. And that effect could then change the splits (or possibly non-splits) at Nodes 2 and 3 and so on, with the those changes cascading down to the lowest levels of the resulting tree. Note that not only might the split points in the nodes change, but the membership of the nodes could also change. A training set data point that had been in Node 2 may now be in Node 3. In other words:

> Decision trees can be very sensitive to slight changes in the inputs. That means they are very sensitive to sampling variation—that is, **decision trees have a high variance.**

Recall that splitting a node reduces bias and that, typically, reducing bias also increases variance. But for the reason given above, variance may be especially problematic in DT settings.

In this chapter, we treat two major methods for handling this problem, *bagging/random forests* and *boosting*. Both take this point of view: "Variance too high? Well, that means the sample size is too small, so let's generate more trees!" But how?

6.2 Bagging: Generating New Trees by Resampling

The term *bagging* refers to an ML version of a handy tool from modern statistics known as the *bootstrap*. This consists of drawing many random subsamples from our data, applying our given estimator to each subsample, and then averaging (or otherwise combining) the results. Here we apply the bootstrap to decision trees.

Starting with our original data, once again considered a sample from some population, we'll generate s new samples from the original dataset. We generate a new sample by randomly sampling m of our n data points—*with* replacement. (We may get a few duplicates.) We'll fit a tree to each new sample, thus achieving the above goal of generating more trees, and combine the results in a manner to be presented shortly. The quantities s and m here are—you guessed it—hyperparameters.

6.2.1 Random Forests

Say we have a new case to be predicted. We will then *aggregate* the *s* trees by forming a prediction for each tree and then combining all those predicted values to form our final prediction as follows:

- In a numeric-*Y* setting, the combining would take the form of averaging all the predictions. In the taxi data, for example (see Section 5.3), each tree would give us a predicted trip time, and our final predicted trip time would be the average of all those individual predictions.

- In a classification setting, such as the vertebrae example we covered in Section 2.3, we could combine by using a *voting* process. For each tree, we would find the predicted class, NO, DH, or SL, and then see what class received the most "votes" among the various trees. That would be our predicted class. Or, we could find the estimated class probabilities for this new case, for each tree, and then average the probabilities. Our predicted class would be whichever one has the largest average.

So, we do a bootstrap and then aggregation, hence the short name *bagging*. It is also commonly known as *random forests*, a specific implementation by Leo Breiman. (The earliest proposal along these lines seems to be that of Tin Kam Ho. She called the method *random decision forests*.) That approach places a limit on the number of features under consideration for splitting at any given node, with a different candidate set at each step.

Why might this strategy, which is using a different candidate set of features each time, work? Ordinary bagging can result in substantially correlated trees because it tends to choose the same features every time. It can be shown that the average of positively correlated numbers has a higher variance than the average of independent numbers. Thus the approach in which we limit the candidate feature set at each step hopefully reduces variance.

6.2.2 The qeRF() Function

The qe*-series of functions actually includes several for random forests. For a given application, one may be more accurate or faster than others, but they all use the general random forest paradigm described previously. We'll use qeRF() here.

Recall that the qe* functions all have the following arguments:

data   A data frame containing our training data.

yName   The name of the column in data containing *Y*, the outcome variable to be predicted. The user distinguishes between numeric-*Y* and classification settings by having this column be numeric or an R factor, respectively.

holdout   The size of the optional holdout set.

Application-specific arguments   For example, as the number k of nearest neighbors in the case of qeKNN().

Each qe* function is a wrapper interface to a function in a standard R ML package. In the case of random forests, qeRF() is a wrapper for randomForest in the package of the same name. The call form is:

```
qeRF(data, yName, nTree = 500, minNodeSize = 10,
    holdout = floor(min(1000,0.1 * nrow(data))))
```

The application-specific arguments are nTree, which is the number of boot-strapped trees to generate, and minNodeSize, which is similar to minsplit in ctree().

6.2.3   Example: Vertebrae Data

Let's look again at the vertebrae dataset from Section 2.3, now applying random forests instead of k-NN. We'll predict the same hypothetical new case as in that earlier example:

```
# fit RF model
> rfout <- qeRF(vert,'V7',holdout=NULL)
# new case to predict
> z <- vert[1,-7]
> z$V2 <- 18
# predict
> predict(rfout,z)
$predClasses
[1] "DH"

$probs
      DH    NO    SL
2 0.532 0.378 0.09
attr(,"class")
[1] "matrix" "array"  "votes"
```

With k-NN, we had predicted the same class, DH, but with slightly different class probabilities:

```
> predict(kout,z)
$predClasses
[1] "DH"

$probs
      DH  NO  SL
[1,] 0.6 0.2 0.2
```

The difference between the two sets of probabilities is due both to the fact that we used two different ML algorithms and to the small n in this dataset (310), which caused large sample variability.

We used the default values here for nTree and minNodeSize. We could explore a few other pairs of these hyperparameters and then compare the performance of random forests and k-NN on this dataset.

6.2.4   Example: Remote-Sensing Soil Analysis

Here we will analyze the African Soil Property dataset from Kaggle.[1] From the data site:

> Advances in rapid, low cost analysis of soil samples using infrared spectroscopy, georeferencing of soil samples, and greater availability of earth remote sensing data provide new opportunities for predicting soil functional properties at unsampled locations.... Digital mapping of soil functional properties, especially in data sparse regions such as Africa, is important for planning sustainable agricultural intensification and natural resources management.

We wish to predict various soil properties without directly testing the soil.

One important property of this dataset that we have not encountered before is that it has $p > n$ (that is, more columns than rows). The original first column, an ID variable, has been removed.

```
> dim(afrsoil)
[1] 1157 3599
```

Traditionally, the statistics field has been wary of this kind of setting, as linear models (Chapter 8) do not work there. One must first do dimension reduction. Tree-based methods do this as an integral aspect of their operation, so let's give it a try using qeRF().

Here are the names of the columns:

```
> names(afrsoil)
...
[3547] "m659.543" "m657.615" "m655.686" "m653.758" "m651.829" "m649.901"
[3553] "m647.972" "m646.044" "m644.115" "m642.187" "m640.258" "m638.33"
[3559] "m636.401" "m634.473" "m632.544" "m630.616" "m628.687" "m626.759"
[3565] "m624.83"  "m622.902" "m620.973" "m619.045" "m617.116" "m615.188"
[3571] "m613.259" "m611.331" "m609.402" "m607.474" "m605.545" "m603.617"
[3577] "m601.688" "m599.76"  "BSAN"     "BSAS"     "BSAV"     "CTI"
[3583] "ELEV"     "EVI"      "LSTD"     "LSTN"     "REF1"     "REF2"
[3589] "REF3"     "REF7"     "RELI"     "TMAP"     "TMFI"     "Depth"
[3595] "Ca"       "P"        "pH"       "SOC"      "Sand"
```

---

1. *https://www.kaggle.com/c/afsis-soil-properties/data*

Columns 1 through 3594 are the X variables, with cryptic code names. The remaining columns are Y, some with more easily guessable names. We'll predict pH, the soil acidity.

This kind of setting is considered tough. There is a major potential for overfitting since, with so many features, one or more of them may accidentally look to be a strong predictor due to p-hacking (Section 1.13). Let's see how well qeRF() does here.

```
> set.seed(9999)
> rfo <- qeRF(afrsoil[,c(1:3578,3597)],'pH',holdout=500)
> rfo$testAcc
[1] 0.3894484
> rfo$baseAcc
[1] 0.6858574
```

Use of the features has cut MAPE almost in half. Note the range under the pH scale used here:

```
> range(afrsoil$pH)
[1] -1.886946  3.416117
```

We are now ready to predict, say, on a hypothetical new case like that of row 88 in the training data:

```
> predict(rfo,afrsoil[88,1:3594])
      88
0.6068828
```

We would predict a pH level of about 0.61.

6.3 Boosting: Repeatedly Tweaking a Tree

Imagine a classification problem with just two classes, so $Y = 1$ or 0, and just one feature, X, say, age. We fit a tree with just one level. Suppose our rule is to guess $Y = 1$ if $X > 12.5$ and guess $Y = 0$ if $X \leq 12.5$. *Boosting* would involve exploring the effect of small changes to the 12.5 threshold on our overall rate of correct classification.

Consider a data point for which $X = 5.2$. In the original analysis, we'd guess Y to be 0. And, here is the point, if we were to move the threshold to, say, 11.9, we would *still* guess $Y = 0$. But the move may turn some misclassified data points near 12.5 to correctly classified ones. If more formerly misclassified points become correctly classified than vice versa, it's a win.

So the idea of boosting is to tweak the original tree, thus forming a new tree, then in turn tweaking that new tree, forming a second new tree, and so on. After generating s trees (s is a hyperparameter), we predict a new case by plugging it into all those trees and somehow combining the resulting predicted values.

6.3.1   Implementation: AdaBoost

The first proposal made for boosting was *AdaBoost*. The tweaking involves assigning weights to the points in our training set, which change with each tree. Each time we form a new tree, we fit a tree according to the latest set of weights, updating them with each new tree.

In a numeric-Y situation, to predict a new case with a certain X value, we plug that value into all the trees, yielding s predicted values. Our final predicted value in a numeric-Y setting is a weighted average of the individual predictions. In a classification setting, we would take a weighted average of the estimated probabilities of $Y = 1$ to get the final probability estimate, or use weighted voting.

To make this idea concrete, below is an outline of how the process could be implemented with ctree(). It relies on the fact that one of the arguments in ctree(), named weights, is a vector of nonnegative numbers, one for each data point. Say our response is named y, with features x. Denote the portion of the data frame d for x by dx.

In the pseudocode below, we will maintain two vectors of weights:

1. wts will store the current weightings of the various rows in the training data. Recall that as the boosting process evolves, we will weight some rows more heavily than others according to their current impact on misclassification.

2. alpha will store the current weights of our various trees. Recall that in the end, when we do prediction, we will place more weight on some trees than others.

Here is an outline of the algorithm:

```
ctboost <- function(d,s) {
   # uniform weights to begin
   wts <- rep(1/n,n)
   trees <- list()
   alpha <- vector(length=s)  # alpha[i] = coefficient for tree i
   for(treeNum in 1:s) {
      trees[[i]] <- ctree(y ~ x,data=d,weights=wts)
      preds <- predict(trees[[i]],dx)
      # update wts, placing larger weight on data points on which
      # we had the largest errors (regression case) or which we
      # misclassified (classification case)
      wts <- (computation not shown)
      # find latest tree weight
      alpha[i] <- (computation not shown)
   }
   l <- list(trees=trees,treeWts=alpha)
   class(l) <- 'ctboost'
   return(l)
}
```

And to predict a new case, `newx`:

```
predict.ctboost <- function(ctbObject,newx)
{
    trees <- ctbObject$trees
    alpha <- ctbObject$alpha
    pred <- 0.0
    for (i in 1:s) {
        pred <- pred + alpha[i] * predict(trees[[i]],newx)
    }
    return(pred)
}
```

Since this book is aimed to be nonmathematical, we omit the formulas for `wts` and `alpha`. It should be noted, though, that `alpha` is an increasing sequence, so when we predict new cases, the later trees play a larger role.

The `qeML` package has a function for AdaBoost, `qeAdaBoost()`. But it is applicable to classification settings only, so let's go right to the next form of boosting.

6.3.2   Gradient Boosting

In statistics/ML, there is the notion of a *residual*—that is, the difference between a predicted value and an actual value. *Gradient boosting* works by fitting trees to residuals. Given our dataset, a rough description of the process is as follows:

1.   Start with some initial tree. Set *CurrentTree* to it.
2.   For each of our data points, calculate the residuals for *CurrentTree*.
3.   Fit a tree *to the residuals*—that is, take our residuals as the "data" and fit a tree T on it. Set *CurrentTree = T*.
4.   Go to Step 2.

These steps are iterated for the number of trees specified by the user. Then, to predict a new case, we plug it into all the trees. The predicted value is simply the sum of the predicted values from the individual trees.

At any given step, we are saying, "Good, we've got a certain predictive ability so far, so let's work on what is left over—that is, our current errors." Hence our predicted value for any new case is the sum of what each tree predicts for that case.

6.3.2.1   The qeGBoost() Function

The qe* function for gradient boosting is `qeGBoost()`, a wrapper for `gbm()` in the package of the same name. Its call form is:

```
qeGBoost(data, yName, nTree = 100, minNodeSize = 10, learnRate = 0.1,
    holdout = floor(min(1000, 0.1 * nrow(data))))
```

This is similar to qeRF() but with a new argument, the *learning rate*. That rate is a common notion in ML and will be explained shortly.

NOTE   *A number of gradient boosting packages are available for R. We chose the gbm package for its simplicity. Just as was the case above for random forests, other packages may be faster or more accurate on some datasets, notably qeXGBoost. Here, qeGBoost() sticks to the "quick and easy" philosophy of the qe*-series, but the reader is encouraged to explore other packages as an advanced topic.*

6.3.3 Example: Call Network Monitoring

Let's first apply boosting to a dataset titled Call Test Measurements for Mobile Network Monitoring and Optimization,[2] which rates quality of service on mobile calls. The aim is to predict the quality rating.

6.3.3.1 The Data

Here is an introduction to the data:

```
> ds <- read.csv('dataset.csv',stringsAsFactors=TRUE)
> names(ds)
[1] "Date.Of.Test"          "Signal..dBm."
[3] "Speed..m.s."           "Distance.from.site..m."
[5] "Call.Test.Duration..s." "Call.Test.Result"
[7] "Call.Test.Technology"   "Call.Test.Setup.Time..s."
[9] "MOS"
> ds <- ds[,-1]
> head(ds)
  Signal..dBm. Speed..m.s. Distance.from.site..m. Call.Test.Duration..s.
1          -61       68.80                1048.60                     90
2          -61       68.77                1855.54                     90
3          -71       69.17                1685.62                     90
4          -65       69.28                1770.92                     90
5         -103        0.82                 256.07                     60
6          -61       68.86                 452.50                     90
  Call.Test.Result Call.Test.Technology Call.Test.Setup.Time..s. MOS
1          SUCCESS                 UMTS                     0.56 2.1
2          SUCCESS                 UMTS                     0.45 3.2
3          SUCCESS                 UMTS                     0.51 2.1
4          SUCCESS                 UMTS                     0.00 1.0
5          SUCCESS                 UMTS                     3.35 3.6
6          SUCCESS                 UMTS                     0.00 1.0
...
```

Here Y is MOS, the quality of service.

---

2. *https://www.kaggle.com/valeriol93/predict-qoe*

How big is it?

```
> dim(ds)
[1] 105828       8
```

Now, let's fit the model.

6.3.3.2   Fitting the Model

With over 100,000 data points and just 8 features, overfitting should not be an issue in this dataset. It easily satisfies our rough rule of thumb, $p < \sqrt{n}$ (Section 3.1.3). So, let's not bother with a holdout set. There is still some randomness in the algorithm, though, so for consistency, let's set the random seed.

```
> set.seed(9999)
> gbout <- qeGBoost(ds,'MOS',nTree=750,holdout=NULL)
```

The default value for nTree is only 100, but we tried a much larger number, 750, for reasons that will become clear below.

Let's do a prediction. Say we have a case like ds[3,] but with distance being 1,500 and duration 62:

```
> ds3 <- ds[3,-8]
> ds3[,3] <- 1500
> ds3[,4] <- 62
> predict(gbout,ds3)
[1] 2.462538
```

6.3.3.3   Hyperparameter: Number of Trees

But should we have used so many trees? After all, 750 may be overfitting. Maybe the later trees were doing "noise fitting." The package has a couple of ways of addressing that issue, one of which is to use the auxiliary function gbm.perf(). Applied to the output of gbm(), it estimates the optimal number of trees.

As noted, qeGBoost() calls gbm() and places the output of the latter in the gbmOuts component of its own output. So, we are able to call gbm.perf():

```
> gbm.perf(gbout$gbmOuts)
```

See the output graph in Figure 6-1. The dashed vertical line shows the estimated "sweet spot"—that is, the best number of trees, 382 in this case. (This value is also printed to the R console.)

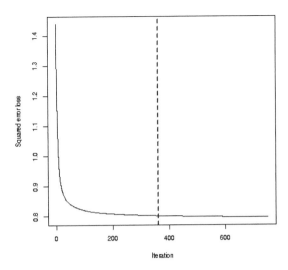

Figure 6-1: Output from gbm.perf

But we need not refit the model. We can change the number of trees in the prediction:

```
> predict(gbout,ds3,newNTree=382)
[1] 2.45214
```

Since we did not form a holdout set, we'll need to calculate MAPE manually:

```
> mean(abs(preds - ds[,8]))
[1] 0.6142699
```

Details on other features of the gbm package are in its documentation.

6.3.4 Example: Vertebrae Data

Boosting can be used in classification settings as well as numeric-*Y* cases. (And its usage is probably much more common on the classification side.) Here is qeGBoost() applied to the the vertebrae data (see Section 2.3).

```
> set.seed(9999)
> gbout <- qeGBoost(vert,'V7')
```

And, say we were to predict a new case like that of row 12 in the training set:

```
> predict(gbout,vert[12,-7])
$predClasses
[1] "DH"

$probs
```

```
                DH          NO          SL
[1,] 0.6283904 0.3694108 0.002198735

attr(,"class")
[1] "qeGBoost"
```

We predict DH, with an estimated probability of about 0.63. (Unfortunately, gbm.perf() is not available for the multiclass case.)

6.3.5   Bias vs. Variance in Boosting

Boosting is "tweaking" a tree, potentially making it more stable, especially since we are averaging many trees, thus smoothing out "For want of a nail..." problems. So, it may reduce variance. By making small adjustments to a tree, we are potentially developing a more detailed analysis, thus reducing bias.

But all of that is true only "potentially." Though the tweaking process has some theoretical basis, it still can lead us astray, actually *increasing* bias and possibly increasing variance too. If the hyperparameter s is set too large, producing too many trees, we may overfit.

6.3.6   Computational Speed

Boosting can take up tons of CPU cycles, so we may need something to speed things up. The n.cores argument in gbm() tries to offload computation to different cores in your machine. If you have a quad core system, you may try setting this argument to 4 or even 8 (and then call gbm() directly rather than through qeGBoost()).

6.3.7   Further Hyperparameters

Boosting algorithms typically have a number of hyperparameters. We have already mentioned nTree (n.trees in gbm()), which is the number of trees to be generated.

Another hyperparameter is minNodeSize (n.minobsinnode in gbm()), which is the minimum number of data points we are willing to have in one tree node. As we saw in Chapter 5, reducing this value will reduce bias but increase variance.

The shrinkage hyperparameter is so important in the general ML context that we'll cover it in a separate subsection, next.

6.3.8   The Learning Rate

The notion of a learning rate comes up often in ML. We'll describe it here in general and then explain how it works for gradient boosting. We'll see it again in our material on support vector machines (Chapter 10) and neural networks (Chapter 11).

This section has a bit of math in it, in the form of curves and lines tangent to them, which is an exception to the avowedly nonmathematical nature of this book. But there are still no equations, and even math-averse readers should be able to follow the discussion.

6.3.8.1   General Concepts

Recall that in ML methods we are usually trying to minimize some loss function, such as MAPE, or the overall misclassification error OME. Computationally, this minimization can be a challenge.

Consider the function graphed in Figure 6-2. It is a function of a one-dimensional variable x, whereas typically our x is high-dimensional, but it will make our point.

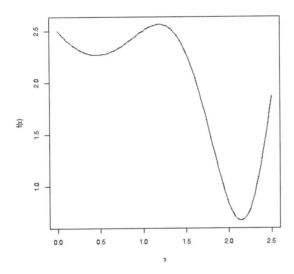

Figure 6-2: A function to be minimized

There is an overall minimum at approximately $x = 2.2$. This is termed the *global minimum*. But there is also a *local minimum*, at about $x = 0.4$; that term means that this is the minimum value of the function only for points near—"local to"—0.4. Let's give the name x_0 to the value of x at the global minimum.

To us humans looking at the graph, it's clear where x_0 is, but we need our software to be able to find it. That may be problematic. Here's why.

Most ML algorithms use an *iterative* approach to finding the desired minimum point x_0. This involves a series of guesses for x_0. The code starts with an initial guess, g_0, say, randomly chosen, then evaluates $f(g_0)$. Based on the result, the algorithm then somehow (see below) updates the guess to g_1. It then evaluates $f(g_1)$, producing the next guess, g_2, and so on.

The algorithm keeps generating guesses until they don't change much, say, until $|g_{i+1} - g_i| < 0.00000001$ for Step i. We say that the algorithm has *converged* to this point. Let's give the name c to that value of i. It then reports x_0, the global minimum point, to be the latest guess, g_c.

So, what about that "somehow" alluded to above? How does the algorithm generate the next guess from the present one? The answer lies in the *gradient*. In our simple example here with x being one-dimensional, the gradient is the slope of the function at the given point—that is, the slope of the tangent line to the curve.

Say our initial guess $g_0 = 1.1$. The tangent line is shown in Figure 6-3. The line is pointing upward to the right—that is, it has a positive slope—so it tells us that by going to the left we will go to smaller values of the function. We want to find the point at which $f()$ is smallest, and the tangent line is saying, "Oh, you want a smaller value than $f(1.1)$? Move to the left!" But actually we should be moving to the right, toward 2.2, where the global minimum is.

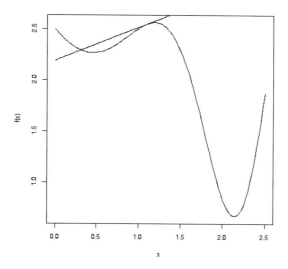

Figure 6-3: A function to be minimized, plus the tangent

So, the reader can already see that iterative algorithms are fraught with danger. Worse, it also adds yet another hyperparameter: we must decide not only *in which direction* to move for our next guess but also *how far* to move in that direction. The learning rate addresses the latter point.

As noted, we should be moving to the right from 1.1, not to the left. The function $f(x)$ is fooling the algorithm here. Actually, in this scenario, our algorithm may converge to the wrong point. Or it may not even converge at all and just wander aimlessly.

This is why typical ML packages allow the user to set the learning rate. Small values may be preferable, as large ones may result in our guesses lurching back and forth, always missing the target. On the other hand, if it is too small, we will just inch along, taking a long time to get there. Or worse, we converge to a local minimum.

Once again, we have a hyperparameter that we need to be at a "Goldilocks" level—not too large and not too small—and may have to experiment with various values.

6.3.8.2 The Learning Rate in gbm

This is the `shrinkage` argument in `gbm()`, called `learnRate` in `qeGBoost()`. Say we set it to 0.2. Recall the pseudocode describing gradient boosting in Section 6.3.2. The revised version is this:

1. Start with an initial tree. Set *CurrentTree* to it.

2. For each of our data points, calculate the residuals for *CurrentTree*.

3. Fit a tree *to the residuals*—that is, take our residuals as the "data" and fit a tree T on it. Set *CurrentTree* to the old *CurrentTree*, plus `shrinkage * T`.

4. Go to Step 2.

Here, `shrinkage * T` means multiplying all the values in the terminal nodes of the tree by the factor `shrinkage`. In the end, we still add up all our trees to produce the "supertree" used in the prediction of new cases.

Again, a small value of `shrinkage` is more cautious and slower, and it may cause us to need more trees in order to get good predictive power. But it may help prevent overfitting.

6.4 Pitfall: No Free Lunch

> *There is no such thing as a free lunch.*
> —Old economics saying

Though Leo Breiman had a point on the considerable value of AdaBoost (especially in saying "off the shelf," meaning usable with just default values of hyperparameters), that old saying about no free lunch applies as well. As always, applying cross-validation and so on is indispensable to developing good models.

Similar advice concerns another famous Breiman statement: that it is impossible to overfit using random forests. The reader who has come this far in this book will immediately realize that Breiman did not mean his statement in the way some have interpreted it. Any ML method may overfit. What Breiman meant was that it is impossible to set the value of *s*, the number of trees, too high. But the trees themselves still can overfit, for example, by having too small a minimum value for the number of data points in a node or, for that matter, by including too many features.

7

FINDING A GOOD SET OF HYPERPARAMETERS

As discussed in earlier chapters, especially Section 3.2.1, most analysts' approach to the problem of determining good values of hyperparameters is to use cross-validation. In this chapter, we'll learn to use a qeML function, qeFT(), that greatly facilitates the process.

7.1 Combinations of Hyperparameters

Note that typically we are talking about *sets* of hyperparameters. Suppose, for instance, that we wish to use PCA in a k-NN setting. Then we have two hyperparameters: the number of neighbors k and the number of principal components m. Thus we are interested in finding a good *combination* of a k value and an m value.

In many cases, the combinations are larger than just pairs. With qeDT(), for instance, there are hyperparameters alpha, minsplit, minbucket, maxdepth, and mtry. We thus wish to find a good set of five hyperparameters.

Many ML methods have even more hyperparameters. The more hyperparameters an ML method has, the more challenging it is to find a good combination of values. The qeML function qeFT() is aimed at facilitating this search.

NOTE   *Before continuing, note that though ML discussions–as well as some software documentation–will often refer to finding the **best** hyperparameter combination, this is typically an illusion. Due to p-hacking (see Section 1.13), the best combination for a given training set may not be the best for predicting new data, which is what counts. Nevertheless, by the end of this chapter, you'll have the tools to dependably determine **good** combinations.*

7.2   Grid Searching with qeFT()

Many ML packages include functions to do a *grid search*, which means evaluating all possible hyperparameter combinations. However, the number of combinations is typically so large that a full grid search would take a prohibitive amount of time to run.

Some grid search software libraries attempt to solve this problem by evaluating only combinations that seem promising, via an iterative search moving through narrow parts of the grid. At each iteration, the algorithm updates its guess as to what to try next. This saves time but can move in the wrong direction and, again, is vulnerable to p-hacking problems.

The qeML function qeFT() takes a more cautious approach. It generates a large number of random hyperparameter combinations, with the number being specified by the user, and evaluates them according to the relevant loss criterion (MAPE for numeric-*Y* settings or OME for classification settings). It tabulates and displays the results and includes a graphical display option. And, most importantly and uniquely, it guards against p-hacking, as will be explained shortly.

The qeFT() function is a qe-series wrapper for a regtools function, fineTuning(). Recall that another term for hyperparameters is *tuning parameters*. The function name is a pun on the old radio days, when tuning to the precise frequency of your favorite station was known as "fine-tuning."

7.2.1   How to Call qeFT()

Here is the basic qeFT() call form:

```
qeFT(data,yName,qeftn,pars,nCombs=NULL,nTst,nXval,showProgress=TRUE)
```

Let's look at the roles of the arguments:

data   As in all of the qe*-series, our input data.

yName   As in all of the qe*-series, the name of our *Y* column.

qeftn   ML function name, such as qeKNN.

pars   R list specifying which qeftn hyperparameter values we wish to consider, such as *k* in k-NN.

nCombs   Number of random combinations of the hyperparameters to evaluate. If NULL, then all possible combinations will be run.

nTst   Size of the holdout sets.

nXval   Number of holdout sets to run for each hyperparameter combination.

showProgress   For the impatient; print results as they become available.

In short, we run the specified ML function qeftn on nCombs combinations of hyperparameters using ranges shown in pars. For each combination, we generate nXval training/test partitions of the data, with the test portion being of size nTst. We then tabulate the resulting MAPE or OME values across all combinations of hyperparameters.

Note the difference between qeFT() and the replicMeans() function introduced in Section 3.2.2. The latter deals with the problem that the analyst may feel that a single holdout set is not enough to accurately assess performance. The qeFT() function does this too, via the argument nXval, but it does much more, automating the search process.

7.3   Example: Programmer and Engineer Data

Returning to the US census data on programmers' and engineers' salaries in the year 2000 (see Section 3.2.3), let's find good hyperparameters to predict wage income.

```
> set.seed(9999)
> ftout <- qeFT(data=pef,yName='wageinc',qeftn='qeKNN',
+    pars=list(k=5:25),nTst=1000,nXval=5)
> ftout
$outdf
    k  meanAcc       CI   bonfCI
1   5 22991.82 23402.16 23693.80
2   7 23168.20 24038.72 24657.43
3   9 23302.83 23829.56 24203.92
4  14 23384.68 23857.61 24193.75
5  10 23471.30 24095.60 24539.30
6   6 23635.61 24538.43 25180.09
7  25 23767.42 24651.47 25279.81
8  15 23843.55 24633.13 25194.31
9   8 23921.75 24846.51 25503.77
10 22 23924.46 24271.38 24517.95
11 16 24036.80 24784.32 25315.61
12 20 24120.60 24996.35 25618.78
13 11 24168.83 25639.28 26684.37
14 13 24192.18 24693.87 25050.43
15 12 24256.22 24690.67 24999.46
16 17 24261.34 24934.30 25412.59
17 18 24375.20 24576.41 24719.41
```

```
18 23 24376.66 25109.56 25630.46
19 24 24619.82 25249.43 25696.91
20 21 24693.10 25456.93 25999.81
21 19 24842.66 25564.61 26077.72

$nTst
[1] 1000

...
```

The only hyperparameter argument here is k. We've specified its range as 5:25—that is, we try $k = 5$, $k = 6$, and so on, up through $k = 25$. Since we've left out the nCombs argument, we investigated all 21 of these by default.

The meanAcc is the primary result, giving us the mean testAcc over all cross-validation runs. We will explain the CI and bonfCI columns in the next section.

7.3.1 Confidence Intervals

At first it would seem that $k = 5$ neighbors is best. Indeed, that is our guess as to the optimal k for our setting here (meaning this n, this feature set, this sampled population, and so on). But we should be careful. Here is why.

Any testAcc value output from a qe*-series function is random, due to the randomness of the holdout sets. With qeFT(), we look at many holdout sets and average the result to obtain meanAcc. Since all the holdout sets are random, then so is meanAcc. Of course, the larger the nXval, the better the accuracy.

Thus the meanAcc column is only approximate. The idea of the CI column is to get an idea as to the accuracy of that approximation. Specifically, the values in the CI column are the right endpoints of approximate 95 percent confidence intervals (CIs) for the true mean accuracy of any given combination. (For those who know statistics, these are *one-sided* CIs, of the form $(-\infty, a)$.)

In our case here, the meanAcc value for 7 neighbors is well within that CI for 5 neighbors. It's really a toss-up between using 5 or 7 neighbors, and their meanAcc numbers are not too far apart anyway. Thus we should not take the apparent superiority of $k = 5$ literally.

In other words, the CI column "keeps us honest," serving to remind us that meanAcc is only approximate and giving us some idea whether the apparent top few performers are distinguishable from each other.

But there's more. When we construct a large number of CIs, their overall validity declines due to p-hacking (see Section 1.13). CIs that are set individually at a nominal 95 percent level have a much lower overall confidence level. To see this, imagine tossing 10 coins. The individual probability of heads is 0.5 for each coin, but the probability that *all* of them come up heads is much lower. Similarly, if we have ten 95 percent CIs, the probability that they are *all* correct is much less than 95 percent.

The bonfCI column adjusts for that, using something called *Bonferroni-Dunn* CIs. In other words, that column gives us CIs that take into account that we are looking at many random CIs. We thus really should look more at that column than the CI one.

In our case here, the adjusted CI bounds are only a little larger than the original ones. This means we are not in much danger of p-hacking in this simple example. But as discussed in Section 1.13, it could be an issue with an ML algorithm having many hyperparameters. In such a setting, it is quite possible that we will pounce on a seemingly "best" combination that actually is quite unrepresentative and thus much inferior to some other alternatives.

We have no way of knowing that is the case, of course, but a good rule of thumb is to consider taking the more moderate combination among several with similar meanAcc values rather than extremely large or small values of the hyperparameters.

For instance, consider neural networks (we will look at these further in Chapter 11), which typically have a number of hyperparameters, including:

- number of layers
- number of neurons per layer
- dropout rate
- learning rate
- momentum
- initial weights

In order to investigate a broad variety of hyperparameter combinations, we would need to set the nCombs argument in qeFT() to a very large number, putting us at significant risk of finding a combination that is not actually very effective but that accidentally looks great. The bonfCI column warns us of this; the higher the discrepancy between it and the CI column, the greater the risk.

On the other hand, we are merely seeking a *good* combination of hyperparameters, not the absolute best. For any particular combination, the bonfCI figure is giving us a reasonable indication as to whether this combination will work well in predicting future cases. As with many things in ML, there is no magic formula for how to deal with the CIs, but they can act as informal aids to our thinking.

NOTE   *Here's a bit of history on Bonferroni–Dunn intervals: Traditionally, only the name Bonferroni is used, in honor of the Italian mathematician who developed the probability inequality central to the CIs. However, as a former student of Professor Olive Jean Dunn, I have been pleased to find that her name is now often included, as she was the one who proposed using the inequality for constructing CIs.*

7.3.2   The Takeaway on Grid Searching

The takeaway here is that we cannot take the ordering of results in a grid search literally. The first few "best" results may actually be similar. Moreover, the apparent "best" may actually be unrepresentative. Settle on a "good" combination that is hopefully not too extreme rather than trying to optimize.

7.4   Example: Programmer and Engineer Data

Let's try predicting occupation instead of wage income.

```
> ftout <- qeFT(data=pef,yName='occ',qeftn='qeKNN',pars=list(k=1:25),
  nTst=1000,nXval=5)
> ftout
$outdf
```

	k	meanAcc	CI	bonfCI
1	4	0.4656	0.4774134	0.4862065
2	7	0.4688	0.4756510	0.4807504
3	3	0.4726	0.4850419	0.4943029
4	2	0.4746	0.4846176	0.4920740
5	1	0.4766	0.4866176	0.4940740
6	5	0.4782	0.4827307	0.4861032
7	8	0.4990	0.5082016	0.5150508
8	6	0.5016	0.5179475	0.5301156
9	11	0.5150	0.5273033	0.5364611
10	9	0.5162	0.5239988	0.5298037
11	10	0.5292	0.5376199	0.5438871
12	14	0.5326	0.5425630	0.5499789
13	13	0.5332	0.5411714	0.5471048
14	15	0.5374	0.5522555	0.5633130
15	12	0.5402	0.5546542	0.5654131
16	17	0.5416	0.5499582	0.5561795
17	16	0.5422	0.5568134	0.5676908
18	24	0.5514	0.5632823	0.5721268
19	18	0.5570	0.5706960	0.5808905
20	20	0.5576	0.5682114	0.5761100
21	19	0.5600	0.5699275	0.5773169
22	21	0.5656	0.5766019	0.5847911
23	22	0.5674	0.5797099	0.5888727
24	25	0.5738	0.5844089	0.5923055
25	23	0.5758	0.5904321	0.6013233

The CIs, especially the Bonferroni–Dunn ones—which, as noted, are more reliable—suggest that any of the first k values have about the same predictive ability. The bonfCI value for 4 neighbors extends to include the meanAcc value for 5 neighbors.

Note the role of nXval here. We simply used too few cross-validations. We should try more, but if not, the values of k, 1, 2, 3, 4, and 7, look about the same. Conservatively, we might choose to use 3 or 4 neighbors.

7.5 Example: Phoneme Data

This dataset, which is included in the regtools package, seeks to predict one of two phoneme types from five sound measurements. Let's take a look:

```
> head(phoneme)
         V1        V2        V3        V4        V5 lbl
0  0.489927 -0.451528 -1.047990 -0.598693 -0.020418   1
1 -0.641265  0.109245  0.292130 -0.916804  0.240223   1
2  0.870593 -0.459862  0.578159  0.806634  0.835248   1
3 -0.628439 -0.316284  1.934295 -1.427099 -0.136583   1
4 -0.596399  0.015938  2.043206 -1.688448 -0.948127   1
5  0.164735 -0.642728 -0.980619 -0.386415 -0.242046   1
> dim(phoneme)
[1] 5404    6
```

The Y column here is lbl. As noted, it has two levels, so this is a two-class classification problem.

Let's try qeDT() on this data. As noted, the various hyperparameters interact with each other, so at first, we might not try using all of them. We might just use, say, alpha, minbucket, and maxdepth.

We need to specify ranges that we want to investigate for each of these parameters. Once again, there is no formula for deciding this, and one must gain insight from experience. But as an example, let's try 0.01, 0.05, 0.10, 0.25, 0.50, and 1 for alpha, and 1, 5, and 10 for minbucket, and so on, as seen in the call:

```
> z <- qeFT(phoneme,'lbl','qeDT',list(alpha=c(0.01,0.05,0.10,0.25,0.50,1),
    minbucket=c(1,5,10),maxdepth=c(3,8),minsplit=c(1,5,10),mtry=c(0,3)),
    50,1000,5,showProgress=T)
> z
$outdf
   alpha minbucket maxdepth minsplit mtry meanAcc        CI    bonfCI
1   1.00         1        8        5    0  0.1150 0.1284351 0.1401622
2   1.00         5        8       10    0  0.1176 0.1224275 0.1266412
3   1.00         5        8        1    0  0.1180 0.1238801 0.1290127
4   0.25         1        8        5    0  0.1218 0.1344352 0.1454640
5   1.00        10        8        1    3  0.1276 0.1403232 0.1514289
6   0.10         1        8        1    0  0.1310 0.1412380 0.1501744
7   1.00        10        8       10    3  0.1336 0.1380151 0.1418689
8   0.05         5        8       10    0  0.1338 0.1386500 0.1428834
9   0.05         5        8        1    0  0.1358 0.1429046 0.1491060
10  0.50         1        8        5    3  0.1362 0.1507200 0.1633940
11  0.01         1        8       10    0  0.1376 0.1416952 0.1452698
```

12	0.10	10	8	10	0	0.1408	0.1442374	0.1472378
13	0.50	5	8	5	3	0.1448	0.1543984	0.1627765
14	0.05	1	8	1	0	0.1466	0.1511066	0.1550404
15	0.25	5	8	10	3	0.1480	0.1609606	0.1722736
16	0.01	5	8	10	0	0.1486	0.1535665	0.1579015
17	0.10	10	8	1	3	0.1502	0.1631963	0.1745404
18	0.25	10	8	1	3	0.1536	0.1682711	0.1810770
19	0.25	5	8	5	3	0.1548	0.1731395	0.1891475
20	0.10	1	8	1	3	0.1552	0.1629286	0.1696747
...								
46	0.50	10	3	10	3	0.2210	0.2279024	0.2339274
47	0.10	10	3	10	3	0.2216	0.2274476	0.2325518
48	0.50	10	3	1	3	0.2224	0.2302890	0.2371751
49	0.25	1	3	10	3	0.2228	0.2301494	0.2365645
50	0.01	5	3	5	3	0.2238	0.2333700	0.2417233

Recall the role of nCombs. If we set it to NULL, that means we want qeFT() to try all possible combinations of our specified hyperparameter ranges. It turns out that there are 216 combinations (not shown). But we had set nCombs to 50, so qeFT() ran 50 randomly chosen combinations among the 216, and thus we see only 50 rows in the output here.

The more hyperparameters an ML algorithm has, and the more values we try for each one, the more possible combinations we have. In some cases, there are just too many to try them all, hence the non-NULL use of nCombs.

Note, too, that the more hyperparameter combinations we run, the greater the risk of p-hacking. It is here that the bonfCI column is most useful. The fact that, in the output above, the bonfCI column is very close to the CI column in most cases tells us that p-hacking is probably not an issue for this data.

Now, what might we glean from this output?

1. Hyperparameter tuning matters. The lowest OME values were about half of the largest ones.

2. Since the first three CI values are very close and within each other's CIs, any of the first three hyperparameter combinations should be good.

3. The first 20 hyperparameter combinations all had a value of 8 for maxdepth. This suggests that we might do even better with a value larger than 8.

4. Larger values of alpha seemed to do better. This suggests that we try some additional large values. For instance, we didn't try any values between 0.50 and 1, so 0.75 might be worth a try.

5. The top three combinations all had `mtry` = 0, while the bottom ones had a value of 3 for that hyperparameter. We probably should do more detailed investigation here.

6. The hyperparameters do interact. Look at line 6, for instance. The value of `alpha` was smaller than in most top lines, putting a damper on the node-splitting process, but this was compensated for in part by small values of `minsplit` and `minbucket`, which encourage lots of node splitting. Such negative "correlations" are clear in the graphical display capability of `qeFT()` (not shown).

7.6 Conclusions

No doubt about it, finding a good set of hyperparameters is one of the major challenges in ML. But in this chapter we've seen tools that can be used for this purpose, and we can be reasonably confident that we've made a good choice.

PART III

METHODS BASED ON LINEAR RELATIONSHIPS

These chapters begin with the classic linear and logistic models, which assume the regression function has a linear form. We then move to the more modern variant, the LASSO, which, oddly enough, deliberately shrinks the coefficients in the linear model.

8

PARAMETRIC METHODS

Recall the term *regression function*, first introduced in Section 1.6 and denoted by $r(t)$. It's the mean Y in the subpopulation defined by the condition $X = t$. The example we gave then involved bike ridership data:

> A regression function has as many arguments as we have features. Let's take humidity as a second feature, for instance. To predict ridership for a day with temperature 28 and humidity 0.51, we would use the mean ridership in our dataset, among days in which temperature and humidity are approximately 28 and 0.51. In regression function notation, that's $r(28, 0.51)$.

Basically, ML methods all are techniques to estimate the regression function from sample data. With k-NN, we would estimate $r(28, 0.51)$ in the bike ridership example by calculating the mean ridership among the days in the neighborhood of (28,0.51). With trees, we would plug (28,0.51) into our tree, follow the proper branches, and then calculate the mean ridership in the resulting leaf node, which acts like a neighborhood.

So far, we have not made any assumptions about the shape of the regression function graph. In this chapter, we will assume the shape is that of a straight line, or planes and so on in higher dimensions.

The so-called *linear model* is quite old, a couple of centuries old, actually. It can work fairly well in "easy" prediction applications, and even in some "advanced" ones. Indeed, we will see in Section 8.13 that a variant of the linear model can often outperform more sophisticated ML models.

The linear model should thus be in every analyst's toolkit. But an even more compelling reason to know the linear model is that it forms the basis of some of the most popular and powerful ML algorithms, including the LASSO, support vector machines, and neural networks, which we will cover in the succeeding chapters of this book.

8.1   Motivating Example: The Baseball Player Data

We'll soon introduce the qe*-series function for linear models, qeLin(). But to understand what it does, let's start with a simple setting in which we have only one feature and use it to motivate the concept of a linear model.

Recall the dataset mlb in Section 1.8 that is included with regtools. Let's restrict attention to just heights and weights of the players:

```
> data(mlb)
> hw <- mlb[,2:3]
```

Here, X and Y will be height and weight, respectively.

8.1.1   A Graph to Guide Our Intuition

So, we are predicting weight from height. In the $r()$ notation, that means that if we wish to predict the weight of a new player whose height is 71 inches, we need to estimate $r(71)$. This is the mean weight of all players in the subpopulation of players having height 71.

We don't know population values, as we only have a sample from the population. (As noted earlier, we consider our data to be a sample from the population of all players, past, present, and future.) How, then, can we estimate $r(71)$? The natural estimate is the analogous sample quantity, the mean weight of all height 71 players in our sample:

```
# find indices of data rows having height 71
> ht71 <- which(hw$Height == 71)
# find the average weight in those rows
> mean(hw$Weight[ht71])
[1] 190.3596
```

Recalling that the "hat" notation means "estimate of," we have that $\hat{r}(71) = 190.3596$. With deft usage of R's tapply() function, we can get all the estimated $r()$ values:

```
> meanWts <- tapply(hw$Weight,hw$Height,mean)
> meanWts
        67        68        69        70        71        72        73        74
  172.5000  173.8571  179.9474  183.0980  190.3596  192.5600  196.7716  202.4566
        75        76        77        78        79        80        81        82
  208.7161  214.1386  216.7273  220.4444  218.0714  237.4000  245.0000  240.5000
        83
  260.0000
```

This says, "Group the weight values by height, and find the mean weight in each group." By the way, note that the heights are available as the names of the weight items:

```
> meanWts['70']
     70
183.098
```

Let's plot the estimated mean weights against height:

```
> plot(names(meanWts),meanWts)
```

Figure 8-1 shows the result.

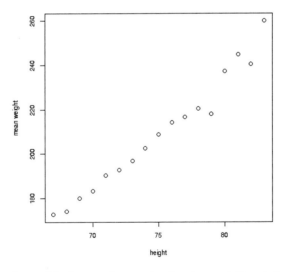

Figure 8-1: Estimated regression function, weight vs. height

Remarkably, the points seem to nearly lie on a straight line. This suggests a model for $r(t)$,

$$r(t) = b + mt \tag{8.1}$$

for some unknown values of the slope m and intercept b that we will estimate from the data. We are assuming that the graph of $r(t)$ is *some* straight line, though we don't know which one—that is, we don't know b and m. This is the linear model.

Keep in mind $r(t)$ is the *mean Y* for the subpopulation $X = t$, so we are modeling *mean Y* and not *Y* itself. We are not saying Equation 8.1 gives us the weight of individual players, though we do use the equation as the basis of our predictions.

8.1.2 View as Dimension Reduction

If Equation 8.1 is a valid model, we have greatly simplified our problem.

Ordinarily, we would need to estimate many different values of $r(t)$, such as those for t equal to 68, 69, 70, 71, 72, 73, and so on, say, 15 or 20 of them. But with the above model, *we need to estimate only two numbers, m and b*. As such, this is a form of dimension reduction.

8.2 The lm() Function

Assuming the linear model (again, we'll address its validity shortly), we can use R's lm() function to estimate m and b:

```
> lmout <- lm(Weight ~ .,data=hw)
> lmout

Call:
lm(formula = Weight ~ ., data = hw)

Coefficients:
(Intercept)        Height
   -151.133         4.783
```

So, $\widehat{m} = 4.783$ and $\widehat{b} = -151.133$.

Let's see what this call is saying:

```
lm(Weight ~ .,data=hw)
```

Here we are requesting that R fit a linear model to our data frame hw, predicting weight. The dot (.) means "all other columns," which, in this case, is just the height column.

To predict the weight of a new player of height 71, we would compute:

$$\widehat{r}(71) = \widehat{b} + \widehat{m} \cdot 71 = -151.133 + 4.783 \times 71 = 188.46 \tag{8.2}$$

But hey, we should have the computer do this computation rather than do it by hand:

```
> predict(lmout,data.frame(Height=71))
       1
188.4833
```

The slight discrepancy is due to a roundoff error in the computation by hand, where our data was given only to a few digits.

8.3 Wrapper for lm() in the qe*-Series: qeLin()

The lm() function is so basic in R that everyone should see it at least once, so we used it in the last section. But for simplicity and uniformity, we will use its qe*-series wrapper, qeLin().

Here's how to do the above computations in qeLin():

```
> qelout <- qeLin(hw,'Weight',holdout=NULL)
> qelout$coef
(Intercept)       Height
-151.133291    4.783332
> predict(qelout,data.frame(Height=71))
      2
188.4833
```

Most applications have more than just one feature. We cover the general case next.

8.4 Use of Multiple Features

We can, and typically do, fit the model to more than one feature.

8.4.1 Example: Baseball Player, Continued

Say we add in age, so our linear model is:

$$\text{mean weight} = b + m_1 \text{ height} + m_2 \text{ age} \tag{8.3}$$

For the purpose of terminology (used here and later), let's write this as

$$\text{mean weight} = b \cdot D + m_1 \text{ height} + m_2 \text{ age} \tag{8.4}$$

where D is an artificial variable that is always equal to 1. Then we say that mean weight is a *linear combination* of the variables D, *height*, and *age*. This is just a term meaning that to get mean weight, we multiply each of the three variables D, *height*, and *age* by the corresponding coefficients b, m_1, and m_2 and sum up the result.

We now are using columns 4, 5, and 6 of mlb, so we fit the model as follows, say, for age 28:

```
> qelout <- qeLin(mlb[,4:6],'Weight',holdout=NULL)
> predict(qelout,data.frame(Height=71,Age=28))
      11
187.4603
```

8.4.2 Beta Notation

Since the reader of this book will likely see other discussions, say, on the web, it should be mentioned that it's traditional to use the Greek letter β for the coefficients. For instance, Equation 8.3 would be written as:

$$\text{mean weight} = \beta_0 + \beta_1 \text{ height} + \beta_2 \text{ age} \tag{8.5}$$

We will estimate β_0, β_1, and β_2 from our sample data, as seen in Section 8.4.4. And, recalling that we use the hat notation for estimates, our estimated coefficients will be denoted by $\widehat{\beta}_0$, $\widehat{\beta}_1$, and $\widehat{\beta}_2$.

8.4.3 Example: Airbnb Data

The short-term housing firm Airbnb makes available voluminous rental data. Here we look at some data from San Francisco.[1] (The dataset used here, from February 1, 2019, appears to no longer be available.) It will not only provide another example of the linear model, but it also will illustrate some data-cleaning issues.

8.4.3.1 Data Preparation

After downloading the data and reading it into R (details not shown), we had a data frame Abb, which still required a lot of attention.

Many of the features are textual, for example:

```
> Abb[1,]$house_rules
[1] "* No Pets - even visiting guests for a short time period. * No Smokers..."
```

We will treat the topic of text data later in this book but removed it for this example.

Another problem is that prices include dollar signs and commas, for example:

```
> Abb[1,]$monthly_price
[1] "$4,200.00"
```

Dealing with such issues tends to take up a remarkably large portion of a data scientist's job. Here we wrote a function to convert a column d of such numbers to the proper form, using a couple of R's character string manipulation facilities:

```
convertFromDollars <- function(d) {
    d <- as.character(d)
    # replace dollar sign by ''
    d <- sub('\\$','',d,fixed=F)
    # replace commas by ''
    d <- gsub(',','',d)
    d <- as.numeric(d)
```

---

1. *http://insideairbnb.com/get-the-data/*

```
    # some entries were ''; replace by NAs
    d[d == ''] <- NA
    d
}
```

And, not surprisingly, this dataset seems to have its share of erroneous entries:

```
> table(Abb$square_feet)
```

0	1	2	14	120	130	140	150	160	172	175	195	250	280	300	360
2	3	2	1	1	1	3	2	1	1	1	1	2	2	4	2

400	450	500	538	550	600	650	700	750	780	800	810	815	840	850	853
1	2	8	1	1	4	1	3	5	1	4	1	1	1	1	1

890	900	950	1000	1012	1019	1100	1200	1390	1400	1490	1500	1600	1660	1750	1800
1	2	3	9	1	1	2	9	1	2	1	7	1	1	1	3

1850	1900	1996	2000	2100	2200	2250	2600	3000
1	1	1	4	3	2	1	1	4

For instance, areas of 1 and 2 square feet are listed, obviously incorrect. We will not pursue this further here, but clearly we would have a lot more work to do if this were not merely an example for the book.

After data cleaning, the data frame looks like this:

```
> head(Abb)
  zipcode bathrooms bedrooms square_feet weekly_price monthly_price
1   94117       1.0        1          NA         1120          4200
2   94110       1.0        2          NA         1600          5500
3   94117       4.0        1          NA          485          1685
4   94117       4.0        1          NA          490          1685
5   94117       1.5        2          NA           NA            NA
6   94115       1.0        2          NA           NA            NA
  security_deposit guests_included minimum_nights maximum_nights
1              100               2              1             30
2               NA               2             30             60
3              200               1             32             60
4              200               1             32             90
5                0               2              7           1125
6                0               1              2            365
  review_scores_rating
1                   97
2                   98
3                   85
4                   93
5                   97
6                   90
```

We are now ready to perform the analysis.

8.4.4 Applying the Linear Model

Here is the call, omitting the square footage and weekly price columns:

```
> linout <- qeLin(Abb[,-c(4,5)],'monthly_price',holdout=NULL)
> linout$coef
       (Intercept)          zipcode94103          zipcode94104
      -4.485690e+03         -4.441996e+02          6.364539e+02
       zipcode94105          zipcode94107          zipcode94108
       1.012009e+03         -2.846037e+02         -1.649897e+03
       zipcode94109          zipcode94110          zipcode94111
      -3.945963e+02         -1.113476e+03          1.619558e+03
       zipcode94112          zipcode94114          zipcode94115
      -2.304310e+03         -2.607913e+02         -3.881351e+02
       zipcode94116          zipcode94117          zipcode94118
      -1.959336e+03         -1.543353e+02         -1.362785e+03
       zipcode94121          zipcode94122          zipcode94123
      -1.315474e+03         -1.434050e+03          1.639610e+03
       zipcode94124          zipcode94127          zipcode94131
      -2.309765e+03         -2.127720e+03         -1.525655e+03
       zipcode94132          zipcode94133          zipcode94134
      -1.675761e+03          6.496800e+02         -1.370148e+03
       zipcode94158             bathrooms             bedrooms
      -2.509281e+03          2.025493e+02          1.540830e+03
    security_deposit       guests_included        minimum_nights
       3.462443e-01          3.663498e+02         -6.400597e-01
      maximum_nights  review_scores_rating
      -2.371457e-04          6.613115e+01
```

As is common in R, the estimated coefficients are displayed here in *scientific notation*, in which, for instance, $1.605326e + 03 = 1.605326 \times 10^3 = 1605.326$. So, for instance, $\widehat{\beta}_0$ is about −4,486, $\widehat{\beta}_1$ is about −444, and so on.

Note that lm() (via its wrapper qeLin()) has converted the ZIP code feature, an R factor, to dummy variables. Recall that typically we have one fewer dummy than the number of categories—in this case, the number of ZIP codes. R leaves out the first one here, which is 94102.

Since our focus in this book is on prediction rather than causal interpretation, the estimated coefficients are of lesser interest. Furthermore, one must be very careful in interpreting coefficients. Nevertheless, some comments regarding the coefficients are in order, next.

8.5   Dimension Reduction

Let's discuss this fundamental ML topic in the context of linear models and the Airbnb example in the previous section.

8.5.1 Which Features Are Important?

As noted in Section 3.1.1, there are more than 40,000 ZIP codes in the United States; this is typically far too many to use directly. In San Francisco, the number is manageable, but still we may wish to drop the ones that seem unimportant to our predictions.

On the other hand, as real estate agents say, "Location, location, location." ZIP code should matter a lot, and the estimated coefficients at least seem to confirm this. For instance, according to the coefficient estimates given earlier, a property in ZIP code 94105, on average, commands a price premium of about $1,012, while one in 94107 will, on average, cost about $285 below market, holding all other variables fixed. But what are the terms *premium* and *cost less* relative to here? Since ZIP code 94102 was omitted, we see that 94105 costs about $1,012 more on average than 94102–the ZIP code term in $\widehat{r}(t)$ would be about $1 \cdot 1012$ for a property in that ZIP code, while it would be 0 for one in 94102, since there is no dummy variable for that ZIP code. Similarly, 94107 runs about $444 below 94102, and so on. In other words, 94102 becomes the baseline ZIP code.

But . . . note the phrasing above: "the estimated coefficients at least *seem* to confirm this." After all, we are working with *estimates* of finite accuracy. This is a vital point to take into account, which we will do next.

On the other hand, the amount of `security_deposit` seems not to matter much at all, so we should consider dropping it from our analysis. Recall that having more features means less bias but more variance. Since the effect of a security deposit in prediction values seems small, dropping this feature should add very little bias. The same statement holds for the features `minimum_nights` and `maximum_nights`.

8.5.2 Statistical Significance and Dimension Reduction

In the previous section, we suggested several features to drop from our analysis. But we did so only on the basis of a "feeling." It is natural to desire some magic formula that will determine which features to retain and which to remove. But alas, as has been explained in this book, no such magic formula exists. We have cited a few methods, such as cross-validation and PCA, that are commonly used, but again, these are not magic, foolproof solutions.

In this section, we look at the use of *statistical significance* for dimension reduction in parametric models. *We do not recommend it*, and it is less favored than in the past, but it is still popular among many analysts. Thus, it is imperative to cover the technique here.

First, we will need to introduce a new R generic function (Section 1.5.1). In addition to `print()`, `plot()`, and `predict()`, another common generic function in R is `summary()`. It does what its name implies; that is, it provides a summary of the object.

Recall that a generic function is tailored to the class of the object at hand. What is the class of our object here, `linout`?

```
> class(linout)
[1] "qeLin" "lm"
```

So, if we make the call summary(linout), the R interpreter will first check for a function summary.qeLin(). Since the qeML package has no such function, the interpreter will next look for summary.lm(), which does exist. Let's see what the function gives us:

```
> summary(linout)
...
Coefficients:
                      Estimate Std. Error t value Pr(>|t|)
(Intercept)         -4.486e+03  1.478e+03  -3.034 0.002479 **
zipcode94103        -4.442e+02  5.177e+02  -0.858 0.391094
zipcode94104         6.365e+02  2.131e+03   0.299 0.765227
zipcode94105         1.012e+03  7.071e+02   1.431 0.152724
zipcode94107        -2.846e+02  4.906e+02  -0.580 0.561978
zipcode94108        -1.650e+03  6.354e+02  -2.597 0.009566 **
zipcode94109        -3.946e+02  4.955e+02  -0.796 0.426025
zipcode94110        -1.113e+03  4.280e+02  -2.601 0.009435 **
zipcode94111         1.620e+03  1.014e+03   1.598 0.110396
zipcode94112        -2.304e+03  4.761e+02  -4.840 1.52e-06 ***
zipcode94114        -2.608e+02  4.425e+02  -0.589 0.555770
zipcode94115        -3.881e+02  4.666e+02  -0.832 0.405719
zipcode94116        -1.959e+03  7.028e+02  -2.788 0.005412 **
zipcode94117        -1.543e+02  4.441e+02  -0.348 0.728269
zipcode94118        -1.363e+03  5.560e+02  -2.451 0.014434 *
zipcode94121        -1.315e+03  6.422e+02  -2.048 0.040819 *
zipcode94122        -1.434e+03  5.437e+02  -2.638 0.008493 **
zipcode94123         1.640e+03  5.507e+02   2.977 0.002985 **
zipcode94124        -2.310e+03  6.552e+02  -3.525 0.000444 ***
zipcode94127        -2.128e+03  6.051e+02  -3.516 0.000459 ***
zipcode94131        -1.526e+03  5.024e+02  -3.037 0.002459 **
zipcode94132        -1.676e+03  7.745e+02  -2.164 0.030746 *
zipcode94133         6.497e+02  5.402e+02   1.203 0.229402
zipcode94134        -1.370e+03  8.837e+02  -1.550 0.121376
zipcode94158        -2.509e+03  1.546e+03  -1.623 0.104905
bathrooms            2.025e+02  1.323e+02   1.531 0.125996
bedrooms             1.541e+03  1.071e+02  14.385  < 2e-16 ***
security_deposit     3.462e-01  9.820e-02   3.526 0.000443 ***
guests_included      3.663e+02  5.897e+01   6.212 7.92e-10 ***
minimum_nights      -6.401e-01  2.670e+00  -0.240 0.810569
maximum_nights      -2.371e-04  2.132e-03  -0.111 0.911465
review_scores_rating 6.613e+01  1.432e+01   4.617 4.44e-06 ***
...
```

One particular type of information computed here is standard errors, discussed next.

8.5.2.1 Standard Errors

You can see above that a *standard error* is reported for each estimated coefficient $\widehat{\beta}_i$. It's the estimated standard deviation of $\widehat{\beta}_i$ over all possible samples for whatever population is being sampled. This gives us an idea as to how accurate $\widehat{\beta}_i$ is, using the following reasoning.

If the standard error is small, it says that if we had had a different set of sample data from the given population, $\widehat{\beta}_i$ probably would have come out to about the same value as what we got. In other words, we can treat $\widehat{\beta}_i$ as representative.

We can form an approximate 95 percent confidence interval (CI) for β_i by adding and subtracting 1.96 times the standard error of $\widehat{\beta}_i$.

For instance, consider the dummy variable `zipcode94134`. The estimated beta coefficient for this variable is −$1,370. This is relative to whichever ZIP code is the base, meaning the one for which there is no dummy variable. (Recall from Section 1.4 that with a categorical feature, we have one fewer dummy than the number of categories.) As noted earlier, the omitted ZIP code is 94102. So, for a given security deposit, guest policy, and so on, this neighborhood is estimated to be more than $1,000 cheaper than the baseline. But look at the CI:

$$-1370 \pm 1.96 \times 883.7 = (-3102.1, 362.1) \tag{8.6}$$

The CI suggests that this neighborhood actually could be hundreds of dollars more *expensive* than the base.

8.5.2.2 Significance Tests

That last example suggests that the status of `zipcode94134` as a predictor of rent is inconclusive. We should thus seriously consider dropping it from our model. Remember the notion of the Bias-Variance Trade-off means that if a feature is not very helpful, then including it in our model may degrade our predictive ability.

But let's consider another ZIP code, say, 94132. Here the CI is

$$-1676 \pm 1.96 \times 774.5 = (-3194.0, -158.0) \tag{8.7}$$

which is entirely in negative territory. For this reason, it is flagged with an asterisk.

What do all those asterisks mean? Why are there double asterisks for some coefficients? Our focus in this book is not on statistics, but it is important for the reader to have at least an overview of the situation since it is common to use the asterisks as a guide for dimension reduction.

Roughly speaking, if the CI does not contain 0, the coefficient is flagged with an asterisk. It rates *two* asterisks if 0 is well outside the interval and three if the CI is far, far away from 0. A coefficient with one asterisk is termed *significant* (that is, significantly different from 0); one with two asterisks is called *highly significant*, and three asterisks wins a coefficient the accolade *very highly significant*.

Well then, what constitutes "well outside the interval" and "far, far away from 0"? This is determined by the p-value. A p-value under 0.05 is significant, and it is highly or very highly significant if it is under 0.01 or 0.001, respectively.

The p-value is a certain probability whose convoluted definition we will skip. (Recall this term from Section 5.5.) Suffice it to say, under this approach to dimension reduction, one discards any feature with no asterisks, such as zipcode94134, and retains the others in the model. If one wants to exercise a little more caution, one might retain only the coefficients with at least two asterisks.

Today, many analysts, including myself, consider this approach to be flawed. Let's see why. The short answer is that p-values are too dependent on the number of data points n. Actually, the standard error is inversely proportional to $\sqrt{n}$. This has quite an implication, as follows.

Suppose, hypothetically, that the estimated coefficient for, say, zipcode94132 had been 1.4, with a standard error of 0.9. That would give us a confidence interval of:

$$(-0.4, 3.2) \tag{8.8}$$

This contains 0, hence no asterisks. And that's probably a good thing, since this feature seems to have no real predictive power: being in that ZIP code makes an estimated difference in rent of only a dollar or so.

But what if we were fortunate to have 25 times as much data? Then $\sqrt{n}$ would increase by a factor of 5, so the standard error would shrink by a factor of 5, coming out at approximately 0.18. It would change somewhat, as would the coefficient estimate 1.4, but in rough terms our CI would now be something like:

$$1.4 \pm 1.96 \times 0.18 = (1.05, 1.75) \tag{8.9}$$

Ah, now it's significant! Yay! But ... the estimated coefficient would still be something like $1.40—less than $2! That variable can hardly help us predict rent. In other words, the so-called significant nature of that feature could really lead us astray.

Use of significance tests and p-values is frowned upon by many statisticians (including this author).[2] The tests are especially unreliable in prediction applications. With large datasets, *every* feature will be declared "very highly significant" (three asterisks) regardless of whether the feature has substantial predictive power. A feature with a very small regression coefficient could be declared "significant," in spite of being essentially useless as a predictor.

---

2. *https://www.amstat.org/asa/files/pdfs/P-ValueStatement.pdf*

8.5.2.3 Pitfall: NA Values and Impact on n

As shown above, this dataset also includes a number of NA values. We didn't have to deal with this directly, since `lm()`, which `qeLin()` wraps, automatically restricts its computations to complete cases. Nevertheless, as noted in Section 4.1, if a dataset contains many NAs, this is yet another reason to seek dimension reduction, as doing so may increase the number of complete cases. This means less variance, which is very desirable. Some experimentation here reveals that removal of the most NA-prone features, beyond the ones we've already deleted, does not help increase data size in this particular case, but it is an important general principle.

8.5.2.4 Pitfall: Difficulty of Forming Holdout Sets with Many-Level Categoricals

In our earlier Airbnb analysis, problems occur if we form a holdout set:

```
> linout <- qeLin(Abb[,-c(4,5)],'monthly_price')
holdout set has  707 rows
Error in model.frame.default(Terms, newdata,
   na.action = na.action, xlev = object$xlevels) :
  factor zipcode has new levels 94014
> linout <- qeLin(Abb[,-c(4,5)],'monthly_price')
holdout set has  707 rows
Error in model.frame.default(Terms, newdata,
   na.action = na.action, xlev = object$xlevels) :
  factor zipcode has new levels 94014, 94106
```

Of course, since the holdout set is chosen randomly, there may be a different result each time. But we see that in each of our two tries here, we had at least one error, "factor zipcode has new levels." What is happening here?

The problem is that certain ZIP codes, such as 94014, appear in only a few data points. Apparently there were no 94014 cases in each training set here, so *lm() was "surprised" to see one in the holdout set.*

The only solution would be to remove all cases with 94014 (and possibly others) from the data before running `qeLin()`.

8.6 Least Squares and Residuals

Even though the computational details underlying `lm()` are beyond the scope of this book, it's important to have a rough idea of what is involved, as similar computations will arise later in the book. This will bring in the notion of *least squares*. That, in turn, will lead to the idea of *residuals*, which are important in their own right.

For simplicity, let's consider the context of Section 8.2 here. The quantities $\widehat{m}$ and $\widehat{b}$ and so on are computed using the famous *ordinary least squares (OLS)* method, which works as follows.

Imagine that after we compute $\widehat{m}$ and $\widehat{b}$, we go back and "predict" the weight of the first player in our sample data. As implied by the quotation marks, this would be silly; after all, we already know the weight of the first player, 180:

```
> data(mlb)
> mlb[1,]
          Name Team Position Height Weight   Age
1 Adam_Donachie  BAL  Catcher     74    180 22.99
  PosCategory
1     Catcher
```

But think through this exercise anyway. It will turn out to be the basis for how things work, both for linear models and all the ML methods in the remainder of the book.

Our predicted value would be $\widehat{b} + \widehat{m} \cdot 71$. Thus our prediction error would be:

$$180 - (\widehat{b} + \widehat{m} \cdot 71)$$

This is the *residual* for that row in the dataset. (Recall that this was briefly mentioned in Section 6.3.2.) We'll square that error rather than using it in its raw form, as we will be summing errors and don't want positive and negative ones to cancel. Now we "predict" all the other data points as well, and add up the squared errors:

$$[180 - (\widehat{b} + \widehat{m} \cdot 71)]^2 + [215 - (\widehat{b} + \widehat{m} \cdot 74)]^2 + \dots + [195 - (\widehat{b} + \widehat{m} \cdot 73)]^2 \quad (8.10)$$

Now here is the point: the way lm() finds $\widehat{b}$ and $\widehat{m}$ is to set them to whatever values minimize the sum of squares (Equation 8.10). In other words, think of the expression as a function of two variables, $\widehat{b}$ and $\widehat{m}$, and then minimize the expression with respect to those two variables. (Readers who know calculus may have spotted the fact that we set the two derivatives equal to 0 and solve for $\widehat{b}$ and $\widehat{m}$.)

Since we are minimizing a sum of squares, the estimated coefficients are said to be the *least squares estimates*. (The word *ordinary* is often added, as ordinary least squares is distinct from some variants that we will not discuss here.)

8.7 Diagnostics: Is the Linear Model Valid?

> *All models are wrong, but some are useful.*
> —George Box, famous early statistician

The linearity assumption is pretty strong. When is it appropriate? Let's take a closer look.

8.7.1 Exactness?

The reader may ask, "How can the linear model in Equation 8.1 be valid?" Yes, the points in Figure 8-1 look like they are kind of on a straight line, but not exactly so. There are two important answers:

- As the quote from George Box points out, no model is *exactly* correct. Commonly used physics models ignore things like air resistance and friction, and even models accounting for such things still don't reflect all possible factors. A linear approximation to the regression function $r(t)$ may do a fine job in prediction even if the model is not perfect.

- Even if Equation 8.1 were exactly correct, the points in Figure 8-1 would not lie exactly on the line. Remember, $r(71)$, for instance, is only the *mean* weight of all players of height 71. Most individual players of that height are heavier or lighter than that value, so their data points will not fall exactly on that line and, in fact, may be far from it in some cases. And the same point holds for the mean weights that we plotted in Figure 8-1; each of those means were based on only a few players.

By the way, classical linear model methodology makes some assumptions beyond linearity, such as Y having a normal distribution in each subpopulation. But these are not relevant to our prediction context. (Actually, even for statistical inference, the normality assumption is not important in large samples.)

8.7.2 Diagnostic Methods

Over the years, analysts have developed a number of methods to check the validity of the linear model. Several are described in my book *Statistical Regression and Classification: From Linear Models to Machine Learning* (CRC Press, 2017).

Again, since we are interested in prediction rather than causal analysis, we will not cover this material here. As long as the outcome variable is an increasing or decreasing function of the features—for example, mean human weight is an increasing function of height—a linear model should do fairly well in prediction-oriented applications. With linear polynomial models (see Section 8.11), this can be refined.

8.8 The R-Squared Value(s)

Recall that the estimated coefficients are calculated by minimizing the sum of squared differences between actual and predicted Y values (see Section 8.6). R^2 is the squared correlation between actual and predicted Y.

It can be shown that this can be interpreted as the proportion of variation in Y due to X. (As always, X refers collectively to all our features.) As such, we have $0 \le R^2 \le 1$, with a value of 1 meaning that X perfectly predicts Y. However, there is a big problem here, as we are predicting the same data that we used to estimate our prediction machine, the regression coefficients. If we are overfitting, then R^2 will be overly optimistic.

This, of course, is the motivation for using holdout data. Thus `qeLin()` reports not only the standard R^2 but also the R^2 calculated on the holdout set (stored in the `holdoutR2` component of the `qeLin()` return value). The latter is more reliable. Furthermore, if there is a large discrepancy between the two, it suggests that we are overfitting.

Most linear regression software libraries also report the *adjusted* R^2 value. The word *adjusted* here alludes to the fact that the formula attempts to correct for overfitting. The `qeLin()` reports this too, and again a large discrepancy between this value and the first R^2 value suggests we are overfitting.

8.9 Classification Applications: The Logistic Model

The linear model is designed for regression applications. What about classification? A generalization of the linear model, unsurprisingly called the *generalized linear model*, handles that. Here we will present one form of the model, the *logistic* model.

Recall the discussion at the beginning of Chapter 2, which pointed out that in classification settings, where Y is either 1 or 0, the regression function becomes the probability of $Y = 1$ for the given subpopulation. If we fit a purely linear model with `lm()`, the estimated regression values may be outside the interval $[0,1]$ and thus not represent a probability. We could, of course, truncate any value predicted by `lm()` to $[0,1]$, but the *logistic* model provides a better approach.

The model takes its name from the logistic function $l(t) = 1/(1 + e^{-t})$. Since that function takes values in $(0,1)$, it is suitable for modeling a probability. We still use a linear form but run the form through the logistic function to squeeze it into $(0,1)$ for probability modeling.

Say we wish to predict gender from height. Our model might be:

$$\text{probability}(\text{male} \mid \text{height}) = \frac{1}{1 + \exp\left[-(\beta_0 + \beta_1 \text{ height})\right]}$$

Here β_0 and β_1 are, again, population values, which we estimate from our data.

The logistic and linear models are basically similar: in the linear model, β_i is the impact that the ith feature has on mean Y, while in the logit case, β_i is the impact that the ith feature has on the probability that $Y = 1$. (Some analysts view logit in terms of a linear model of the *log-odds ratio*, $\log(P(Y = 1|X) / [1 - P(Y = 1|X)])$.)

The logistic model is often called the *logit* model for simplicity.

8.9.1 The glm() and qeLogit() Functions

In R, the standard function for the generalized linear model is glm(). In the logistic case, that function is wrapped by the qeML package function qeLogit(). The call form for the latter is:

```
qeLogit(data,yName,
    holdout = floor(min(1000, 0.1 * nrow(data))),yesYVal = NULL)
```

The first three arguments are as in the other qe*-series functions. The last argument, yesYVal, is needed in the 2-class case. It specifies the value of Y that we wish to be coded as $Y = 1$.

8.9.2 Example: Telco Churn Data

In Section 2.2, we used k-NN to analyze some customer retention data. Let's revisit that data, now using a logistic model. Recall that the Churn variable has values 'Yes' and 'No'.

```
# data prep as before, not shown
> set.seed(9999)
> glout <- qeLogit(tc,'Churn',holdout=NULL,yesYVal='Yes')
```

Our model is:

$$\text{probability of churn} = \frac{1}{1 + \exp\left(-[\beta_0 + \beta_1 \cdot \text{Male} + \beta_2 \cdot \text{SeniorCitizen} + \ldots]\right)}$$

Let's predict a new case that is similar to, say, the 333rd one in our dataset but with a different gender:

```
> names(tc)
 [1] "gender"          "SeniorCitizen"   "Partner"           "Dependents"
 [5] "tenure"          "PhoneService"    "MultipleLines"     "InternetService"
 [9] "OnlineSecurity"  "OnlineBackup"    "DeviceProtection"  "TechSupport"
[13] "StreamingTV"     "StreamingMovies" "Contract"          "PaperlessBilling"
[17] "PaymentMethod"   "MonthlyCharges"  "TotalCharges"      "Churn"
> newx <- tc[333,-20]   # exclude Y
> newx
    gender SeniorCitizen Partner Dependents tenure PhoneService MultipleLines
333 Male               0      No         No     46          Yes           Yes
    InternetService OnlineSecurity OnlineBackup DeviceProtection TechSupport
333     Fiber optic             No          Yes              Yes          No
    StreamingTV StreamingMovies Contract PaperlessBilling
333         Yes              No One year              Yes
              PaymentMethod MonthlyCharges TotalCharges
333 Credit card (automatic)           94.9      4422.95
> newx$gender <- 'Female'
> predict(glout,newx)
```

```
$predClasses
[1] "No"

$probs

       [,1]
[1,] 0.2307227
```

We guess that the customer will stay put—that is, not jump to another service provider—with a jump probability of only about 23 percent.

We also get a warning message:

```
Warning messages:
1: In predict.lm(object, newdata, se.fit, scale = 1, type = if (type ==  :
  prediction from a rank-deficient fit may be misleading
2: In predict.lm(object, newdata, se.fit, scale = 1, type = if (type ==  :
  prediction from a rank-deficient fit may be misleading
```

This is a technical issue, occurring when the features are highly correlated. Here glm() has actually skipped over some of the features that are in essence redundant.

Sometimes glm() will give us a warning message like:

```
glm.fit: fitted probabilities numerically 0 or 1 occurred
```

Again, this is a technical issue, which we will not pursue here. The reader may proceed as usual.

On the other hand, a warning that one cannot ignore is "failed to converge." This will not happen with lm(), the R function wrapped by our qeLinear(), but it may occasionally occur with logit. This is usually remedied by performing some dimension reduction.

8.9.3   Multiclass Case

If there are more than two classes, we have two options. For concreteness, consider the vertebrae data from Section 2.3. There we had three classes, DH, NO, and SL. For now, just consider using glm() directly rather than its wrapper, qeLogit().

One vs. All (OVA) method   Here we run glm() once for each class. We first run logit with DH playing the role of *Y*. Then we do this with NO serving as *Y* and then finally the same for SL. That gives us three sets of coefficients—in fact, three return objects from glm(), say, DHout, NOout, and SLout. Then when predicting a new case newx, we run:

```
predict(DHout,newx,type='response')
predict(NOout,newx,type='response')
predict(SLout,newx,type='response')
```

This gives us three probabilities. We take as our prediction whichever class has the highest probability.

All vs. All (AVA) method   Here we run glm() once for each *pair* of classes. First, we restrict the data to just DH and NO, putting SL cases aside for the moment, and take *Y* as DH. Then we focus on just DH and SL, taking *Y* to be DH again. Finally, we put DH aside for the moment, running with NO and SL and taking *Y* to be NO. Again, that would give us three objects output from glm().

Then we would call predict() three times on newx. Say the outcome with the first object is less than 0.5. That means between DH and NO, we would predict this new case to be NO—that is, NO "wins." We do this on all three objects, and whichever class wins the most often is our predicted class.

The qeLogit() function uses the OVA approach. Since qeLogit() is a wrapper for glm(), we do not see the actions of the latter, and they are used only as intermediate internal computations. However, if desired, the results of the calls to glm() can be accessed in the glOuts component of the object returned by qeLogit().

8.9.4   *Example: Fall Detection Data*

This dataset is included in qeML, originally from Kaggle.[3] From the site:

> Falls are a serious public health problem and possibly life threat-ening for people in fall risk groups. We develop an automated fall detection system with wearable motion sensor units fitted to the subjects' body at six different positions.

There are six activity types, thus six classes, coded 0 (Standing), 1 (Walking), 2 (Sitting), 3 (Falling), 4 (Cramps), and 5 (Running). Let's see how well we can predict the class:

```
> data(falldetection)
> fd <- falldetection
> head(fd)
  ACTIVITY    TIME      SL      EEG BP  HR CIRCULATION
1        3 4722.92 4019.64 -1600.00 13  79         317
2        2 4059.12 2191.03 -1146.08 20  54         165
3        2 4773.56 2787.99 -1263.38 46  67         224
4        4 8271.27 9545.98 -2848.93 26 138         554
5        4 7102.16 14148.80 -2381.15 85 120         809
6        5 7015.24 7336.79 -1699.80 22  95         427
> fd$ACTIVITY <- as.factor(fd$ACTIVITY)  # was integer, need factor for qe*
> set.seed(9999)
> fd$ACTIVITY <- as.factor(fd$ACTIVITY)
```

---

3. Unfortunately, this data seems to be no longer available.

```
> fdout <- qeLogit(fd,'ACTIVITY')
> fdout$testAcc
[1] 0.593
> fdout$baseAcc
[1] 0.7186972
> table(fd$ACTIVITY)

   0    1    2    3    4    5
4608  502 2502 3588 3494 1688
```

We are correctly predicting only about 40 percent of the cases with our logit model, but that's better than the 28 percent correct we'd get just guessing every case to be of Class 3, the most common class.

Let's predict a hypothetical new case, say, like the first row in the data but with BP equal to 28:

```
> newx <- fd[1,-1]
> newx
     TIME      SL    EEG BP HR CIRCULATION
1 4722.92 4019.64 -1600 13 79         317
> newx$BP <- 28
> newx
     TIME      SL    EEG BP HR CIRCULATION
1 4722.92 4019.64 -1600 28 79         317
> predict(fdout,newx)
$predClasses
[1] "2"

$probs
          0         1         2         3         4          5
[1,] 0.2294015 0.1111428 0.2324076 0.1605359 0.1830733 0.08343888
```

Such a case would result in a prediction of Class 2, with a probability of about 23 percent.

8.10   Bias and Variance in Linear/Generalized Linear Models

As discussed in Chapter 3, the more features we use, the smaller the bias but the larger the variance. With parametric models, such as those in this chapter, the larger variance comes in the form of less-stable estimates of the coefficients, which, in turn, make later predictions less stable.

Once again, note that high variance for a coefficient estimate means that the value of that estimate will vary a lot from one sample to another. That large oscillation, in turn, means that the estimated coefficient vector will be less likely to be near the true population value.

Here we present a concrete example illustrating the fact that the variance increases with the complexity of the model.

8.10.1 Example: Bike Sharing Data

We can make that point about instability of predictions more concrete using the regtools function stdErrPred(). This function finds the standard error of a predicted value obtained from lm(). Recall from Section 8.5.2.1 that the standard error of an estimator is the estimated standard deviation of that estimator. A larger standard error thus means more variability of the estimator from one sample to another.

We'll fit two models, one with a smaller feature set and the other with a somewhat larger one, and then do the same prediction on each; just as an example, we'll predict the third data point in the dataset. We will print out the two predictions and, most important, the standard error of the two predictions.

```
> data(day1)
> e1 <- day1[,c(4,10,12,13,16)]
> e2 <- day1[,c(4,10,12,13,16,6,7)]   # add holiday, weekday columns
> names(e1)
[1] "yr"        "temp"      "hum"       "windspeed" "tot"
> names(e2)
[1] "yr"        "temp"      "hum"       "windspeed" "tot"       "holiday"
[7] "weekday"
> set.seed(9999)
> e1out <- qeLin(e1,'tot')
> e2out <- qeLin(e2,'tot')
> newx1 <- e1[3,-5]   # exclude tot
> newx2 <- e2[3,-5]   # exclude tot
> predict(e1out,newx1)
      31
1818.779
> predict(e2out,newx2)
       3
1689.054
> stdErrPred(e1out,newx1)
[1] 97.77229
> stdErrPred(e2out,newx2)
[1] 108.3989
```

So the prediction from the larger feature set has a larger standard error. The standard error is the standard deviation of an estimator—in this case, our estimate of prediction accuracy. So here we see the Bias-Variance Trade-off in action. The larger model, though more detailed and thus less biased, does have a larger variance.

Does that mean that we should use the smaller feature set? No. In order to see if we've hit the switchover point, we'd need to use cross-validation. But the reader should keep this concrete illustration of the trade-off in mind.

8.11   Polynomial Models

Surprisingly, one can use linear regression methods to model nonlinear effects. We'll see how in this section. Why is this important?

- A polynomial model can often match or even outperform many of the more glamorous ML models.

- Polynomials will play an important role in our chapter on support vector machines (Chapter 10), and even in our treatment of neural networks (Chapter 11), where there is a surprising connection to polynomials.

8.11.1   Motivation

We've used the example of programmer and engineer wages earlier in this book (see Section 3.2.3). Consider the graph of wage income against age shown in Figure 8-2. There seems to be a steep rise in a worker's 20s, then a long leveling off, with a hint even of a decline after age 55 or so. This is definitely not a linear relationship.

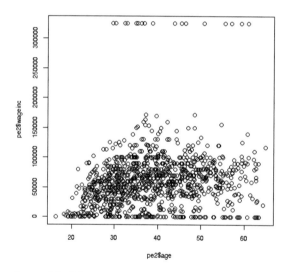

Figure 8-2: Wage income vs. age

Or consider Figure 8-3, for the bike sharing data, graphing total ridership against temperature. The nonlinear relationship is even clearer here. (We seem to see two groups here, possibly for the registered and casual riders.) No surprise, of course—people don't want to go bike riding if the weather is too cold or too hot—but again, the point is that a linear model would seem questionable.

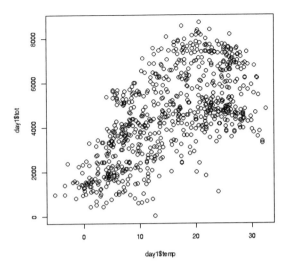

Figure 8-3: Ridership vs. temperature

Fortunately, these nonlinear effects actually *can* be accommodated with linear models.

8.11.2 Modeling Nonlinearity with a Linear Model

Starting simple, suppose in the bike rental data we wish to predict total ridership tot, using temperature temp as our sole feature, but want a quadratic model:

$$mean\ tot = b + c\ temp + d\ temp^2 \qquad (8.11)$$

This is still a linear model! Sure, there is a squared term there for temp, so we say the model is nonlinear *in terms of* temp. But it is still linear in b, c, and d. We are modeling mean tot as a linear combination of three things: 1, temp, and $temp^2$ (thinking of b as $b \times 1$).

Then we could simply add a $temp^2$ column and call qeLin():

```
> data(day1)
> day1tottemp <- day1[,c(10,16)]  # just tot, temp
> head(day1tottemp)
      temp  tot
1 8.175849  985
2 9.083466  801
3 1.229108 1349
4 1.400000 1562
5 2.666979 1600
6 1.604356 1606
> day1tottemp$tempSqr <- day1tottemp$temp^2
> head(day1tottemp)
```

```
      temp   tot   tempSqr
1 8.175849   985  66.844507
2 9.083466   801  82.509355
3 1.229108  1349   1.510706
4 1.400000  1562   1.960000
5 2.666979  1600   7.112777
6 1.604356  1606   2.573958
> qeLin(day1tottemp,'tot')
...

Coefficients:
(Intercept)          temp       tempSqr
   1305.597       346.422        -6.815
```

We see that $\widehat{b}$ = 1305.597, $\widehat{c}$ = 346.422, and $\widehat{d}$ = −6.815.

But this is inconvenient. Not only would we need to add that squared column manually, but we also would have to remember to add it later to new cases that we wish to predict.

Worse, we would need to add the *cross-product* terms. Say we are predicting total ridership from both temperature and humidity. In that case, Equation 8.11 would include a product of these two features, becoming:

$$mean\ tot = b + c\ temp + d\ temp^2 + e\ hum + f\ hum^2 + g\ temp \times hum \qquad (8.12)$$

If we have a lot of features, adding these terms manually would become a real nuisance.

A more subtle problem concerns dummy variables. Since 0^2 = 0 and 1^2 = 1, we see that the square of any dummy is itself. So adding squared terms to our model for dummies would be redundant.

To avoid such issues, the qeML package has the qePolyLin() function, which takes care of these things for us automatically. Its basic call form is:

```
qePolyLin(data, yName, deg = 2, maxInteractDeg = deg,
    holdout = floor(min(1000,0.1 * nrow(data))))
```

The argument deg is the degree of the polynomial, and maxInteractDeg is the maximum interaction degree term; for instance, *temp* × *hum* is considered to be of degree 2 in Equation 8.12. Of course, if we have just a single feature, there are no interaction terms.

It gives the same fit as the one we got above manually (of course). Let's again predict tot from temp:

```
> day1tottemp <- day1[,c(10,16)]
> qepout <- qePolyLin(day1tottemp,'tot',deg=2,holdout=NULL)
```

Let's take a look at the resulting estimated coefficients:

```
> names(qepout)
 [1] "bh"           "deg"           "maxInteractDeg" "modelFormula"
 [5] "XtestFormula" "retainedNames" "standardize"    "x"
 [9] "y"            "classif"       "trainRow1"
> qepout$bh
             [,1]
[1,] 1305.597268
[2,]  346.421623
[3,]   -6.815313
```

Prediction is as usual, for example, for a 12-degree day:

```
> predict(qepout,data.frame(temp=12))
[1] 4481.252
```

Let's see if the quadratic model predicts better:

```
> set.seed(9999)
> qePolyLin(day1tottemp,'tot',deg=2,holdout=100)$testAcc
[1] 1214.063
> set.seed(9999)   # to get the same holdout set
> qeLin(day1tottemp,'tot',holdout=100)$testAcc
[1] 1250.177
```

Yes, the MAPE value was smaller for the quadratic model, though as always, it must be added that we should use `replicMeans()` to be sure (see Section 3.2.2).

8.11.3   Polynomial Logistic Regression

Recall that the logit model starts with a linear combination of the features and then runs it through the logistic function $l(t) = 1/(1 + e^{-t})$ to squeeze it into [0,1]. That means we can add polynomial terms as in the linear model. The `regtools` function `qePolyLog()` does this.

8.11.4   Example: Programmer and Engineer Wages

Let's predict occupation by applying nonpolynomial logit first:

```
> data(pef)
> set.seed(9999)
> qeLogit(pef,'occ')$testAcc
[1] 0.646
```

About 35 percent right, which is not too bad, considering there are 6 classes. But maybe a quadratic model—that is, adding terms such as the squares of income and age—would improve things. Let's see:

```
> set.seed(9999)
> qePolyLog(pef,'occ',2)$testAcc
[1] 0.619
```

This is a slight improvement. But is it a sampling accident? We could use the qeCompare() function to compare different degrees while using many holdout sets to address sampling issues (see Section 8.13).

8.12   Blending the Linear Model with Other Methods

Problems tend to occur with k-NN around the fringes of a dataset. As a simple concrete example, let's again consider predicting human weight from height in the Major League Baseball Player data from Section 1.8.

Here's a summary of the data:

```
> table(mlb$Height)
```

67	68	69	70	71	72	73	74	75	76	77	78	79	80	81	82	83
2	7	19	51	89	150	162	173	155	101	55	27	14	5	2	2	1

Suppose we wish to predict the weight of a new player whose height is 68.2 and use k-NN. This height is on the low end of our training data, so most of the nearest neighbors will be taller than this. Taller people tend to be heavier, and the dataset neighbors of our new point will mostly be taller than this new player and thus likely heavier. The result will be that our prediction will be biased upward; we will tend to predict a larger weight than this player's true value. Similarly, if our new case has height, say, 81.5, our prediction will be biased downward.

One remedy is to fit a linear model within the neighborhood. Say we are predicting a new case x and use $k = 25$ neighbors. Then, instead of averaging the weights of those 25 neighboring players, we invoke lm() on that neighborhood data. We then predict x from the output of lm(). The linearity of this process will result in more realistic predictions at the fringes of the data.

The point, then, is that instead of using the mean to smooth the data in a neighborhood, we could use lm(). Or, if we are worried about the effects of outliers, we might try median().

There is an argument called smoothingFtn in the regtools function kNN() (which is wrapped by qeKNN()) that lets us specify some kind of smoothing other than the usual mean. The default is smoothingFtn = mean; to use median smoothing, we would specify smoothingFtn = median. For linear smoothing, we would use smoothingFtn = loclin.

Recall that decision trees (and thus random forests and tree-based boosting as well) form neighborhoods too. They thus are subject to the same problem—that is, bias in neighborhoods that are near the edges of the data.

Thus the same local-linear idea could be applied here. The CRAN package grf does this; it is wrapped by `qeRFgrf()`.

8.13   The qeCompare() Function

In our experiment in Section 8.11.4, a quadratic model did appear to help, with a slightly lower OME than that of the ordinary logit. An extensive investigation would involve `fineTuning()`, with cross-validation trials, and possibly exploring polynomial degrees other than 1 or 2.

But remember, "qe" stands for "quick and easy." The qeML function `qeCompare()` can be used for quick comparisons between models. (Of course, for large datasets, it won't be so quick.)

Let's use it to compare ordinary logistic regression with a quadratic version for the vertebrae data. While we are at it, let's compare to the other methods we've had in the book so far.

```
> qeCompare(vert,'V7',c('qeLogit','qePolyLog','qeKNN','qeRF','qeGBoost'),100)
      qeFtn     meanAcc
1   qeLogit 0.13677419
2 qePolyLog 0.09129032
3     qeKNN 0.23741935
4      qeRF 0.15741935
5  qeGBoost 0.16322581
```

What happened here?

- Here we generated 100 random holdout sets (of size 73, the default for this dataset). The same holdout set is used for all methods. (The `qeCompare()` function has an optional random-number seed argument, but we've taken the default value of 9999.)

- We are using default hyperparameters for each of the functions. The `qeCompare()` function has an optional `opts` argument to set non-default values, such as `nTree` for `qeRF()`.

- We found OME values for each method.

The quadratic logit not only outperformed the ordinary logit, but it also turned out to be the best of the bunch! Yes, it outperformed the fancy ML methods. Of course, each method was run with the default hyperparameters, and things could change with other values.

8.13.1   Need for Caution Regarding Polynomial Models

The polynomial degree is a hyperparameter. In our example of predicting occupation in Section 8.11.4, we might, say, try a cubic (degree-3) model

```
qePolyLog(pef,'occ',3)
```

or even set degree to 4, 5, and so on.

However, with higher and higher degrees, we do need to watch for over-fitting, as the number of terms increases very rapidly with degree. Let's illustrate that point by checking the number of β coefficients in each model for varying degree, as shown in Table 8-1. This requires some digging into the output objects. It would be a distraction to explain that here, but for the interested reader, this is in the component `$glmOuts[[1]]`. One must then exclude the intercept term.

Table 8-1: Complexity of Polynomial Models

Degree	Coefficients
1	6
2	22
3	50
4	90
5	143

Remember, these are the values of p, our number of features, after we add in polynomial terms. Our sample size n remains at 20,090. At some point while increasing the degree, we will overfit.

If we follow the rough rule of thumb that we need to have $p < \sqrt{n}$, this suggests a limit of something like $p < 141$, corresponding to using at most a degree-4 model. But this is, after all, only a rule of thumb. It may be the case that, say, OME starts increasing after just a degree-2 model. The reader is urged to try polynomials of various degrees, on this dataset and others, noting the OME values that result.

We note the following:

- Polynomial models may be able to hold their own against, or even outperform, their more esoteric ML counterparts.

- Use of polynomial models is attractive in that there is only one hyperparameter (the degree), and also because the calculation (in the case of `qePolyLin()`) is noniterative and thus has no convergence issues.

- As with any ML method, one must always keep in mind the possibility of overfitting.

Unfortunately, many treatments of ML overlook polynomial models. But they can be quite powerful and should definitely be in the analyst's toolkit.

8.14   What's Next

The linear model is the oldest form of ML. As we have seen, it still can be quite powerful, outperforming "modern" ML methods in some cases. But in some settings, it can be made even better by, oddly, "shrinking" $\widehat{\beta}$. This is the topic of the next chapter.

9

CUTTING THINGS DOWN TO SIZE: REGULARIZATION

A number of modern statistical methods "shrink" their classical counterparts. This is true for ML methods as well. In particular, the principle may be applied in:

- Boosting (covered in Section 6.3.8)
- Linear models
- Support vector machines
- Neural networks

In this chapter, we'll see why that may be advantageous and apply it to the linear model case. This will also lay the foundation for material in future chapters on support vector machines and neural networks.

9.1 Motivation

Suppose we have sample data on human height, weight, and age. We denote the population means of these quantities by μ_{ht}, μ_{wt}, and μ_{age}. We estimate them from our sample data as the corresponding sample means, $\overline{X}_{ht}$, $\overline{X}_{wt}$, and $\overline{X}_{age}$.

We then add just a bit more notation, grouping these quantities into vectors

$$\mu = (\mu_{ht}, \mu_{wt}, \mu_{age}) \tag{9.1}$$

and

$$\overline{X} = (\overline{X}_{ht}, \overline{X}_{wt}, \overline{X}_{age}) \tag{9.2}$$

Amazingly, *James–Stein theory* says the best estimate of μ might NOT be $\overline{X}$. It might be a shrunken-down version of $\overline{X}$, say, $0.9\overline{X}$:

$$(0.9\overline{X}_{ht}, 0.9\overline{X}_{wt}, 0.9\overline{X}_{age}) \tag{9.3}$$

And the higher the dimension (3 here), the more shrinking needs to be done.

The intuition is this: for many samples, there are a few data points that are extreme on the fringes of the distribution. These points skew our estimators in the direction of being too large. So, it is optimal to shrink the estimators.

Note that, usually, different components of a vector will be shrunken by different amounts. Instead of Equation 9.3, the best estimator might be:

$$(0.9\overline{X}_{ht}, 1.2\overline{X}_{wt}, 0.023\overline{X}_{age}) \tag{9.4}$$

In this example, the second component actually expanded rather than shrank. Shrinking refers to the overall size of the vector (defined in the next section) and not the individual components.

How much shrinking should be done? In practice, this is typically decided by our usual approach of cross-validation.

Putting aside the mathematical theory—it's quite deep—the implication for us in this book is that, for instance, the least squares estimator $\widehat{\beta}$ of the population coefficient vector β in the linear model is often too large and should be shrunken. Most interesting, *this turns out to be a possible remedy for overfitting*.

9.2   Size of a Vector

Is the vector (15.2,3.0,−6.8) "large"? What do we mean by its size, anyway?

There are two main measures, called ℓ_1 and ℓ_2, that are denoted by the "norm" notation, $|| \ ||$ (two pairs of vertical bars). So the two norms are denoted $|| \ ||_1$ and $|| \ ||_2$. For the example above, the ℓ_1 norm is

$$||(15.2, 3.0, -6.8)||_1 = |15.2| + |3.0| + |-6.8| = 25 \tag{9.5}$$

that is, the sum of the absolute values of the vector elements. Here is the ℓ_2 case:

$$||(15.2, 3.0, -6.8)||_2 = \sqrt{15.2^2 + 3.0^2 + (-6.8)^2} = 16.9 \tag{9.6}$$

This is the square root of the sums of squares of the vector elements. (Readers who remember their school geometry may notice that in 2 dimensions, this is simply the length of the diagonal of a right triangle—the famous Pythagorean theorem.)

9.3 Ridge Regression and the LASSO

For years, James–Stein theory was mainly a mathematical curiosity suitable for theoretical research but not affecting mainstream data analysis. There was some usage of *ridge regression*, to be introduced below, but even that was limited. The big change came from the development of the *Least Absolute Shrinkage and Selection Operator (LASSO)* and its adoption by the ML community.

9.3.1 How They Work

Recall the basics of the least squares method for linear models, say, for the case of one feature: we choose $\hat{\beta} = (\hat{m}, \hat{b})$ to minimize the sum of squared prediction errors, as in Equation 8.10. For convenience, here is a copy of that expression:

$$[180 - (\hat{b} + \hat{m} \cdot 71)]^2 + [215 - (\hat{b} + \hat{m} \cdot 74)]^2 + \ldots + [195 - (\hat{b} + \hat{m} \cdot 73)]^2 \quad (9.7)$$

The idea of ridge regression was to "put a damper" on that by adding vector size limitation. We now minimize Equation 9.7, *subject to the following constraint*:

$$||(\hat{m}, \hat{b})||_2 \leq \eta \quad (9.8)$$

Here $\eta > 0$ is a hyperparameter set by the user, say, via cross-validation. The minimizing values of $\hat{b}$ and $\hat{m}$ are the ridge coefficients.

Here is the intuition behind such an approach. We are basically saying we wish to minimize the sum of squares as before *but* without allowing $(\hat{m}, \hat{b})$ to get too large. It's a compromise between, on the one hand, predicting the Y_i well and, on the other, limiting the size of $(\hat{m}, \hat{b})$. (We hope that the shrinking will improve our prediction of future cases.) The hyperparameter η controls that trade-off.

It can be shown that this constrained minimization problem is equivalent to choosing $\hat{b}$ and $\hat{m}$ to minimize the quantity:

$$[180 - (\hat{b} + \hat{m} \cdot 71)]^2 + [215 - (\hat{b} + \hat{m} \cdot 74)]^2 + \ldots \quad +[195 - (\hat{b} + \hat{m} \cdot 73)]^2 + \lambda ||(\hat{m}, \hat{b})||_2^2 \quad (9.9)$$

Here $\lambda > 0$ is a hyperparameter that takes the place of η, which, again, is typically set via cross-validation.

This formulation (Equation 9.9) is actually the standard definition of ridge regression. The η version is easier to explain in terms of the James–Stein context, but this λ formulation should also make intuitive sense: that last term "penalizes" us in our minimizing the sum of squares. The larger we set λ, the greater the penalty, forcing us to limit the size of $(\hat{m}, \hat{b})$.

The LASSO version is almost the same as ridge but with an ℓ_1 "damper" term rather than ℓ_2. It finds the values of $\hat{b}$ and $\hat{m}$ that minimize:

$$[180 - (\hat{b} + \hat{m} \cdot 71)]^2 + [215 - (\hat{b} + \hat{m} \cdot 74)]^2 + \ldots \quad +[195 - (\hat{b} + \hat{m} \cdot 73)]^2 + \lambda ||(\hat{m}, \hat{b})||_1 \quad (9.10)$$

In terms of η, for LASSO we minimize

$$|180 - (\widehat{b} + \widehat{m} \cdot 71)| + |215 - (\widehat{b} + \widehat{m} \cdot 74)| + \ldots + |195 - (\widehat{b} + \widehat{m} \cdot 73)| \quad (9.11)$$

subject to:

$$||(\widehat{m}, \widehat{b})||_1 \leq \eta \quad (9.12)$$

9.3.2 The Bias-Variance Trade-off, Avoiding Overfitting

A major reason that the idea of shrinkage—often called *regularization*—has had such an impact on statistics and ML is that it is a tool to avoid overfitting. Here are the issues:

- On the one hand, we want to make the prediction sum of squares as small as possible, which can be shown to eliminate bias.

- On the other hand, recall from Section 8.8 that the sum of squares can be overly optimistic and thus smaller than we would get in predicting new cases in the future. A small value for that sum of squares may come with a large variance, due in part to the influence of extreme data points, as discussed earlier. Shrinkage reduces variance—a smaller quantity varies less than a larger one—thus partially neutralizing the pernicious effects of the extreme points.

So the hyperparameter λ is used to control where we want to be in that Bias-Variance Trade-off. Overfitting occurs when we are on the wrong side of that trade-off.

The bottom line: shrinkage reduces variance, and if this can be done without increasing bias much, it's a win.

Again, regularization is used not only in the linear model, the case studied in this chapter, but also in support vector machines, neural nets, and so on. It can even be used in principal component analysis.

9.3.3 Relation Between λ, n, and p

Again, the Bias-Variance Trade-off notion plays a central role here, with implications for dataset size. The larger n is (that is, the larger the sample size), the smaller the variance in $\widehat{\beta}$, which means the lesser the need to shrink.

In other words, for large datasets, we may not need regularization. But recall from Chapter 3 that "large n" here is meant both in absolute terms and relative to p—for example, by the $\sqrt{n}$ criterion following Equation 3.2. So, a very large dataset may still need regularization if there are numerous features.

In any event, the surest way to settle whether shrinkage is needed in a particular setting is to try it, once again, with cross-validation.

9.3.4 Comparison, Ridge vs. LASSO

The advantage of ridge regression is that its calculation is simple. There is an explicit, closed-form solution—that is, it is noniterative; the LASSO requires iterative computation (though it does not have convergence problems).

But the success of the LASSO is due to its providing a *sparse* solution, meaning that often many of the elements of $\widehat{\beta}$ are 0s. The smaller we set η, the more 0s we have. We then discard the features having $\widehat{\beta}_i = 0$, thereby achieving dimension reduction. Note that, of course, the resulting nonzero $\widehat{\beta}_i$ values are different from the corresponding OLS values.

9.4 Software

Once again, we will use a qe*-series function, qeLASSO(), with the following call form:

```
qeLASSO(data,yName,alpha = 1,
    holdout = floor(min(1000, 0.1 * nrow(data))))
```

The function wraps cv.glmnet() in the glmnet package. That package allows the user to specify either ridge regression or LASSO via the argument alpha, setting that value to 0 or 1, respectively; the default is LASSO. One can also set alpha to an intermediate value, combining the two approaches, something termed the *elastic net*.

The cv.glmnet() algorithm will start with a huge value of λ and then progressively reduce λ. This corresponds to starting with a very tiny value of η and progressively increasing it. Since a very tiny value of η means that no features are allowed, progressively increasing it means we start adding features. It is all arranged so that we add one feature at a time. The algorithm computes MSPE or OME at each step, using its own built-in cross-validation. The return value of the qeLASSO() wrapper is actually the object returned by cv.glmnet(), with a few additional components, such as testAcc.

That object will include one set of results for each value of λ run by the code. So, there will be one $\widehat{\beta}$ vector for each λ. However, when we do subsequent prediction, the code uses the specific value of λ that had the smallest mean cross-validated prediction error.

9.5 Example: NYC Taxi Data

Let's return to the New York City taxi data from Section 5.3.

```
> yellout <- qeLASSO(yell10k,'tripTime')
> yellout$testAcc
[1] 258.4983
> yellout$baseAcc
[1] 442.4428
```

We see that the features definitely are helpful in prediction, yielding a large reduction in MAPE relative to just using the overall mean for prediction.

Recall that the LASSO typically yields a sparse $\hat{\beta}$, meaning that most of the coefficients are 0s. In this way, the LASSO can be used for dimension reduction, in addition to being used as a predictive model in its own right. Let's explore this for the taxi data by inspecting the coefs component of the output.

Note first that, as usual, the features that are R factors are converted to dummy variables. How many are there?

```
> length(yellout$coefs)
[1] 475
```

Considering that the original dataset had only 5 features, 475 is quite a lot! But remember, two of our features were the pickup and dropoff locations, of which there are hundreds, and thus hundreds of dummies.

Well, which coefficients are nonzero?

```
> yellout$coefs
475 x 1 sparse Matrix of class "dgCMatrix"
                          1
(Intercept)       401.500380
passenger_count       .
trip_distance     128.666529
PULocationID.1        .
PULocationID.3        .
PULocationID.4        .
PULocationID.7        .
PULocationID.8        .
...
PULocationID.130      .
PULocationID.131      .
PULocationID.132 -263.807074
PULocationID.133      .
...
PULocationID.263      .
PULocationID.264      .
DOLocationID.1      -4.005357
DOLocationID.3        .
...
DOLocationID.262      .
DOLocationID.263      .
DOLocationID.264      .
PUweekday           3.030196
> sum(yellout$coefs != 0)
[1] 11
```

Only 11 coefficients are nonzero, including pickup location 132 and dropoff location 1. That's impressive dimension reduction.

9.6 Example: Airbnb Data

Let's revisit the Airbnb dataset analyzed in Section 8.4.3, where we are predicting monthly rent.

```
> Abb$square_feet <- NULL
> Abb$weekly_price <- NULL
> Abb <- na.exclude(Abb)
> z <- qeLASSO(Abb,'monthly_price',holdout=NULL)
```

The `qeLASSO()` function wraps `cv.glmnet()`. The latter has a generic `plot()` function, which we can access here:

```
> plot(z)
```

The plot, shown in Figure 9-1, displays the classic Bias-Variance Tradeoff, which is essentially U-shaped. As λ increases to the right (lower horizontal axis; the log is used), the number of nonzero coefficients (upper horizontal axis) decreases. At first, this produces reductions in MSPE. However, after we hit about 26 nonzero coefficients, this quantity rises. In bias-variance terms, increasing λ brought large reductions in variance with little increase in bias. But after hitting 26 features, the bias became the dominant factor.

At any rate, using 26 features, corresponding to $\lambda \approx e^4 = 53.9$, seems best, yielding a very substantial improvement in prediction accuracy. (Standard errors are also shown in the vertical bars extending above and below the curve.)

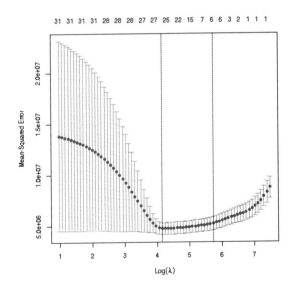

Figure 9-1: MSPE, Airbnb data

Let's try a prediction, say, taking row 18 from our data and changing the security deposit to $360 and the rating to 92. What would be our predicted value for the rent?

```
> x18 <- Abb[18,-4]
> x18[4] <- 360
> x18[8] <- 92
> predict(z,x18)
          1
[1,] 3750.618
```

How much did our shrinkage approach change the coefficients compared to the OLS output in Section 8.4.4? Well, for example, the estimated average premium for living in ZIP code 94123 was $1,639.61 with the OLS model. What is it now, using LASSO?

```
> z$coefs
...
zipcode.94118           .
zipcode.94121           .
zipcode.94122           .
zipcode.94123        698.6044574
zipcode.94124           .
zipcode.94127           .
...
```

Ah, so it did shrink. On the other hand, LASSO shrinks the vector, not necessarily individual elements, which could even grow a bit. Of course, many elements were indeed shrunken all the way to 0.

Recall how the process works: it begins with no features in the model at all, which corresponds to a huge value of λ. At each step, λ is reduced, possibly resulting in our acquiring a new feature. We can also view the order in which the features were brought into the model:

```
> z$whenEntered
          bedrooms        guests_included    security_deposit
                 2                     10                  13
   zipcode.94112   review_scores_rating       zipcode.94123
                15                     16                  17
   zipcode.94133          zipcode.94105       zipcode.94117
                22                     24                  24
   zipcode.94124          zipcode.94127       zipcode.94114
                24                     25                  26
   zipcode.94111          zipcode.94131            bathrooms
                27                     27                  27
   zipcode.94110          zipcode.94116       zipcode.94102
                28                     29                  30
   zipcode.94108          zipcode.94122       zipcode.94118
                30                     30                  31
```

zipcode.94132	zipcode.94107	zipcode.94121
31	33	34
zipcode.94158	zipcode.94115	zipcode.94134
35	37	37
zipcode.94104	zipcode.94109	minimum_nights
44	56	57
maximum_nights		
57		

Not too surprisingly, the first feature chosen by the process was the number of bedrooms. But perhaps less intuitively, the process's second choice was a dummy variable regarding guests. Our example above, a dummy for ZIP code 94123, came in at the 17th step. One might view this ordering as a report on the importance of each selected feature.

NOTE *Since our emphasis in this book is on prediction from data rather than description of data, we have not discussed the issue of feature importance before now. We only present it here as an aid to understanding how LASSO works. However, it is available in some of the packages used in this book. For instance, see the* importance() *function in the* randomForests *package.*

9.7   Example: African Soil Data

As noted in Section 6.2.4, the importance of the African soil dataset is that it has $p > n$, with the number of features being almost triple the number of data points. This is considered a very difficult situation.

Remember, to many analysts, the very essence of LASSO is dimension reduction, so it will be very interesting to see how LASSO does on this data.

9.7.1   LASSO Analysis

Again, we will predict soil acidity, pH:

```
> afrsoil1 <- afrsoil[,c(1:3578,3597)]
> z <- qeLASSO(afrsoil1,'pH',holdout=NULL)
```

The nzero component of the output tells us how many features the process has chosen at each step:

```
> z$nzero
 s0  s1  s2  s3  s4  s5  s6  s7  s8  s9 s10 s11 s12 s13 s14 s15 s16 s17 s18 s19
  0   2   2   2   4   4   5   5   6   6   6   7   8   8  10  12  17  16  14  13
s20 s21 s22 s23 s24 s25 s26 s27 s28 s29 s30 s31 s32 s33 s34 s35 s36 s37 s38 s39
 13  13  12  15  15  15  15  12  13  13  13  13  13  14  16  15  16  16  17  18
s40 s41 s42 s43 s44 s45 s46 s47 s48 s49 s50 s51 s52 s53 s54 s55 s56 s57 s58 s59
 21  21  22  22  24  24  24  24  40  25  26  28  35  44  35  41  40  42  44  42
s60 s61 s62 s63 s64 s65 s66 s67 s68 s69 s70 s71 s72 s73 s74 s75 s76 s77 s78 s79
 43  56  50  70  61  66  64  62  57  58  64  73  79  84  85  85  97  97 102  82
```

s80	s81	s82	s83	s84	s85	s86	s87	s88	s89	s90	s91	s92	s93	s94	s95	s96	s97	s98	s99
85	80	81	70	58	77	83	80	77	80	82	93	99	86	141	131	177	140	142	156

And the `lambda` component gives the corresponding λ values:

```
> z$lambda
 [1] 0.342642919 0.327069269 0.312203466 0.298013337 0.284468171 0.271538653
 [7] 0.259196803 0.247415908 0.236170473 0.225436161 0.215189739 0.205409033
[13] 0.196072876 0.187161061 0.178654302 0.170534188 0.162783146 0.155384401
[19] 0.148321940 0.141580479 0.135145428 0.129002860 0.123139480 0.117542601
[25] 0.112200108 0.107100440 0.102232560 0.097585932 0.093150501 0.088916667
[31] 0.084875267 0.081017555 0.077335183 0.073820179 0.070464938 0.067262198
[37] 0.064205027 0.061286810 0.058501230 0.055842258 0.053304142 0.050881386
[43] 0.048568749 0.046361224 0.044254035 0.042242621 0.040322628 0.038489903
[49] 0.036740477 0.035070566 0.033476554 0.031954993 0.030502590 0.029116200
[55] 0.027792824 0.026529597 0.025323786 0.024172781 0.023074090 0.022025337
[61] 0.021024252 0.020068667 0.019156515 0.018285822 0.017454703 0.016661360
[67] 0.015904076 0.015181211 0.014491201 0.013832554 0.013203843 0.012603708
[73] 0.012030850 0.011484029 0.010962062 0.010463820 0.009988223 0.009534243
[79] 0.009100897 0.008687247 0.008292398 0.007915496 0.007555724 0.007212305
[85] 0.006884495 0.006571584 0.006272895 0.005987782 0.005715628 0.005455844
[91] 0.005207868 0.004971162 0.004745215 0.004529538 0.004323663 0.004127146
[97] 0.003939561 0.003760502 0.003589581 0.003426429
```

The corresponding graph is shown in Figure 9-2.

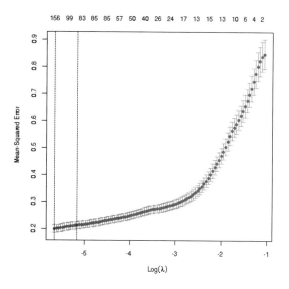

Figure 9-2: African soil data

Here we have a rather incomplete result. The smallest MSPE came from the smallest λ value tried by the software (0.003426429), but the curve seems to suggest that even smaller values would do better. So, we might rerun with a custom set of λ values, rather than using the default value sequence.

Nevertheless, even if we choose to settle for $\lambda = 0.003426429$, that value would be pretty good. LASSO retained 156 features out of the original 3,578. That's quite a dimension reduction.

9.8 Optional Section: The Famous LASSO Picture

This section has a bit more mathematical content, and it can be safely skipped, as it is not used in the sequel. However, readers who are curious as to why the LASSO retains some of the original features but excludes others may find this section helpful.

As mentioned, a key property of the LASSO is that it usually provides a *sparse* solution for $\widehat{\beta}$, meaning that many of the $\widehat{\beta}_i$ values are 0. In other words, many features are discarded, thus providing a means of dimension reduction. Figure 9-3 shows why. Here is how it works.

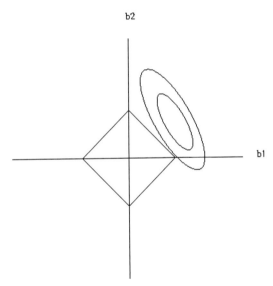

Figure 9-3: Feature subsetting nature of the LASSO

Figure 9-3 is for the case of $p = 2$ predictors, whose coefficients are b_1 and b_2. (For simplicity, we assume there is no constant term b_0.) Let U and V denote the corresponding features. Write $b = (b_1, b_2)$ for the vector of the b_i.

Without shrinkage, we would choose b to minimize the sum of squared errors:

$$SSE = (Y_1 - b_1 U_1 - b_2 V_1)^2 + \ldots + (Y_n - b_1 U_n - b_2 V_n)^2 \qquad (9.13)$$

The horizontal and vertical axes are for b_1 and b_2, as shown. The key point is that for any value that we set in Equation 9.13 for SSE, the points (b_1, b_2) that solve the resulting equation form an ellipse. The value of (b_1, b_2) computed by the LASSO is just one point in the given ellipse; lots of other (b_1, b_2) values yield the same SSE.

As we vary the SSE value, we get various concentric ellipses, two of which are shown in Figure 9-3. Larger values of SSE correspond to larger ellipses.

Now, what happens when we give the LASSO algorithm a value of λ or η? As noted earlier, either quantity can be used, but it will be easier to assume the latter. So, what will the LASSO algorithm do when we give it a value of η?

- The algorithm will minimize SSE, subject to the constraint:

$$|b_i| \leq \eta, \; i = 1, 2 \qquad (9.14)$$

  Let's denote that minimum value of SSE by SSE_{alg}, and denote the corresponding (b_1, b_2) value by $(b_1, b_2)_{alg}$.

- On the one hand, the point $(b_1, b_2)_{alg}$ will be on the ellipse associated with SSE_{alg}.

- On the other hand, Equation 9.14 says that $(b_1, b_2)_{alg}$ must be somewhere in the diamond in the picture, whose corners are at $(\eta, 0)$, $(0, \eta)$, and so on.

- So, $(b_1, b_2)_{alg}$ must lie on an ellipse that intersects with the diamond.

- But remember, we want SSE to be as small as possible, subject to Equation 9.14. Recall, too, that smaller SSE values correspond to smaller ellipses. So the ellipse for SSE_{alg} must *just barely touch the diamond*, as seen in the outer ellipse in Figure 9-3.

- In the figure, the "just barely touch" point is at one of the corners of the diamond. And each of the corners has either b_1 or b_2 equal to 0—sparsity!

- Is that sparsity some kind of coincidence? No! Here's why: depending on the relative values of our input data (U_i, V_i), the ellipses in the picture will have different orientations. The ones in the picture are pointing approximately "northwest and southeast." But it is clear from inspection that most orientations will result in the touch point being at one of the corners and hence a sparse solution.

Thus the LASSO will usually be sparse, which is the major reason for its popularity. And what about ridge regression? In that case, the diamond becomes a circle, so there is no sparseness property.

9.9 Coming Up

Next, we take an entirely different approach. With k-NN and decision trees, no linearity was used, and then this property was explicitly assumed. In Part IV, we cover methods in which linearity is used, but only indirectly.

PART IV

METHODS BASED ON SEPARATING
LINES AND PLANES

The methods we've looked at so far were developed by statisticians or, in the case of boosting, by both statisticians and ML researchers. In this part, the two methods under discussion, support vector machines and neural networks, originated solely in the ML world.

Both of these methods are used primarily in classification applications. Support vector machines are predicated on there being a line (in two dimensions—that is, two features) or a hyperplane (three or more features) that (mostly) separates the data by class. The coefficients in these lines or hyperplanes will work somewhat like those in linear models, though in a more complex manner. The coefficients are obtained by minimizing a sum similar to that of linear models, though again more complex.

Neural networks will also share these similarities. Using the most popular *activation function* ReLU(), the feature space is also broken up into portions defined by hyperplanes (though the original goal is not expressed in those terms), and again a certain sum is minimized.

10

A BOUNDARY APPROACH: SUPPORT VECTOR MACHINES

Support vector machines (SVMs), together with neural networks (NNs), are arguably the two most "purist" of ML methods, motivated originally by artificial intelligence—that is, nonstatistical concepts. We'll cover SVMs in this chapter and NNs in the next. SVMs are best known for classification applications. They can be used in regression settings as well, but we will focus on classification.

Keep in mind this chapter will be a tad more mathematical than the others. Staying true to the nonmath spirit of the book, though, equations will be kept to the absolute minimum. SVM is such a powerful, generally usable method that understanding a bit of math here is an excellent investment of time. Even reading the documentation of SVM software requires some understanding of the structural underpinnings of the method.

10.1 Motivation

Everything about SVM involves boundary lines separating one class from another. To motivate that, we will first do a boundary analysis using the logistic model and then later bring in SVM. It will be important to keep in mind that throughout this section, we are simply exploring, to motivate SVM.

10.1.1   Example: The Forest Cover Dataset

Let's revisit the forest cover data from Section 5.4. Here we will construct a motivational graph, so we will need to look at only a small subset of the data. First, to avoid the "black screen problem," in which we have so many points that the graph becomes an amorphous mess, we will graph a random subset of just 500 data points. Second, to keep things to a visualizable two dimensions, we will use just two features.

The qeML package includes a dataset forest500, consisting of a random 500 rows of the original data. Now, what about the columns? We could try the Feature Ordering by Conditional Independence (FOCI) approach from Section 4.5.1:

```
> data(forest500)
> qeFOCI(forest500,'V55')$sel
     index names
 1:     1    V1
 2:     6    V6
...
```

We might run the function again, as there is some randomness involved, but let's go with the above for our example and, as always, get acquainted with the data:

```
> f500 <- forest500[,c(1,6,55)]
> head(f500)
      V1   V6 V55
1: 3438 1033   1
2: 3165 3961   2
3: 3020 5407   2
4: 3244  911   2
5: 2754 1463   2
6: 3008 1275   2
> table(f500$V55)
  1   2   3   4   5   6   7
194 238  29   3   5  10  21
```

As seen above, there are seven cover types, meaning this is a multiclass problem. Here we'll look at a two-class version, in which we wish to predict whether we have cover type 1 versus all others. The regtools::toSubFactor() function is handy for that kind of thing.

```
> f500$V55 <- regtools::toSubFactor(f500$V55,list('1'))
> head(f500)
      V1   V6       V55
1: 3438 1033         1
2: 3165 3961   zzzOther
3: 3020 5407   zzzOther
4: 3244  911   zzzOther
5: 2754 1463   zzzOther
6: 3008 1275   zzzOther
```

Let's see what the data looks like:

```
> plot(f500[,1:2],pch=ifelse(f500[,3] == '1',0,3))
```

This code generates the plot shown in Figure 10-1.

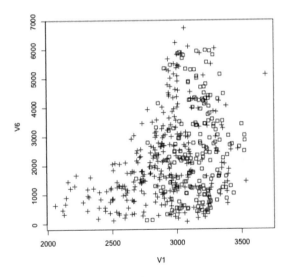

Figure 10-1: Forest cover data

We want to plot columns 1 and 2, hence the expression f500[,c(1,2)]. But we want to visually distinguish between the two classes, say, using squares and plus signs as symbols. In base-R graphics, plotting symbols are specified via the pch (point character) argument, and it turns out that the numerical codes were 0 and 3.[1] The squares are the cover type 1 points, and pluses are non–type 1.

There seems to be no sharp tendency in the graph (that is, no trend of separation of the two groups). We see squares and pluses all over the graph.

---

1. *https://www.r-bloggers.com/2021/06/r-plot-pch-symbols-different-point-shapes-in-r/*

However, the plus signs seem to fall to the left and more on the upward side, versus more to the right for the squares.

We would like to draw a line in Figure 10-1, such that most pluses are on one side of the line and most squares are on the other side. The reader can take a sneak peak at Figure 10-2 to see where we are headed. But where did the line come from? Actually, one can use a logit model here. This should not be too surprising, as you will recall that the logit model has a linear form at its core.

Here is how such a line can be drawn. Let's fit the model:

```
> w <- qeLogit(f500,'V55',holdout=NULL,yesYVal='1')
```

Normally, in prediction contexts we are not interested in the estimated logistic model coefficients $\widehat{\beta}_i$. Here, however, we will want to draw a separating line in Figure 10-1 using these coefficients. How do we obtain them from the output object w?

Recall from Section 8.9.3 that multiclass applications of the logit model use either a One vs. All (OVA) or an All vs. All (AVA) approach; qeLogit() uses OVA. It thus runs one logit model for each class, placing the glm() outputs in the glmOuts component of the qeLogit() output.

However, the two-class model is a little different. To avoid essentially running the same model twice—for the forest cover data, type 1 versus non-type 1—qeLogit() runs it just once. In other words, we'll look at w\$glmOuts[[1]].

To obtain the coefficients, we turn to coef(), yet another generic function like the ones we've seen before, such as print() and plot(). This function extracts the estimated coefficients:

```
> cf <- coef(w$glmOuts[[1]])
 (Intercept)              v1               v2
-1.684947e+01   5.389779e-03   1.469269e-05
```

Now recall again that the logistic model routes the linear model into the logistic function, $\ell(t) = 1/(1 + e^{-t})$; the placeholder t is set to the linear form. The above output gives the estimated probability of type-1 cover for a location having feature values of $v1$ and $v6$ as:

$$\text{estimated } P(\text{type-1 cover} \mid v1, v6) = \frac{1}{1 + e^{[-(-1.68 + 0.0054\, v1 + 0.000014\, v6)]}} \quad (10.1)$$

Say we guess the location to have type-1 cover or not depending on whether the estimated probability in Equation 10.1 is greater than 0.5 or not. Setting that equation to 0.5, things look formidable at first but become simple when we note the fact that $e^0 = 1$. In other words, if the exponent

$$-1.68 + 0.0054\, v1 + 0.000014\, v6 = 0 \quad (10.2)$$

then the right-hand side of Equation 10.1 is equal to 0.5, which is just what we want, a straight line forming the decision boundary.

So the line in Equation 10.2 forms the boundary between predicting type-1 or non-type-1 cover. That is the equation of a straight line, which is plotted in Figure 10-2. We superimposed that line onto Figure 10-1 by using R's abline() function, which plays exactly the role implied by the name—that is, adding a line to an existing plot:

```
# arguments are intercept and slope
> abline(a=-cf[1]/cf[3], b=-cf[2]/cf[3])
```

The result is shown in Figure 10-2. It happens to be almost vertical, which is not surprising since the coefficient of V6 is so small, but no matter. Data points to the right of the line are predicted to be of type-1 cover, with a non-type-1 prediction for those to the left.

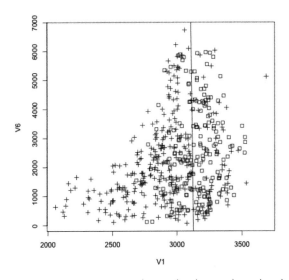

Figure 10-2: Forest cover data with a logistic boundary line

Clearly, quite a few data points are misclassified—that is, plus signs to the right of the line and squares to the left. We probably could reduce the number of misclassified points by increasing the number of features we use—we had only $p = 2$ features here—but there still would be some misclassified points.

This motivates the basic goal of SVM:

We wish to find a line that separates our classes well and then use that line to predict new cases in the future by determining which side of the line they fall on. Our line typically will not fully separate our classes, so we will have some misclassification errors, just as with any ML method. But hopefully a carefully chosen line will serve us well.

With $p = 3$ features, the line becomes a plane in three dimensions, difficult to visualize, and if we have more than three features, it is impossible to visualize. But by always keeping in mind the two-feature case and its geometric interpretation, we will have the intuition to use SVM effectively.

One more point before getting into the details: Why not simply use the above logit scheme to create our boundary line? What might be the advantage of using an SVM-produced line? The answer is that logit is very confining. It specifies a particular form for the regression function, involving the exponential function and so on as in Equation 10.1, and though this might be a good assumption in some applications, it might not be so in others.

By contrast, aside from the implicit assumption that the best interclass boundary is a straight line rather than some other curve (even this condition can be dropped, as we will see later), SVM makes no assumptions, so it is more flexible and may produce a better fit (just as is the case for k-NN, random forests, and so on, which make even fewer assumptions).

10.2   Lines, Planes, and Hyperplanes

Let's explore that geometric view a bit further.

The derivation above always holds with a logistic model; prediction of $Y = 1$ versus $Y = 0$ will always boil down to computing a linear function of the features. If we have $p = 2$ (that is, two features, such as $v1$ and $v6$), the boundary between predicting $Y = 1$ and $Y = 0$ is a straight line of the form

$$c_1\, v1 + c_2\, v6 = c_3 \tag{10.3}$$

as we saw in Equation 10.2. If $p = 3$, say, adding the $v8$ feature, the boundary takes the form of a plane, with the form

$$c_1\, v1 + c_2\, v6 + c_3\, v8 = c_4 \tag{10.4}$$

As noted above, this is hard to visualize. As also noted, for $p > 3$, we can't visualize the setting at all. But we are still working with a linear form in the features, whose behavior is like that of a line or plane. Since it is plane-like, we call it a *hyperplane*. For technical accuracy, we'll use the acronym LPH (line/plane/hyperplane) rather than merely saying "line," but readers should always think in terms of lines in the $p = 2$ case to guide their intuition.

10.3   Math Notation

Central to any discussion of SVM—including reading the documentation for SVM software—is the "dot product" notation. Though the name and math formula may sound intimidating, it's just a way of stating things more succinctly. We first discuss how to change much of the SVM notation to vector form and then introduce dot products.

10.3.1   Vector Expressions

As can be seen from Equations 10.3 and 10.4, an LPH can be represented by its coefficient vector—for example, (c_1, c_2, c_3, c_4) in Equation 10.4. It's customary in SVM to write things in terms of equality to 0, so, for instance, we rewrite Equation 10.4 as

$$c_1 v1 + c_2 v6 + c_3 v8 - c_4 = 0 \tag{10.5}$$

and set:
$$w = (c_1, c_2, c_3,), \quad w_0 = -c_4 \tag{10.6}$$

The vector w and the number w_0 compose our description of the LPH.

So, we would summarize Equation 10.2 by writing:
$$w = (0.0054, 0.000014), \quad w_0 = 1.68 \tag{10.7}$$

10.3.2 Dot Products

The underlying theory of SVM makes heavy use of calculus and linear algebra. As noted, such mathematics is far beyond the scope of this book. However, it will be productive and easy to use some notation from that subject—just notation and nothing conceptual other than a little algebra.

Our goal will be to come up with a simple, compact way to determine on which side of the boundary line or LPH a new case falls so that we may easily predict its class.

The *dot product* between two vectors $u = (u_1, \ldots, u_m)$ and $v = (v_1, \ldots, v_m)$ is simply a sum of products:
$$u \bullet v = u_1 v_1 + \ldots + u_m v_m \tag{10.8}$$

For example, let's take the dot product of w in Equation 10.7 with the vector $(1,-4)$:
$$w \bullet (1, -4) = 0.0054 \times 1 + 0.000014 \times (-4) = 0.005344 \tag{10.9}$$

It is helpful to recast Equation 10.1 in our new dot product notation:
$$\text{estimated } P(\text{type-1 cover} | v1, v6) = \frac{1}{1 + e^{-[w \bullet (v1, v6) + w_0]}} \tag{10.10}$$

Note some algebraic properties:

- $e^0 = 1$
- $e^t > 1$ for $t > 0$
- $e^{-t} < 1$ for $t > 0$
- $\frac{1}{1 + e^{-t}} > 0.5$ for $t > 0$

Thus, in Equation 10.10,
$$\text{estimated } P(\text{type-1 cover} | v1, v6) > 0.5, \quad \text{if } w \bullet (v1, v6) + w_0 > 0 \tag{10.11}$$

and
$$\text{estimated } P(\text{type-1 cover} | v1, v6) < 0.5, \quad \text{if } w \bullet (v1, v6) + w_0 < 0 \tag{10.12}$$

So, faced with a new case to predict, we simply look at the sign—positive and negative—of $w \bullet (v1, v6) + w_0$. If positive, the new case is more likely (probability more than 0.5) to have cover type 1, while in the negative case, that probability is less than 0.5. In other words, we predict cover type 1 for the new case if $w \bullet (v1, v6) + w_0 > 0$, and otherwise predict non-type 1.

This again is saying that we guess cover type 1 if our new case to be predicted falls to the right of the line or non-type 1 if it is on the left. And our SVM boundary is the vector x that makes:

$$w_0 + w \bullet x = 0 \tag{10.13}$$

Again, this is just notation, but in math, it is often the case that convenient notation helps clarify things. Drawing lines is visualizable for applications with $p = 2$ features, but drawing planes is hard to visualize if $p = 3$, and if $p > 3$, visualization is impossible. What's nice about the dot product notation is that we know which way to guess the class of a new case by simply noting whether $w \bullet (v1, v6) + w_0$ is positive or negative.

By the way, SVM theorists also like to code the two classes as $Y = +1$ and $Y = -1$ rather than 1 or 0, as is standard in statistics. We'll continue to use the latter coding in general but will turn to the former in this chapter.

10.3.3   SVM as a Parametric Model

We have referred to linear and logistic models as *parametric* in that the regression function is modeled as being determined by a finite number of values $\beta_0, \beta_1, \ldots, \beta_p$. This is in contrast to, for example, k-NN methods, which make no assumptions regarding the form of the regression function.

One implication of Equation 10.13 is that SVM too is a parametric model. Instead of assuming a parametric form for the regression function, here we assume a parametric form for the boundary line between the two classes.

10.4   SVM: The Basic Ideas—Separable Case

As noted earlier, the line we drew in Figure 10-2 did not cleanly separate the two classes. There were plus signs and squares on both sides of the line. This is typical, not only for logit-produced lines but also for lines created by SVM—our focus here. However, the SVM method is easier to explain if we first consider datasets for which the two classes are cleanly separable, so most books begin with that case, as we will here.

For clarity, we will continue to focus on the two-class case, as with the type-1/non-type-1 cover example above. And again, we will continue looking at the case of $p = 2$ features, where the LPH is a line.

Note that all our references to "the data" here will be in terms of the training data. We find a boundary line for the training data and then predict future cases according to that line. Similarly, when we speak of separability of "the data," we mean the training data.

10.4.1 Example: The Anderson Iris Dataset

Edgar Anderson's data on iris flowers, included in R, has been the subject of countless examples in books, websites, and so on. There are three classes: *setosa*, *versicolor*, and *virginica*.

This dataset is included in R:

```
> head(iris)
  Sepal.Length Sepal.Width Petal.Length Petal.Width Species
1          5.1         3.5          1.4         0.2  setosa
2          4.9         3.0          1.4         0.2  setosa
3          4.7         3.2          1.3         0.2  setosa
4          4.6         3.1          1.5         0.2  setosa
5          5.0         3.6          1.4         0.2  setosa
6          5.4         3.9          1.7         0.4  setosa
```

Note that what we do in this section will be mainly for motivating the subsequent material. For day-to-day SVM computation, you'll use qeSVM(). So, in the example here, in which we do some non-SVM analysis for motivational purposes, we will omit some of the code and algebra.

As mentioned, for this example, we'd like data in which the two classes are cleanly separated by a straight line. This is the case if we take our two iris classes as setosa and nonsetosa, with the features taken to be the Sepal.Length and Petal.Width columns.

Let's first plot the data.

```
> j2 <- iris[,c(2,4,5)]  # sepal width, petal width, species
# set up species code, 1 for setosa, 0 for nonsetosa
> head(j2)
  Sepal.Width Petal.Width Species
1         3.5         0.2  setosa
2         3.0         0.2  setosa
3         3.2         0.2  setosa
4         3.1         0.2  setosa
5         3.6         0.2  setosa
6         3.9         0.4  setosa
> j2$Species <- toSubFactor(j2$Species,'setosa')
> j2[c(7,77),]
   Sepal.Width Petal.Width  Species
7          3.4         0.3   setosa
77         2.8         1.4 zzzOther
> plot(j2[,1:2],pch=3*as.numeric(j2[,3]))
```

This produces the graph in Figure 10-3.

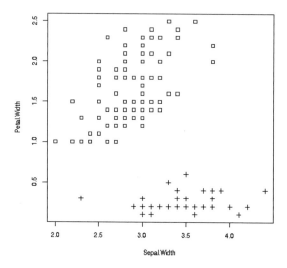

Figure 10-3: Setosa and nonsetosa

One can easily draw a line between the two classes—in fact, many lines. But, which line is optimal?

10.4.2   Optimizing Criterion

Choosing our boundary line amounts to choosing the coefficient vector w and the w_0 term. In other words, the situation is similar to that of the linear and generalized linear models, where we choose the estimated coefficients $\widehat{\beta}_i$. (Actually, w and w_0 are estimates as well, but to avoid clutter, we do not use the hat notation.) Now recall that with a linear model, the way we choose our coefficients $\widehat{\beta}_i$ is through an optimization problem: we minimize a certain sum of squares.

SVM still minimizes a certain sum, but it uses a different loss function than squared error. Detailing it would take us too far into some arcane math with little, if any, benefit. Fortunately, the math has an easily grasped geometric version, which we will now discuss.

Toward this end, look at Figure 10-4. Here we have "roped off" our two classes (setosas above and nonsetosas below) into what are called *convex hulls*. Again, this is just for illustration purposes; the qeSVM() function will do the computation for us (and with a different method), and we will not compute convex hulls ourselves after this example. We thus omit the code. (One can use the function mvtnorm::chull().)

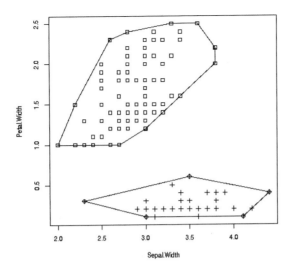

Figure 10-4: SVM convex hulls

It can be shown mathematically that the SVM boundary line is "halfway between" the two convex hulls. More precisely stated, one first finds the two points in the hulls that are closest to each other. Our boundary line is then the perpendicular bisector of the line segment between those two points. We draw that in Figure 10-5, along with two related, dashed lines, which define the "margin" of an SVM fit.

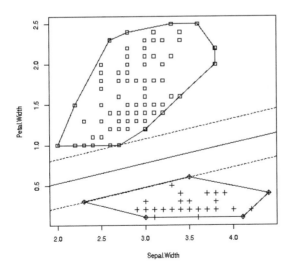

Figure 10-5: SVM margin

Note the following, both here and in general:

- The region between the dashed lines is called the *margin*.

- For separable data, there will be no data points *inside* the margin.

- The points lying *on* the margin are called *support vectors* (the SV in SVM). For this dataset, we have three support vectors, one for the setosas at $(2.7,1.0)$ and two for the nonsetosas at $(2.3,0.3)$ and $(3.5,0.6)$.

- In terms of w and w_0, the value of $w_0 + w \bullet x$ will be:
  - 0 for any point x on the boundary
  - +1 for any support vector in the $Y = +1$ class (setosa in this case)
  - −1 for any support vector in the $Y = -1$ class (nonsetosa in this case)
  - > +1 for any nonsupport vector in the $Y = +1$ class
  - < −1 for any nonsupport vector in the $Y = -1$ class

  By the way, a look at Equation 10.13 shows that the values of w and w_0 are not unique. Multiplying both by, say, 8.8 would still result in 0 on the right-hand side of the equation. So, the convention is to choose them such that the value of $w_0 + w \bullet x$ is +1 or −1 at the support points.

- To predict Y for a new case in which $X = x_{\text{new}}$, we guess Y to be either +1 or −1, depending on whether $w_0 + w \bullet x_{\text{new}}$ is greater than or less than 0. Note that even though our training data is assumed separable here, new data points may fall within the margin.

Keep in mind fitting an SVM model amounts to choosing w and w_0. The above scheme can be shown to be optimal. But wait a minute—what does "optimal" even mean? The criterion for optimality generally used in SVM is this:

We choose w and w_0 in such a way that the margin will have the largest possible width.

In other words, SVM seeks to not only separate the data points of the two classes but also render the two classes as far apart as possible, relative to the boundary. It finds a "buffer zone" between the two classes, maximizing the width of the zone. As noted, that buffer zone is called the margin.

The key idea is that a large margin in the training set means that the two classes are well separated, which hopefully means that new cases in the future will be correctly classified. It turns out that choosing w and w_0 using convex hulls as above (even with $p > 2$) does maximize the margin.

10.4.2.1 Significance of the Support Vectors

The support vectors "support" the fit, in the sense that a change in any of them will change the fit; a change in the other data points will not change the fit (as long as it stays within the hull). Of course, we can also say that *adding* new points won't change the fit either, as long as the new points are within a hull.

An oft-claimed benefit of SVMs is that (at least in the separable case) they tend to produce a sparse fit, in this case, meaning not that most of the components of w are 0s but rather that the essential dimensionality of the fit is low. Viewed another way, the claim is that the more support vectors one has, the greater the risk of overfitting. Evidence for this assertion is weak, I believe, though it may serve as one of several guides to one's model-fitting process.

But that benefit may be illusory. As noted, the source of the sparsity is the dependence of w on a few data points (that is, the support vectors). But what if some of the support vectors are outliers (not representative of the data as a whole) or are even downright erroneous? Many real datasets do have some errors. Our fit then depends heavily on some questionable data.

Furthermore, this high sensitivity of w to just a few data points makes for high sampling variability; a different sample likely has a different set of support vectors. In other words, w has a high variance.

10.5 Major Problem: Lack of Linear Separability

The margin, actually known as the *hard margin*, is only defined in situations in which some line (or LPH) exists that cleanly separates the data points of the two classes. As can be seen in our earlier graphs for the forest cover data, in most practical situations, no such line exists. Even with the iris data, no line separates the versicolor and virginica in columns 1 and 3:

```
> plot(iris[,c(1,3)],pch=as.numeric(iris$Species))
```

See Figure 10-6; pluses and triangles are not cleanly separated.

There are two solutions to that problem: (a) using a *kernel* to transform the data into linear separability or (b) creating a *soft margin*, in which we allow some points to reside within the margin. Typically a combination of these two approaches is used. For instance, after doing a kernel transformation, we still may—in fact, probably will—find that no cleanly separating LPH exists, and thus we will need to resort to also allowing some exceptional points to lie within the margin. However, the fewer the exceptions, the better, so it's best to use both approaches in combination rather than just going directly to a soft margin solution.

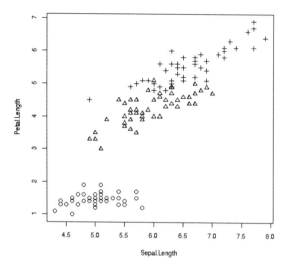

Figure 10-6: Iris data; three classes

10.5.1   Applying a "Kernel"

Here we transform the data, say, by applying a polynomial transformation, and then find an LPH separator on the new data. The degree of the polynomial is then a hyperparameter.

10.5.1.1   Motivating Illustration

To get a feeling as to why kernels can be useful, consider a favorite example in ML presentations: "doughnut-shaped" data. Let's generate some. (The code here is rather arcane and can be safely skipped without affecting the sequel.)

```
# generate 250 pairs of data points centered around (0,0)
> set.seed(9999)
> z <- matrix(rnorm(500),ncol=2)
# form new data by taking only certain points from z
> plus1 <- z[z[,1]^2 + z[,2]^2 > 4,]  # outer ring, class +1
> minus1 <- z[z[,1]^2 + z[,2]^2 < 2,]  # inner disk, class -1
> plus1 <- cbind(plus1,+1)  # add in Y column
> minus1 <- cbind(minus1,-1)  # add in Y column
> head(plus1)  # take a look
            [,1]        [,2] [,3]
[1,]   2.9038161  0.7172792    1
[2,]  -0.4499405  2.0006861    1
[3,]   2.3329026  0.2288606    1
[4,]  -0.2989460  2.3790936    1
[5,]  -2.0778949  0.1488060    1
[6,]  -0.9867098 -2.2020235    1
```

```
> head(minus1)
          [,1]         [,2]  [,3]
[1,]  1.0840991  0.670507239   -1
[2,]  0.8431089 -0.074557109   -1
[3,] -0.7730161 -0.009357795   -1
[4,]  0.9088839 -1.050183477   -1
[5,] -0.1882887 -1.348365272   -1
[6,]  0.9864382  0.936775923   -1
> pm1 <- rbind(plus1,minus1)  # combine into one dataset
> plot(pm1[,1:2],pch=pm1[,3]+2)  # gives us pluses and circles
```

The data is plotted in Figure 10-7. The two classes, drawn with pluses and circles, are clearly separable—but by a circle and not a straight line.

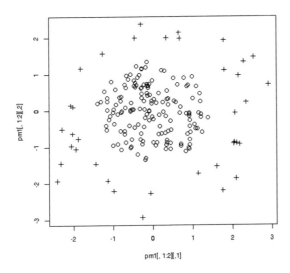

Figure 10-7: "Doughnut" data

But we can fix that by adding a squared term:

```
> pm2 <- pm1[,1:2]^2  # replace each X value by its square
> pm2 <- cbind(pm2,pm1[,3])  # tack on Y to the new datasets
> plot(pm2[,1:2],pch=pm2[,3]+2)
```

We took our original dataset and transformed it, replacing each data point by its square. That square is our new feature, replacing the old one. In the plot of the new data, Figure 10-8, the pluses and circles are easily separated by a straight line.

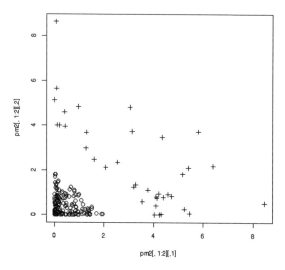

Figure 10-8: "Doughnut" data, transformed

And that is what SVM users typically do: try to find a transformation of the data under which the transformed data will be linearly separable, or at least nearly so. Of course, the SVM software does all the work for us; we don't transform the data by hand, as in the above illustration. This is done with a kernel, as seen in the next section.

10.5.1.2 The Notion of a Kernel

We need to cover one more point before turning to an example on real data. What is a kernel? A *kernel* is a way of transforming our data, again with the goal of making our data separable. But it's a little more specific than that; it's a function $K(u, v)$ whose inputs are two vectors.

This makes sense because we saw in Section 10.3.2 that dot products play a key role in SVM, and, in fact, even more so in the internal computations, which are not covered in this book. Accordingly, many kernels are functions of dot products.

An example is the *polynomial kernel*:

$$K(u, v) = (\gamma u \bullet v + 1)^d \tag{10.14}$$

The quantities d and γ are hyperparameters. In the quadratic case $d = 2$, we achieve essentially the same effect as in the previous section, where we squared the X values. Here we square dot products.

Also in common usage is the *radial basis function (RBF)*:

$$K(u, v) = \exp\left[-\gamma\,||u - v||_2^2\right] \tag{10.15}$$

Here γ is a hyperparameter.

Once again, as with so many ML questions, the answer to the question "Which kernel is best?" is "It depends." The type and size of the dataset, the number of features, and so on all make for variation in performance between kernels.

10.5.2   Soft Margin

As noted, it is rather uncommon to have linearly separable data. Nonseparability is the typical case. How can we handle it, in the sense of tolerating having a few points lying within the margin? Let's consider two approaches.

10.5.2.1   Geometric View

Instead of computing convex hulls, we could work with *reduced convex hulls*. Once again, the mathematical formulation is beyond the scope of this book, but the essence of the procedure is this:

- We replace the two original convex hulls with shrunken versions. (Not only will they be smaller in size, but their shape will tend to be "rounder," or less oblong.)
- The margin will be computed on the basis of the shrunken hulls.
- Then, conduct "business as usual," even though some of the training set data will then fall within the margin.

Of course, the amount of shrinkage is, as always, a hyperparameter to be set by the user, possibly via cross-validation.

10.5.2.2   Algebraic View

The geometric view is intuitive, but the more common approach is via "cost." There is a cost hyperparameter, usually denoted by C. Here is how it works. Denote data point i in our training set by X_i, the vector of features for that data point, and let Y_i be the class label, either +1 or −1.

In the separable case, recall that, for data points on the margin boundary, $w_0 + w \bullet X_i$ is equal to either +1 or −1. For points outside the margin,

$$w_0 + w \bullet X_i \geq 1 \text{ or } \leq -1 \tag{10.16}$$

depending on whether Y_i is +1 or −1. But there is a neat trick to state this requirement more compactly:

$$Y_i(w_0 + w \bullet X_i) \geq 1 \tag{10.17}$$

In the case of a soft margin, we relax that a bit, allowing discrepancies from 1.0, say,

$$Y_3(w_0 + w \bullet X_3) = 0.88 \tag{10.18}$$

and

$$Y_8(w_0 + w \bullet X_8) = -0.71 \tag{10.19}$$

Let d_i denote the discrepancy for data point i so that here $d_3 = 0.12$ and $d_8 = -1.71$. Set $d_i = 0$ if data point i has no discrepancy—that is, if $Y_i(w_0 + w \bullet X_i) \geq 1$.

Note that if $0 < d_i < 1$, then data point i is a margin violation, but it still is on the correct side of the decision boundary—that is, it will be correctly classified. But if $d_i > 1$, the point will be on the other side of the boundary and thus misclassified.

We control the total amount of discrepancy by stipulating that

$$d_1 + d_2 + \ldots + d_n \leq C \qquad (10.20)$$

where the hyperparameter C is our "discrepancy budget." Again, the user sets C.

Note that the d_i are not hyperparameters; they are by-products. The user chooses C. Each potential value of w and w_0 then gives rise to the d_i. The smaller the value we set for C, the fewer the number of data points within the margin—but the narrower the margin. We hope to have a wide margin; the SVM algorithm finds the values of w and w_0 that maximize the width of the margin, subject to the constraint (Equation 10.20).

10.6 Example: Forest Cover Data

Let's give qeSVM() a try:

```
> z <- qeSVM(f500,'V55',holdout=NULL)
```

We can then predict, say, for a new case similar to case 8 in our data, but changing the second feature value to 2,888:

```
> newx <- f500[8,1:2]
> newx
    V1   V6
8 3085 2977
> newx[2] <- 2888
> predict(z,newx)
$predClasses
[1] "zzzOther"

$probs
          1  zzzOther
8 0.4829782 0.5170218
```

We predict non-type-1 cover, though just slightly more likely than type 1.

We're using the default values here, which, among other things, set kernel to radial. If we wish to use just a soft margin (that is, no kernel transformation), we set kernel to linear. The hyperparameter gamma's default value is 1.0. An optional hyperparameter, cost, is the value C in our earlier discussion of soft margins. By the way, qeML() wraps svm in the famous e10171 package.

10.7 And What About That Kernel Trick?

No presentation of SVM would be complete without discussing the famous *kernel trick*, as it is largely responsible for the success of SVM. As usual, we won't delve into the mathematical details—assuming the reader has no burning desire to learn about reproducing kernel Hilbert spaces—but the principle itself has major practical implications.

To motivate this, let's get an idea of how large our dataset can expand to when we transform via polynomials *without* using kernels. Our size measure in the transformed data will be the number of columns.

Let's use the forest cover data again, together with the polyreg package, the latter being used in our counting data columns. (The getPoly() function in polyreg is used by the polynomial models in our qe-series.)

```
> gpout <- polyreg::getPoly(forest500,2)   # input with n = 500, p = 54
P > N. With polynomial terms and interactions, P is 1564.
```

The original dataset had only 54 features, but in the new form we have over 1,500 of them! We would have even more if getPoly() did not avoid creating duplicates—for example, the square of a dummy variable.

So, the new value of p was 1,564, for a dataset with only 500 rows, making it impossible to run. With the original data frame of more than 580,000 rows, the new size would be $581,012 \times 1,564 = 908,702,768$ elements. At 8 bytes per element, that would mean over 7GB of RAM! And it's not just space but also time—the code would run forever.

And that was just for degree 2. Imagine degree-3 polynomials and so on! (Degree 3 turns out to generate 16,897 columns.) So, some kind of shortcut is badly needed. Kernel trick to the rescue!

The key point is that by using the kernel in Equation 10.14, we can avoid having to compute and store all those extra columns. In the forest cover data, we can stick to those original 54 features—the vectors u and v in that expression are each 54 elements long—rather than computing and storing the 1,564. We get the same calculations mathematically as if we were to take u and v to be 1,564-element vectors.

10.8 "Warning: Maximum Number of Iterations Reached"

As with many other ML methods, the computation for SVM is iterative. However, unlike those other methods, SVM should not have convergence problems. The search space has the *convex* property, which basically says it is bowl-shaped and thus easy to find the minimum.

However, that presumes there is something to minimize. As we've seen with using soft margins or kernels, a line may not exist to cleanly separate the classes. For some particular pair of cost value and kernel (and the latter's hyperparameters), it may be that no solution exists. In that case, we will of course have convergence issues, and we will have to try other combinations.

10.9 Summary

This chapter has been a bit more mathematical than the others and perhaps a bit more abstract as well. But really, the basic principles are simple:

- SVM is primarily for classification problems. Using OVA or AVA pairing, SVM can handle any number of classes, but to keep things simple, let's assume two classes here.

- If we have $p = 2$ features, the basic goal is to find a line separating the two classes.

- With $p = 3$, we wish to find a separating plane in three-dimensional space.

- For the cases where $p > 3$, we speak of a separating hyperplane. We cannot visualize these, and instead look at dot products with our hyperplane's w vector. To classify a new case, we take the dot product of that case's feature vector, add w_0, and decide the class based on whether the dot product is greater or less than 0.

- We associate with the separating LPH a pair of LPHs that are parallel to the original one, thus creating the margin. The optimization criterion for choosing w is to maximize the width of the margin.

- Typically the classes overlap, so there is no separating LPH, and we need to resort to artificial means to separate the classes. There are two ways to do this, usually used in combination:
    - We can posit that a separating LPH does exist but is "curvy" rather than straight or flat. We transform the data, using a kernel, in an attempt to at least approximate some of that curviness.
    - We can, to various degrees set by the user, allow data points to reside within the margin.

As noted earlier, SVM is a more complicated tool than the ones we've seen earlier. But it is in wide usage, with many successes to its name, so the extra effort in this chapter is quite worthwhile.

11

LINEAR MODELS ON STEROIDS: NEURAL NETWORKS

The method of neural networks (NNs) is probably the best-known ML technology among the general public. The science fiction–sounding name is catchy—even more so with the advent of the term *deep learning*—and NNs have become the favorite approach to image classification in applications that also intrigue the general public, such as facial recognition.

Yet NNs are probably the most challenging ML technology to use well, with problems such as:

- "Black box" operation, where it's not clear what's going on inside
- Numerous hyperparameters to tune
- Tendency toward overfitting
- Possibly lengthy computation time, with some large-data cases running for hours or even days when large amounts of RAM may be needed
- Convergence issues

Let's see what all the fuss is about.

11.1 Overview

The term *neural network* alludes to an ML method that is inspired by the biology of human thought. In a two-class classification problem, for instance, the predictor variables serve as inputs to a *neuron*, outputting 1 or 0, with 1 meaning that the neuron *fires*—and we decide class 1. NNs consist of several *hidden layers* in which the outputs of one layer of neurons are fed into the next layer and so on, until the process reaches the final output layer. This, too, has been given biological interpretation. The terms *node* and *units* are synonymous with *neurons*.

The method was later generalized, using *activation functions* with outputs other than just 1 and 0 and allowing backward feedback from later layers to earlier ones. This led development of the field somewhat away from the biological motivation, and some questioned the biological interpretation anyway, but NNs have a strong appeal for many in the machine learning community. Indeed, well-publicized large projects using *deep learning* have revitalized interest in NNs.

Figure 11-1, generated by the neuralnet package on our vertebrae data, illustrates how the method works. (We will not be using that package, but it does produce nice displays.)

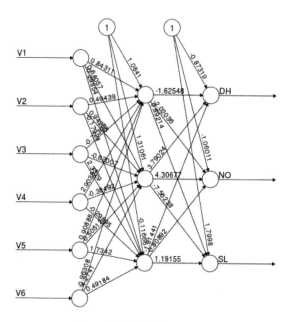

Error: 43.000304 Steps: 1292

Figure 11-1: Vertebrae NN with one hidden layer

Here's the overview:

- A neural network consists of a number of *layers* (three in this case).

- In pictures describing a particular network, there is an input layer on the far left (the vertebrae measurements here) and an output layer on the far right, which, in this case, is giving the class predictions.

- There are one or more *hidden* layers in between, with one in this case.

- The outputs of one layer are fed as inputs into the next layer.

- The output is typically a single number, for regression problems, and c numbers, for c-class classification problems.

- The inputs into a layer are fed through what amounts to a linear model. The outputs of a layer are fed through an *activation function*, which is analogous to kernel functions in SVM, to accommodate nonlinear relations. In Figure 11-1, the activation function used was our old friend the logit, $a(t) = 1/[1 + \exp(-t)]$ (though in an entirely different context; we are *not* performing logistic regression).

How does all this play out in Figure 11-1? Let's look at some of the numbers in the diagram. For example, the input to the first circle, center column is $1.0841 \cdot 1 + 0.84311\ V1 + 0.49439\ V2 + \ldots$, which is a linear combination of the features. A different linear combination is fed into the second circle. The output of each circle is fed into the next layer.

How are the coefficients (*weights*) in these linear combinations computed? We forgo a detailed mathematical answer here, but in essence, we minimize the sum of squared prediction errors in the regression case. In the classification case, we choose the weights to minimize the overall misclassification rate or a variant thereof.

11.2   Working on Top of a Complex Infrastructure

Before we begin, a few words are in order regarding qeNeural(), our qe*-series function for building neural networks.

As we've noted throughout the book, the qe*-series functions are mainly wrappers—that is, convenient wrappers to other functions. This is done so that the series can provide a uniform, quick-and-easy user interface to a variety of ML algorithms.

Our function qeSVM(), for instance, wraps the svm() function in the package e1071. What about qeNeural()? There is quite a tale here! What happens (approximately) is:

- The function qeNeural() wraps the regtools() function krsFit().

- The function krsFit() wraps a number of functions in the R keras package for NNs.

- The R keras package wraps the R tensorflow package.

- The R `tensorflow` package wraps the Python package of the same name.

- And much of `tensorflow` is actually written in the C language.

And much of this, in turn, depends on the function `reticulate()` from the package of the same name. Its role is to translate between R and Python.

Setting this up, then, can be a bit delicate. See the RStudio site for help with your particular platform (for instance, *https://tensorflow.rstudio.com/tutorials/quickstart/beginner.html*). The R interfaces in the above list, as well as `reticulate`, were developed by RStudio.

It's important to keep these points in mind about the "bilingual" nature of the software. For example, one implication is that even if you call `set.seed()` before your NNs run, you still will notice some variation from one run to the next. This will mystify you if you don't know that Python has its own random number generator!

11.3   Example: Vertebrae Data

Say we wish to fit a model and then do prediction. As before, we'll specify no holdout set so that as much data as possible is used in the prediction:

```
> z <- vert[1,-7]  # exclude "Y", which we are predicting
> nnout <- qeNeural(vert,'V7',holdout=NULL)
Epoch 1/30
2/2 [==============================] - 0s 62ms/step - loss: 1.0794 - accuracy: 0
.4274 - val_loss: 1.2847 - val_accuracy: 0.0000e+00
Epoch 2/30
2/2 [==============================] - 0s 19ms/step - loss: 0.9832 - accuracy: 0
.6048 - val_loss: 1.3886 - val_accuracy: 0.0000e+00
...
```

The fitting process is iterative, and a report is given on each iteration or *epoch*. The number of epochs is a hyperparameter. This and the other hyperparameters will be discussed in the next section.

As an example of prediction, consider a patient similar to the first one in our data, but with V2 being 18 rather than 22.55. What would be our predicted class?

```
> z$V2 <- 18
> predict(nnout,z)
$predClasses
[1] "DH"
```

We predict class DH.

11.6.1   L1 and L2 Regularization

Since NNs (typically) minimize a sum of squares, we can apply a penalty term to reduce the size of the solution, just as in the cases of ridge regression and the LASSO. Recall also that in the LASSO, with the ℓ_1 penalty, this tends to produce a sparse solution, with most coefficients being 0s.

Well, that is exactly what we want here. We fear we have too many weights, and we hope that applying an ℓ_1 penalty will render most of them nil.

However, that may not happen with NNs due to the use of nonlinear activation functions. The problem is that the contours in Figure 9-3 are no longer ellipses, and thus the "first contact point" will not likely be at a corner of the diamond.

Nevertheless, ℓ_1 will still shrink the weights, as will ℓ_2, so we should achieve dimension reduction in some sense.

11.6.2   Regularization by Dropout

If a weight is 0, then in a picture of the network, such as Figure 11-1, the corresponding link is removed. So, if the goal is to remove some links, why not simply remove some links directly? Or better yet, remove entire nodes. That is exactly what *dropout* does.

For instance, if our dropout rate is 0.2, we randomly (and temporarily) choose 20 percent of the links from the given layer and remove them. There are further details that we will not list here, but this is the essence of the method.

11.7   Example: Fall Detection Data

Let's revisit the dataset analyzed in Section 8.9.4. We'll do a grid search for a good hyperparameter combination.

Recall that the qeFT() argument pars defines the grid in that it specifies the range of values we wish to explore.

```
> pars <- list(hidden=c('5,5','25,25','100,100','100,0.2,100,0.2',
   '100,0.5,100,0.5','250,0.5,250,0.5'),
   learnRate=c(0.0001,0.0005,0.001,0.005))
> ftout <- qeFT(fd,'ACTIVITY','qeNeural',pars=pars,nTst=250,nXval=25)
```

So, we are varying the number of neurons per layer (5, 100, 250) and the dropout rate (none, 0.2, 0.5). We could also have varied nEpoch and even the activation functions. Note, too, that we could have tried having different numbers of neurons in different layers.

Here are the results:

```
> ftout$outdf
             hidden learnRate  meanAcc        CI     bonfCI
1          100,100      5e-03  0.53256  0.5437322  0.5519608
2    100,0.2,100,0.2    5e-03  0.55896  0.5669100  0.5727654
3    250,0.5,250,0.5    1e-03  0.59480  0.6029615  0.6089727
4    250,0.5,250,0.5    5e-03  0.59696  0.6055761  0.6119221
5          100,100      1e-03  0.60040  0.6106513  0.6182015
6    100,0.2,100,0.2    1e-03  0.60048  0.6074992  0.6126690
7    250,0.5,250,0.5    5e-04  0.60928  0.6154121  0.6199285
8    100,0.5,100,0.5    5e-03  0.60952  0.6176062  0.6235618
9            25,25      5e-03  0.61344  0.6228619  0.6298013
10         100,100      5e-04  0.61744  0.6253014  0.6310915
11   100,0.5,100,0.5    1e-03  0.62120  0.6288043  0.6344051
12   100,0.2,100,0.2    5e-04  0.63056  0.6395884  0.6462380
13   100,0.5,100,0.5    5e-04  0.64048  0.6502662  0.6574739
14           25,25      1e-03  0.64664  0.6539690  0.6593669
15   250,0.5,250,0.5    1e-04  0.65368  0.6603284  0.6652252
16         100,100      1e-04  0.66168  0.6700386  0.6761949
17           25,25      5e-04  0.66528  0.6740087  0.6804375
18   100,0.2,100,0.2    1e-04  0.67240  0.6814274  0.6880762
19             5,5      5e-03  0.68504  0.6927206  0.6983776
20   100,0.5,100,0.5    1e-04  0.69240  0.6989253  0.7037314
21             5,5      1e-03  0.69696  0.7049328  0.7108050
22             5,5      5e-04  0.70368  0.7099837  0.7146265
23           25,25      1e-04  0.70608  0.7143002  0.7203546
24             5,5      1e-04  0.72544  0.7366268  0.7448662
```

The first thing to notice is how much smaller the smallest value is than the largest. In fact, the latter is actually about the same as the base accuracy:

```
> qeNeural(fd,'ACTIVITY')$baseAcc  # any qe* function could be called
[1] 0.7182421
```

Without the features, we would have an error rate of 72 percent.

So, exploring the use of different values of the hyperparameter really paid off here.

But still, interesting patterns emerge here, notably the effect of the learning rate. The smaller values tended to do poorly. Remember, if our learning rate is too small, not only might it slow down convergence, but it also may leave us stuck at a local minimum.

Finally, note that in this case, a smaller value for the dropout rate seemed to produce better results.

11.8 Pitfall: Convergence Problems

As noted, it is often a challenge to configure NN analysis so that proper convergence to a good solution is attained. In some cases, one might even encounter the *broken clock problem*—that is, the network predicts the same value no matter what the inputs are.

Or, one might encounter output like this:

```
Epoch 27/30
618/618 [==============================] -
1s 2ms/step - loss: nan - accuracy: 0.7571 - val _loss: nan - val_accuracy: 0.7520
```

Here nan stands for "not a number." That ominous-sounding message may mean the code attempted to divide by 0, which may be due to the vanishing gradient problem.

The following describes a few tricks we can try, typically specified via one or more hyperparameters.

In some cases, convergence problems may be solved by scaling the data, either using the R scale() function or by mapping to [0,1]. It is recommended that one routinely scale one's data; in qeNeural(), scaling is actually hardwired into the software.

Here are some values to tweak:

Learning rate   Discussed in Section 6.3.8.

Activation function   Try changing to one with a steeper/shallower slope. For example, the function $a(t) = 1/(1 + \exp(-2t))$ is steeper around $t = 0$ than the ordinary logistic function.

Early stopping   In most algorithms, the more iterations the better, but in NNs, many issues depart from conventional wisdom. Running the algorithm for too long may result in convergence to a poor solution. This leads to the notion of *early stopping*, of which there are many variants.

Momentum   The rough idea here is that "We're on a roll," with the last few epochs producing winning moves in the right direction, reducing validation error each time. So, instead of calculating the next step size individually, why not combine the last few step sizes? The next step size will be set to a weighted average of the last few, with heavier weight on the more recent ones. (This hyperparameter is not available in qeNeural() but may be accessed through the keras package directly.)

Note that regression applications, as opposed to classification, may be especially prone to convergence problems, since Y is unbounded.

11.9 Close Relation to Polynomial Regression

In Section 8.11, we introduced polynomial regression, a linear model in which the features are in polynomial form. So, for instance, instead of just having people's heights and ages as features, in a quadratic model we now would also have the squares of heights and ages, as well as a cross-product term, height × age.

Polynomials popped up again in SVM, with polynomial kernels. We might have, for instance, not just height and age but also the squares of heights and ages, as well the height × age term. And we noted that even the use of the radial basis function, a nonpolynomial kernel, is approximately a polynomial due to Taylor series expansion.

It turns out that NNs essentially do polynomial regression as well. To see this, let's look again at Figure 11-1. Suppose we take as our activation function the squaring function t^2. That is not a common choice at all, but we'll start with that and then extend the argument.

So, in the hidden layer in Figure 11-1, a circle forms a linear combination of the inputs and then outputs the square of the linear combination. That means the outputs of the hidden layer are second-degree polynomials in the inputs. If we were to have a second hidden layer, its outputs would be fourth-degree polynomials.

What if our activation function itself were to be a polynomial? Then again, each successive layer would give us higher and higher degree polynomials in the inputs. Since NNs minimize the sum of squared prediction errors, just as in the linear model, you can see that the minimizing solution will be that of polynomial regression.

And what about the popular activation functions? One is the *hyperbolic tangent*, *tanh(t)*, whose graph looks similar to the logistic function. But it too has a Taylor series expansion, so what we are doing is approximately polynomial regression.

ReLU does not have a Taylor series expansion, but we can form a polynomial approximation there too.

In that case, why not just use polynomial regression in the first place? Why NNs? One answer is that it just would be computationally infeasible for large-p data, where we could have a very large number of polynomial terms in calling lm() or glm(). This would cause memory issues. (It's less of a problem for NNs because they find the least squares solutions iteratively. This may cause convergence problems but at least uses less memory.) The kernel trick is very helpful here, and there is even the *kernel ridge regression* method that applies this to linear ridge models, but it turns out that this too is infeasible for large-n cases.

NNs have their own computational issues, as noted, but through trying many combinations of hyperparameters, we may still have a good outcome. Also, if we manage to find a good NN fit on some classes of problems, sometimes we can tweak it to find a good NN fit on some related class (*transfer learning*).

11.10   Bias vs. Variance in Neural Networks

We often refer to the number of hidden layers as the *depth* of a network and the number of units per layer as the *width*. The larger the product of these two (actually depth times the square of the width), the more weights or parameters the network has. As discussed in Section 8.10.1, the more parameters a model has, the more variance increases, even though bias is reduced.

This can be seen as well in light of the polynomial regression connection to NNs described in the previous section. Roughly speaking, the larger the number of hidden layers in an NN, the higher the degree of a polynomial regression approximation. And the higher the degree of a polynomial regression model, the smaller the bias but the larger the variance.

So, NNs are not immune to the Bias-Variance Trade-off. This must be kept in mind when designing an NN's architecture.

11.11   Discussion

NNs have played a major role in the "ML revolution" of recent years, with notable success in certain types of applications. But they can incur huge computational costs, in some cases having run times measured in hours or even days, and can have vexing convergence problems.

In addition, folklore in the ML community suggests that NNs are not especially effective with *tabular data*, meaning the type stored in data frames—that is, every dataset we have seen so far in this book. The reader may wish to reserve NNs for usage in applications such as image recognition and natural language processing, which will be covered in the next two chapters.

PART V

APPLICATIONS

In this part, we present an overview of several of the fields in which ML has had dazzling success. It is, however, just that—*an overview*. A number of entire books have been written on each of these topics.

Truly effective application of ML in these fields often needs advanced techniques, lots of tuning, and some domain expertise. The interested reader is urged to pursue further study of these topics.

12

IMAGE CLASSIFICATION

Probably the most widely celebrated application of NNs is image classification. Indeed, the popularity of NNs today is largely due to some spectacular successes of NNs in image classification contests in the early 2000s. Earlier, the NN field had been treated largely as a curiosity and not a mainstream tool.

And the surge in popularity of NNs for image classification then had a feedback effect: the more NNs did well with images, the more image classification researchers used NNs as their tool, thus the more they refined use of NNs for imaging, which in turn led to more NN success in the contests.

In principle, *any* of the methods in this book could be used on images. The features are the pixel intensities, and the outcome is the class of image. Consider, for instance, the famous MNIST data. Here we have 70,000 images of handwritten digits, with each image having 28 rows and 28 columns of pixels. Each pixel has an intensity (brightness) number between 0 and 255, and we have $28^2 = 784$ pixels, so we have 784 features and 10 classes.

The "secret sauce" for NNs in the image field has been *convolutional* operations, leading to the term *convolutional neural networks (CNNs)*. Actually, those operations were not really new; they borrow from classical image processing techniques. And most important, convolutional operations are not inherent to NNs. They could be used with other ML methods, and in fact, some researchers have developed *convolutional SVMs*. But again, the momentum in the image field is solidly with CNNs.

Thus the focus of this chapter on images will be on NNs. We'll start with a non-NN example to make the point that any ML method might be used and then get into CNNs.

12.1 Example: The Fashion MNIST Data

It's standard to use the MNIST data as one's introductory example, but let's be a little different here. The Fashion MNIST data is of the same size as MNIST (28×28 pixel structure, 10 classes, 70,000 images) but consists of pictures of clothing (10 types) rather than digits. (The dataset is available at *https://github.com/zalandoresearch/fashion-mnist.*)

One important difference is that while MNIST can be considered basically black and white, Fashion MNIST truly has "shades of gray." An example is shown in Figure 12-1. The blurriness is due to the low 28×28 resolution of the image set.

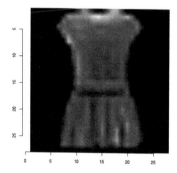

Figure 12-1: A Fashion MNIST image

This makes the dataset more challenging, and accuracy rates are generally somewhat lower for Fashion MNIST than for MNIST.

12.1.1 A First Try Using a Logit Model

The dataset actually comes already partitioned into training and test sets (60,000 and 10,000 rows, respectively), but for convenience, let's just stick to the training set, which I have named ftrn, with columns V1, V2, ..., V785. That last column is the clothing type, with values 0 through 9.

Let's try a logistic model on this data (which, by the way, took about 2 hours to run):

```
> z <- qeLogit(ftrn,'V785')
> z$testAcc
[1] 0.205
> z$baseAcc
[1] 0.8998305
```

So, we were attaining about 80 percent accuracy. The base was only about 10 percent accuracy, which makes sense: there are roughly equal numbers of the 10 clothing types, so random guessing would give us about 10 percent. Thus 80 percent is not bad. But since the world's record best accuracy on this dataset is in the high 90s, we would like to do better.

12.1.2   Refinement via PCA

We might surmise, as we did above, that $p = 784$ is too large and is in need of dimension reduction. One possible remedy would be to use PCA:

```
> z <- qePCA(ftrn,'V785','qeLogit',pcaProp=0.8)
> z$testAcc
[1] 0.172
```

Ah, now we are up to about 83 percent accuracy. (And it took only about a minute to run.)

We could try different values of the number of principal components, but a better approach would likely be to take advantage of what we know about images, as we will now see.

12.2   Convolutional Models

Though the CNN structure may seem complex at first, it actually is based on simple ideas. Let's get started.

12.2.1   Need for Recognition of Locality

It's no coincidence that the picture in Figure 12-1 looks blurry. Remember, these are very low-resolution images (28 × 28 pixels). Yet even though this is tiny as images go, it gives us 784 features. With $n = 70,000$, our "$p < \sqrt{n}$" rule of thumb (Equation 3.2) would suggest a maximum of about 260 features, which is well short of 784. And while that rule is conservative—CNNs do well in spite of ending up with p much greater than n—it's clear that using the 784 pixels as if they were unrelated features is going to impede our ability to predict new cases well.

We need to exploit the *locality* of our images. An image pixel tends to be correlated with its neighboring pixels, and the nature of this relationship should help us classify the image. Is that pixel part of a short straight line, say, or maybe a small circle? The *convolutional model* is designed with this in mind, consisting of various operations that are applied to patches within an image. These patches are often called *tiles*, which we will work with here.

12.2.2 Overview of Convolutional Methods

Let's first sneak a look at the code and run it on the Fashion MNIST data. After that, we'll explain the operations in the code. We'll use code adapted from an RStudio example:

```
# set up 5 image op layers
> conv1 <- list(type='conv2d',filters=32,kern=3)
> conv2 <- list(type='pool',kern=2)
> conv3 <- list(type='conv2d',filters=64,kern=3)
> conv4 <- list(type='pool',kern=2)
> conv5 <- list(type='drop',drop=0.5)

# note that qeNeural() by default sets up two hidden layers; these will
# come after the convolutional ones
> z <- qeNeural(ftrn,'V785',
    conv=list(conv1,conv2,conv3,conv4,conv5),xShape=c(28,28))
> z$testAcc
[1] 0.075
```

Ah, now we are up to more than 92 percent correct classification. And we almost certainly could do even better by tuning the hyperparameters (including changing the number and structure of the image operation layers).

What do we see here?

- Using qeNeural()'s conv argument, we have set up five image-operation layers.

- The image-operation layers are followed by "ordinary" layers (not specified here), thus taking qeNeural()'s default value of two layers of 100 neurons each. The "ordinary" layers are termed *dense* layers or *fully connected* layers.

- The first image-operation layer performs a convolutional operation on the input image, which involves extracting tiles and forming linear combinations of the image intensities within each tile. These linear combinations become outputs of the layer.

- Recall from earlier chapters that in the linear combination, say, $3a - 1.5b + 16.2c$, the numbers 3, −1.5, and 16.2 are called *coefficients*. In the CNN context, they are called *weights*.

- Usually we will use many different sets of weights. The conv2d parameter filters specifies the number of sets of weights that we want for a layer. It acts analogously with the number of neurons in a dense layer.

- The conv2d parameter kern value specifies the tile size, with the value 3 in the first layer meaning 3×3 tiles.

- Another `conv2d` parameter `stride` controls the number of tiles in an image by specifying the amount of overlap a tile has with its neighbors, which will be explained below.

- The argument `xShape` specifies the size of an image, such as 28×28 in the current example.

- For color data of that size, we would denote the situation as $28 \times 28 \times 3$, with the 3 referring to the number of primary colors, red, yellow, and blue. We would have a 28×28 array of red intensities, then another for yellow, and finally one for blue. Then we would set *xShape* to (28,28,3).

- That third coordinate, 3, is called a *channel*. We don't call it "color," because it may not be a color, as will be seen below.

The output of one layer is input to the next, and its dimensions may be, say, $13 \times 13 \times 64$. That would be treated as a 13×13 "image" with 64 "primary colors," both of which are artificial. The point is that, mathematically, any three-dimensional array can be treated this way, and it makes the code simpler to do so. (An array of three or more dimensions is called a *tensor*, hence the name `tensorflow` for the Python package underlying what we do here.)

12.2.3 Image Tiling

The first and third layers in the above code example perform a *convolution* operation. (Readers with a background in probability theory, Fourier analysis, and so on will find that the term is used somewhat differently in ML.) To explain, we first need to discuss breaking an image into tiles.

Consider this toy example of a 6×6 grayscale image:

$$
\begin{pmatrix}
23 & 18 & 1 & 7 & 15 & 23 \\
6 & 7 & 8 & 11 & 7 & 16 \\
18 & 7 & 8 & 25 & 23 & 10 \\
19 & 14 & 24 & 10 & 13 & 18 \\
14 & 10 & 1 & 3 & 15 & 16 \\
15 & 13 & 20 & 3 & 5 & 2
\end{pmatrix}
\tag{12.1}
$$

For example, the intensity of the pixel in row 2, column 4 of the image is 11. In R, we would store this in a matrix of 6 rows and 6 columns. (An R matrix is like a data frame in which the elements are all numeric or all character strings and so on.)

We could break this into non-overlapping tiles of size 3×3:

$$\begin{pmatrix} 23 & 18 & 1 & 7 & 15 & 23 \\ 6 & 7 & 8 & 11 & 7 & 16 \\ 18 & 7 & 8 & 25 & 23 & 10 \\ 19 & 14 & 24 & 10 & 13 & 18 \\ 14 & 10 & 1 & 3 & 15 & 16 \\ 15 & 13 & 20 & 3 & 5 & 2 \end{pmatrix} \tag{12.2}$$

So, our original matrix has been partitioned into four submatrices or tiles.

We can also have overlapping tiles, using a number called the *stride*. In the above example, the stride is 3: The first column of the upper-right tile

$$\begin{pmatrix} 7 \\ 11 \\ 25 \end{pmatrix} \tag{12.3}$$

is 3 columns to the right of the first column of the upper-left tile located in Equation 12.2

$$\begin{pmatrix} 23 \\ 6 \\ 18 \end{pmatrix} \tag{12.4}$$

and so on. Similar statements hold for rows. For example, the first row of the lower-right tile is 3 rows below the first row of the upper-right tile.

With a stride of 1, say, our first 3×3 tile would still be

$$\begin{pmatrix} 23 & 18 & 1 \\ 6 & 7 & 8 \\ 18 & 7 & 8 \end{pmatrix} \tag{12.5}$$

But the second would be just 1 column to the right of the first tile

$$\begin{pmatrix} 18 & 1 & 7 \\ 7 & 8 & 11 \\ 7 & 8 & 25 \end{pmatrix} \tag{12.6}$$

and so on.

The default value of stride in 'conv2d' operations is 1.

12.2.4   *The Convolution Operation*

Say we are using 3×3 tiles. It is convenient to express the coefficients of a linear combination in matrix form too, say, in the weights matrix:

$$\begin{pmatrix} w_{11} & w_{12} & w_{13} \\ w_{21} & w_{22} & w_{23} \\ w_{31} & w_{32} & w_{33} \end{pmatrix} \qquad (12.7)$$

For a given tile:

- The tile's element in row 1, column 1 will be multiplied by w_{11}.
- The tile's element in row 1, column 2 will be multiplied by w_{12}.
- ...
- The tile's element in row 3, column 3 will be multiplied by w_{33}.

All of those products will be summed to produce a single number.

This set of weights is then applied to each tile. Applying to the upper-left tile in Equation 12.2, we have the single number:

$$w_{11}23 + w_{12}18 + w_{13}1 + w_{21}6 + w_{22}7 + w_{23}8 + w_{31}18 + w_{32}7 + w_{33}8 \quad (12.8)$$

We apply the same set of weights to each tile. For instance, applying the weights to the upper-right tile, we have:

$$w_{11}7 + w_{12}15 + w_{13}23 + w_{21}11 + w_{22}7 + w_{23}16 + w_{31}25 + w_{32}23 + w_{33}10 \quad (12.9)$$

We do the same for the lower-left and lower-right tiles, yielding four numbers altogether, which we arrange in a 2×2 matrix. That is output to the next layer.

Now suppose we have, say, 12 filters. That means 12 different sets of weights—that is, 12 different versions of the matrix in Equation 12.7. That means 12 different 2×2 matrices coming out of this layer. Thus the output of this layer is described as $2 \times 2 \times 12$. To be sure, yes, the total output of this layer will be 48 numbers, but we think of them as consisting of 12 sets of 2×2 matrices, hence the $2 \times 2 \times 12$ notation.

Note we are not choosing these weights ourselves. They are chosen by the NN algorithm, which will minimize the overall prediction sum of squares. We choose the *number* of sets, 12 here, but not the sets themselves. The algorithm will try many different collections of 12 sets of weights, in hope of finding a collection that minimizes the prediction sum of squares.

So . . . there is really nothing new. We are taking linear combinations of the inputs and feeding them to the next layer, just as in the last chapter. In the end, the algorithm minimizes the sum of squared prediction errors, just as before.

The difference, though, is the structuring of the data into tiles, exploiting locality. The role of the weights is to determine the relative importance of various pixels, especially in how they work together.

It will be helpful to visualize this as a "building" with 12 "floors." Each "floor" consists of four "rooms," arranged in two rows of two rooms each. We will take this approach below.

Note that we still have the usual Bias-Variance Trade-off as with dense layers: the more filters, the more opportunities to reduce bias, but the more variance we incur in the weights.

12.2.5   The Pooling Operation

Recall the second layer in the example in Section 12.2:

```
conv2 <- list(type='pool',kern=2)
```

This is not a convolutional layer; it's a *pooling* layer.

Pooling involves replacing the elements in a tile by some representative value, say, the mean or the median, or even the maximum value in the tile. The latter is quite common, in fact, and is the one used in the regtools and qeML packages.

The reader may wonder, "Isn't pooling a special case of convolutional operations? For example, isn't taking the mean in a 2×2 tile the same as a convolutional operation with all the weights being 0.25?" The answer is yes, but with one big difference: here the weights are fixed at 0.25; they are not chosen by the algorithm.

Unlike the conv2d operation, where the default stride is 1, for pooling, the default stride is the tile size, specified above as 2.

12.2.6 Shape Evolution Across Layers

Now, what will be the structure of the output from this second layer? Let's reason this out. Here again are the specifications of the first two layers:

```
conv1 <- list(type='conv2d',filters=32,kern=3)
conv2 <- list(type='pool',kern=2)
```

The input to the first layer was 28×28, or $28 \times 28 \times 1$. The first breaks things into 3×3 tiles with a stride of 1. Just as there is a 2×2 array of tiles in Equation 12.2, here we will have a 26×26 array of tiles, again taking into account that the stride is 1.

So in that first layer, each filter will output a total of 26^2 numbers, in 26×26 form. With 32 filters, the total output of that first layer will be $26 \times 26 \times 32$. In the "building" metaphor, this means 32 floors, with each floor having 26 rows of rooms with 26 rooms per row. Note again here that each "room" holds one number.

Now, what then will happen at the second layer? It will receive 32 tiles sized 26×26. What will it do with them?

The tile size used by this layer, as discussed above, is 2×2, with a stride of 2. Applying this to an inputted 26×26 tile, 13 rows of 13 2×2 tiles in each row will be formed. In each 2×2 tile, the maximum value among the 4 numbers will be extracted.

Again using the "building" metaphor, each "floor" will produce $13^2 = 169$ numbers, arranged in 13×13 form. Since we have 32 "floors," the total output of this layer will be in the form $13 \times 13 \times 32$. (The regtools and qeML packages use the two-dimensional form of the pooling operation, so the pooling is done within floors and not across floors.)

12.2.7 Dropout

As with the dense layers, the danger of overfitting—too many neurons per convolutional layer or too many convolutional layers—is high. The antidote is dropout, for example:

```
> conv5 <- list(type='drop',drop=0.5)
```

This specifies randomly deleting 50 percent of the nodes in this layer.

12.2.8 Summary of Shape Evolution

The keras package gives us a summary of our CNN on request:

```
> z$model
Model
Model: "sequential"
```

Layer (type)	Output Shape	Param #
conv2d (Conv2D)	(None, 26, 26, 32)	320
max_pooling2d (MaxPooling2D)	(None, 13, 13, 32)	0
conv2d_1 (Conv2D)	(None, 11, 11, 64)	18496
max_pooling2d_1 (MaxPooling2D)	(None, 5, 5, 64)	0
dropout (Dropout)	(None, 5, 5, 64)	0
flatten (Flatten)	(None, 1600)	0
dense (Dense)	(None, 100)	160100
dense_1 (Dense)	(None, 10)	1010

```
Total params: 179,926
Trainable params: 179,926
Non-trainable params: 0
```

Recall that qeNeural() calls regtools::krsFit(), which in turn makes calls to the R keras package, so this output actually comes from the latter.

That last column shows the number of weights at each layer. For instance, here is where that 320 figure came from: each filter—that is, each set of numbers w_{ij}—is a 3×3 matrix, thus consisting of 9 numbers. There is also an intercept term w_0 (like β_0 in a linear regression model), for a total of 10 weights. Since there were 32 filters, we have 320 weights, as shown in the output table above.

The flatten layer merely converts from our $a \times c$ form to ordinary data. The output of our second pooling layer had form $5 \times 5 \times 64$, which amounts to 1,600 numbers. In order to be used by a dense layer, the data is converted to a single vector of length 1,600.

Altogether, we have $p = 179926$ but only $n = 65000$. So we are definitely overfitting. The fact that many such models have been found to work well is quite a controversy in the ML community!

12.2.9 Translation Invariance

The weight structure lends *translation invariance*—a fancy term that actually has a simple meaning—to our analysis. Say we are using 3×3 for our tile size. That's 9 pixels. For any tile, consider the pixel in the upper-left corner of the tile. Then we have the same weight w_{11} for that pixel, regardless of whether the tile is near the top of the picture, say, or the bottom.

For facial recognition, for instance, this means that, to a large extent, we don't have to worry whether the face is near the top of the picture, near the bottom, or near the middle. (Problems do occur near the edges of the picture, so the property holds only approximately.) The same statement would hold for left-right positioning.

12.3   Tricks of the Trade

Well, then, how in the world is one supposed to come up with the models? How many layers? What kinds of layers? What parameter values?

One might set some of the model on a hunch informed by the nature of the dataset, such as the size of various parts of the image, the image texture, and so on. But at the end of the day, the answer tends to be rather prosaic: after years of experimenting with various architectures (configurations), this one seems to work with certain kinds of images. Some architectures have been successful in wide-enough application that they have acquired names and become standards, such as AlexNet.

12.3.1   Data Augmentation

One approach to dealing with smaller image sets is *data augmentation*. The idea here is simple: form new images from existing ones. One might shift a given image horizontally or vertically, shrink or enlarge the image, flip it horizontally or vertically, and so on. The motivation for this is that, later, we might be asked to classify a new image that is very similar to one in our training set but is, say, much higher or lower within the image frame. We want our algorithm to recognize the new image as being similar to the one in the training set.

This is especially important for medical tissue images, say, from a biopsy, as there is no sense of orientation—no top or bottom, left or right, or back or front. This is in contrast to MNIST, for instance, where a '6' is an upside-down '9' and the two are quite different.

We can perform data augmentation using the OpenImageR package, with its Augmentation() function. In the latter, for instance, we can do a vertical flip operation:

```
> h18f <- Augmentation(matrix(h18,nrow=28),flip_mode='vertical')
> imageShow(matrix(h18f,nrow=28))
```

The keras package also offers data augmentation services, including a *shear* (twist) operation.

12.3.2 Pretrained Networks

A big issue in the image classification community is *transfer learning*. Here the issue is that, instead of starting from scratch in designing a neural network—dense layers, convolutional layers, and details of each—one builds on some network that others have found useful. One then either uses that network as is or takes it as a starting point and does some tweaking.

12.4 So, What About the Overfitting Issue?

As noted in Section 12.2.8, the success of heavily overparameterized networks in image classification seems to contradict the conventional wisdom regarding overfitting. This has been the subject of much speculation in the ML community.

A key point may be that misclassification rates in image contexts tend to be very low, near 0 for highly tuned networks. In that sense, we are essentially in the settings that were termed *separable* in Chapter 10. Some insight into this issue may then be gained by revisiting Figure 10-4 in that chapter.

As was pointed out, there are many lines, infinitely many, in fact, that could be used to distinguish the two classes, and thus be used to predict a new case. SVM chooses a particular line for this—the one halfway between the two closest points in the two classes—but again, one might use many other lines instead.

Indeed, the separator need not be a straight line. It could be a "curvy" line, say, one obtained by using a polynomial kernel with SVM. Because of the clean separation of the two classes, there is plenty of wiggle room in which we could fit a very wiggly curve, say, a polynomial, of very high degree. And the higher the degree, the more coefficients in the equation of the curve—that is, the larger the value of p.

The result: we could fit a curve that has a value of p much greater than n yet still get perfect prediction accuracy. Noting the connection of NNs to polynomial regression (see Section 11.9), we have a plausible explanation for the success of overparameterization in image classification.

12.5 Conclusions

In spite of this book's aim to avoid writing many equations, the topic here is easily the most mathematical of all the chapters. Viewed from a high level, CNNs work from a very simple idea: break an image into tiles and then apply an NN to the tiled data. But the old saying "The devil is in the details" is quite apt here. It can be challenging, for instance, to keep clear in one's mind the dimensionality of chunks of data as we move from layer to layer. Readers who wish to pursue further study beyond the introduction here will find a background in linear algebra and calculus to be quite useful.

13

HANDLING TIME SERIES AND TEXT DATA

A *time series* is a dataset indexed by time, usually at regular time intervals. Here are some familiar examples:

- Stock market data consisting of the price of a given equity on a daily basis, or even hourly, and so on

- Weather data, daily or in even finer granularity

- Demographic data, such as the number of births, say, monthly or even yearly, to plan for school capacity

- Electrocardiogram data measuring electrical activity in the heart at regular time intervals

A special type of time series is that of written or spoken speech. Here "time" is word positioning. If, say, we are working at the sentence level, and a sentence consists of eight words, there would be Word 1, Word 2, and so on through Word 8, with the index 1 through 8 playing the role of "time."

The field of time series methodology has been highly developed by statisticians, economists, and the like. As usual, ML specialists have developed their own methods, mainly as applications of neural networks. The methods known as *recurrent neural networks (RNNs)* and *long short-term memories (LSTMs)* are especially notable.

Both the statistical and ML approaches use very subtle and intricate techniques whose mathematical content is well above the math level of this book. Nevertheless, one can still build some very powerful ML applications while sticking to the basics, and this chapter will have this theme. It will present methods to apply the qe*-series functions to general time series problems, and to a special kind of text recognition setting (that does not make use of the time series nature of the text).

13.1 Converting Time Series Data to Rectangular Form

One often hears the terms *rectangular data* and *tabular data* in discussions of ML, referring to the usual $n \times p$ data frame or matrix of n rows, with each row representing one data point of p features. As a quick non–time series example we've used several times in this book, say we are trying to predict human weight from height and age, with a sample of 1,000 people. Then we would have $n = 1000$ and $p = 2$.

It's clear that the words "rectangular" and "tabular" are allusions to the rectangular shape or table of the associated data frame or matrix. But this is rather misleading. Image data also has the form, such as $n = 70000$ and $p = 28^2 = 784$ for the MNIST data, yet image data is not referred to as rectangular.

In the case of time series, though, one in fact can convert a time series to rectangular form and then apply ML methods, which is what we'll do here.

13.1.1 Toy Example

Say our training set time series x is (5,12,13,8,88,6). For concreteness, let's say this is daily data, so we have six days of data here, which we'll call day 1, day 2, and so on. On each day, we know the series values up to the present and wish to predict the next day.

We'll use a *lag* of 2, which means that we predict a given day by the previous two. In x above, that means we:

- Predict day 3 from the 5 and 12
- Predict day 4 from the 12 and 13
- Predict day 5 from the 13 and 8
- Predict day 6 from the 8 and 88

Think of what the above description ("predicting the 13...") means in terms of our usual "X" (features matrix) and "Y" (outcomes vector) notation:

$$X = \begin{pmatrix} 5 & 12 \\ 12 & 13 \\ 13 & 8 \\ 8 & 88 \end{pmatrix}$$

$$Y = (13, 8, 88, 6)$$

Note that X has only 4 rows, not 6, and Y is of length 4, not 6. That is due to our lag of 2; we need 2 prior data points. So we cannot even start our analysis until day 3.

Here we will deal only with *univariate* time series. But we can also handle the multivariate case—for example, predicting daily temperature, humidity, and wind speed from their previous values.

13.1.2   The regtools Function TStoX()

The function TStoX() does what its name implies—converts a time series to an "X" matrix. "Y" is created too and returned in the final column. For the previous toy example, we have:

```
> x <- c(5,12,13,8,88,6)
> w <- TStoX(x,2)
      [,1] [,2] [,3]
[1,]     5   12   13
[2,]    12   13    8
[3,]    13    8   88
[4,]     8   88    6
```

Our "X" data are then in the first two columns, and "Y" is the third column.

The function returns a matrix, which we can convert to a data frame if we wish:

```
> wd <- as.data.frame(w)
> wd
  V1 V2 V3
1  5 12 13
2 12 13  8
3 13  8 88
4  8 88  6
```

We could then use any of our qe*-series functions, such as random forests:

```
qeRF(wd,'V3',holdout=NULL)
```

In other words, everything was done as before, with one exception: we cannot take our holdout set to be a random subset of the data, as the remaining data would no longer be for consecutive time periods. We will elaborate on this point shortly.

13.2 The qeTS() Function

But, instead of calling, say, qeRF() "by hand," as above, we again have a convenient wrapper, qeTS(), which transforms from time series format to "X, Y" form and then applies our favorite ML method to the result. The wrapper's call form is:

```
qeTS(lag,data,qeName,opts=NULL,
    holdout=floor(min(1000, 0.1 * length(data))))
```

Here qeName is the quoted name of a qe*-series function—for example, 'qeRF'.

The argument opts allows us to use nondefault versions of the arguments of the quoted-name function. For instance, to use k-NN and $k = 10$, write:

```
> eus <- EuStockMarkets  # built-in R dataset
> tsout <- qeTS(5,eus,'qeKNN',opts=list(k=10))  # use k-NN with k = 10
```

A comment should be made regarding holdout. While it plays its usual role in the qe*-series, note that cross-validation is usually difficult in time series contexts. We cannot choose for our holdout set some randomly chosen numbers from our data, since in time series we predict one datum from its immediately preceding, time-contiguous values. But here, we conduct the holdout operation on the output of TStoX(), whose output *is* rows of sets of contiguous values, so it works.

13.3 Example: Weather Data

Here we will use some weather time series data collected by NASA, which is included in regtools.

```
> data(weatherTS)
> head(weatherTS)
      LON       LAT YEAR MM DD DOY   YYYYMMDD RH2M   T2M PRECTOT
1 151.81 -27.47999 1985  1  1   1 1985-01-01 48.89 25.11    1.07
2 151.81 -27.47999 1985  1  2   2 1985-01-02 41.78 28.42    0.50
3 151.81 -27.47999 1985  1  3   3 1985-01-03 40.43 27.53    0.03
4 151.81 -27.47999 1985  1  4   4 1985-01-04 46.42 24.65    0.10
5 151.81 -27.47999 1985  1  5   5 1985-01-05 50.77 26.54    2.13
6 151.81 -27.47999 1985  1  6   6 1985-01-06 58.57 26.81    5.32
```

That last column is precipitation. Let's fit a model for it and then predict the first day after the end of the data, day 4018, based on day 4016 and day 4017:

```
> ptot <- weatherTS$PRECTOT
> z <- qeTS(2,ptot,'qeRF',holdout=NULL)
> length(ptot)
[1] 4017
> predict(z,ptot[4016:4017])
       2
1.087949
```

So, we predict a bit more than 1 inch of rain.

We used a lag of 2 days here. How would other lag values fare? We could use qeFT() here, but things are a bit complicated. For example, there is no yName argument for qeTS(), so instead we use replicMeans() (see Section 3.2.2).

How about a lag of 1 instead of 2? We call replicMeans(), asking it to execute

```
> qeTS(1,ptot,"qeKNN")$testAcc
```

1,000 times and then report the mean of the resulting 1,000 values of testAcc:

```
> replicMeans(1000,'qeTS(1,ptot,"qeKNN")$testAcc')
[1] 2.116511
```

This gives us a Mean Squared Prediction Error of 2.12. Is that good? As usual, let's compare this to how well we can predict from the mean alone:

```
> mean(abs(ptot - mean(ptot)))
[1] 2.626195
```

Ah, we're in business.

What about other lags?

```
> replicMeans(1000,'qeTS(1,ptot,"qeKNN")$testAcc')
[1] 2.116511
> replicMeans(1000,'qeTS(2,ptot,"qeKNN")$testAcc')
[1] 2.051895
> replicMeans(1000,'qeTS(3,ptot,"qeKNN")$testAcc')
[1] 2.033376
> replicMeans(1000,'qeTS(4,ptot,"qeKNN")$testAcc')
[1] 2.067625
> replicMeans(1000,'qeTS(5,ptot,"qeKNN")$testAcc')
[1] 2.092022
> replicMeans(1000,'qeTS(6,ptot,"qeKNN")$testAcc')
[1] 2.085409
> replicMeans(1000,'qeTS(7,ptot,"qeKNN")$testAcc')
[1] 2.093377
> replicMeans(1000,'qeTS(8,ptot,"qeKNN")$testAcc')
[1] 2.118068
```

```
> replicMeans(1000,'qeTS(9,ptot,"qeKNN")$testAcc')
[1] 2.135797
> replicMeans(1000,'qeTS(10,ptot,"qeKNN")$testAcc')
[1] 2.157187
```

It does seem that the lag makes some difference. A lag of 3 days seems best, though as usual, we must keep in mind the effect of sampling variation. (The replicMeans() function also provides a standard error, which is not shown here.)

How about trying some other ML methods? Let's consider a linear model, since most classical time series methods use linear models:

```
> replicMeans(1000,'qeTS(3,ptot,"qeLin")$testAcc')
[1] 2.245138
```

```
> replicMeans(1000,'qeTS(3,ptot,"qePolyLin")$testAcc')
[1] 2.167949
```

As noted, classical time series methods, for example, the *autoregressive* model, are linear. We see that a linear model doesn't work so well on this particular dataset. Fitting a polynomial improves things substantially but still doesn't match k-NN.

Maybe random forests?

```
> replicMeans(1000,'qeTS(3,ptot,"qeRF")$testAcc')
[1] 2.138265
```

It's still not as good as k-NN. However, with hyperparameter tuning in both cases, either method might end up the victor.

13.4 Bias vs. Variance

The value of the lag impacts bias and variance, though in possibly complex ways.

A larger lag clearly increases bias; time periods in the more distant past are likely less relevant. It's similar to the problem of a large k in k-NN.

On the other hand, the variance aspect is tricky. A larger lag smooths out the day-to-day (or other temporal) variation—that is, it reduces variance. But a larger lag also increases p, the number of features, increasing variance. The overall effect is thus complex.

13.5 Text Applications

The field of text analysis is highly complex, similar to that of the image recognition field. As in the latter case, in this book we can only scratch the surface, in two senses:

- We will limit ourselves to document classification, as opposed to, say, language translation.
- We will limit ourselves to the bag-of-words model (see the next section). This approach merely relies on how often various words appear in a document and not on the order in which the words appear.

So, we do not cover advanced methods such as the aforementioned *recurrent neural networks (RNNs)*, or even more advanced methods such as *hidden Markov models (HMMs)*.

13.5.1   The Bag-of-Words Model

Say we wish to do automatic classification of newspaper articles. Our software notices that the words *bond* and *yield* are contained in some document and classifies it in the Financial category.

This is the *bag-of-words model*. We decide on a set of words, the "bag," and compute the frequency of appearance of each word in each document class. These frequencies are often stored in a *document-term matrix (DTM)*, d. The entry d[i,j] is equal to the number of times word j appears in document i in our training set. Or, d[i,j] may simply be 1 or 0, indicating whether word j appears in document i at all.

The matrix d then becomes our "X," with "Y" being the vector of class labels, such as Financial, Sports, and so on. Each row of X represents our data on one document, with a corresponding label in Y.

Again, this is a simple model. Our guess that the document above is in the Financial class may be incorrect if, say, a sentence in the document reads "The bond between family members will typically yield a stable family environment." A more sophisticated analysis would account for, say, the words in between *bond* and *yield*. The bag-of-words model may, in some cases, be less accurate than a time series–based approach. Yet it is easy to implement and performs well in many applications.

13.5.2 The qeText() Function

And, of course, there is a qeML function for this, qeText(). It has this call form:

```
qeText(data, yName, kTop = 50, stopWords = tm::stopwords("english"),
    qeName, opts = NULL, holdout = floor(min(1000, 0.1 * length(data))))
```

In the data argument, there is assumed one row per document, with the column indicated by yName stating the class of each document, such as Financial; the other column (there must be exactly two) stores the document texts. The argument qeName specifies the ML method to be used, and opts specifies optional arguments for that method. The term *stop words* refers to rather insignificant words such as *the* and *is*, which are ignored.

The role of the kTop argument is as follows: the software does a census of all the words in the documents in the training data and selects the kTop most frequent ones to use as features.

13.5.3 Example: Quiz Data

The qeML package has a built-in dataset named quizzes, consisting of the text of quizzes I've given in various courses. One might ask whether one can predict the course from the text.

```
> data(quizzes)
> str(quizzes)
'data.frame':    143 obs. of  2 variables:
 $ quiz  : chr  " Directions: Work only on this sheet (on both sides,
...
...
 $ course: Factor w/ 5 levels "ECS132","ECS145",..: 3 3 3 3 3 3 3 3 3 3 ...
```

There were 143 quiz documents. The eighth of these will have the quiz text stored in quizzes[8,1] as one very long character string:

```
> quizzes[8,1]
...
...
largest thread number.  The code with print out
...
...
```

The course number is in quizzes[8,2]:

```
> quizzes[8,2]
[1] ECS158
Levels: ECS132 ECS145 ECS158 ECS256 ECS50
```

This was ECS 158, Introduction to Parallel Computation.

As an illustration, let's pretend we don't know the class of this document and try to predict it using random forests:

```
> z <- qeText(quizzes,qeName='qeRF')
holdout set has  14 rows

> predict(z,quizzes[8,1])
$predClasses
[1] "ECS158"
$probs
    ECS132 ECS145 ECS158 ECS256 ECS50
11  0.062  0.066  0.812  0.002 0.058
```

The predicted course is ECS 158.

13.5.4   Example: AG News Dataset

This dataset consists of short news articles in four categories: World, Sports, Business, and Sci/Tech. It is obtainable from the CRAN package textdata, which provides interfaces for downloading various text data testbeds:

```
> library(textdata)
> ag <- dataset_ag_news()
Do you want to download:
 Name: AG News
...
> agdf <- as.data.frame(ag)  # qe-series functions require data frames
> agdf[,1] <- as.factor(agdf[,1])   # qe requires a factor Y
```

Let's take a look around:

```
> dim(ag)
[1] 120000     3
> agdf[28,]  # for example
     class                         title
28 Business HP shares tumble on profit news
                                   description
28 Hewlett-Packard shares fall after disappointing third-quarter profits,
while the firm warns the final quarter will also fall short of expectations.
```

Plenty of data here with 120,000 documents. Well, maybe *too* much, as the run time may be long. For a quick example, let's just take 10,000 rows:

```
> smallSet <- sample(1:nrow(agdf),10000)
> agdfSmall <- agdf[smallSet,]
```

So, let's try fitting a model, say, SVM:

```
> w <- qeText(agdfSmall[,c(1,3)],'class',qeName='qeSVM')
holdout set has  1000 rows
Loading required namespace: e1071
> w$testAcc
[1] 0.461
> w$baseAcc
[1] 0.7403333
```

Not too bad. We reduced a base error of 74 percent to 46 percent. The latter is still rather high, so we would next try tweaking the SVM hyperparameters. Note that kTop is also a hyperparameter! We should try different values for it too.

13.6 Summary

We see here that, even without advanced methods, one may be able to fit good prediction models for time series and text data. In both cases, qe*-series functions qeTS() and qeText() enable convenient use of our favorite ML methods.

LIST OF ACRONYMS AND SYMBOLS

k-NN k-nearest neighbors

MAPE Mean Absolute Prediction Error

ML machine learning

n number of data points (rows)

OME overall misclassification error

p number of features (columns)

PC principal component

PCA principal component analysis

$r(t)$ true regression function

SVM support vector machine

UMAP Uniform Manifold Approximation and Projection

B

STATISTICS AND ML
TERMINOLOGY CORRESPONDENCE

class — label

covariate — side information

dummy variable — one-hot coding

intercept term/constant term — bias

model fitting — learning

normal distribution — Gaussian distribution

observations — examples

prediction — inference

predictor variables — features

tuning parameter — hyperparameter

MATRICES, DATA FRAMES, AND FACTOR CONVERSIONS

It is a fact of life in the R world that R's wonderful flexibility in terms of data types also means that serious use needs some skill in converting between types. This appendix will ensure that the reader has this skill.

C.1 Matrices

Although the R *matrix* class might be viewed as more fundamental than data frames, some R users these days are unaware of it. Since any serious usage of ML in R requires knowledge of this class, this appendix will present a brief tutorial.

In keeping with the theme of this book limiting the use of mathematical tools, we will not discuss the mathematical properties of matrices.

An R matrix is essentially a data frame in which all columns are numeric. It uses the same [i,j] notation. Conversions can be made between the two types. Here are some examples:

```
> library(regtools)
> data(mlb)
> head(mlb)
```

	Name	Team	Position	Height	Weight	Age	PosCategory
1	Adam_Donachie	BAL	Catcher	74	180	22.99	Catcher
2	Paul_Bako	BAL	Catcher	74	215	34.69	Catcher
3	Ramon_Hernandez	BAL	Catcher	72	210	30.78	Catcher
4	Kevin_Millar	BAL	First_Baseman	72	210	35.43	Infielder

C.2 Conversions: Between R Factors and Dummy Variables, Between Data Frames and Matrices

In R, a categorical variable has a formal class: *factor*. It actually is one of the most useful aspects of R, but one must be adept at switching back and forth between factors and the corresponding dummy variables.

Similarly, though we mostly work with data frames in this book, there are some algorithms that need matrices, say, because they calculate distances between rows and do matrix multiplication and inversion. You do not need to know what matrix inversion is and so on, but some software packages will require you to present only matrix inputs and not data frames. There is a brief tutorial on matrices at the beginning of this appendix.

Some highly popular R ML packages automatically generate dummies from factors, but others do not. For example, glmnet for LASSO models requires that categorical features be in the form of dummies, while ranger, for random forests, accepts factors.

So it's important to be able to generate dummy variables ourselves. The regtools functions factorToDummies() and factorsToDummies() do this. We discuss the factorToDummies() function in Section 1.9. We use dummy variables throughout the book, including in this appendix.

We also use the built-in R function as.matrix() to convert from data frames to matrices.

```
5      Chris_Gomez  BAL  First_Baseman    73   188 35.71   Infielder
6    Brian_Roberts  BAL Second_Baseman    69   176 29.39   Infielder
> hwa <- mlb[,4:6]
> head(hwa)
  Height Weight   Age
1     74    180 22.99
2     74    215 34.69
3     72    210 30.78
4     72    210 35.43
5     73    188 35.71
6     69    176 29.39
> class(hwa)
[1] "data.frame"
> hwam <- as.matrix(hwa)
> class(hwam)
[1] "matrix" "array"
> head(hwam)
```

```
   Height Weight    Age
1     74     180 22.99
2     74     215 34.69
3     72     210 30.78
4     72     210 35.43
5     73     188 35.71
6     69     176 29.39
> hwam[2,3]
[1] 34.69
> mean(hwam[,3])  # mean age
[1] 28.70835
> mean(hwam$age)  # illegal
Error in hwam$age : $ operator is invalid for atomic vectors
# rbind(), "row bind", combines rows
> m <- rbind(3:5,c(5,12,13))
> m
     [,1] [,2] [,3]
[1,]    3    4    5
[2,]    5   12   13
> class(m)
[1] "matrix" "array"
> m[2,3]
[1] 13
> md <- as.data.frame(m)
> md
  V1 V2 V3
1  3  4  5
2  5 12 13
> class(md)
[1] "data.frame"
> md[2,3]
[1] 13
# the apply() function can be a nice shortcut
> apply(m,1,sum)  # apply sum() to each row (argument 1) of m
[1] 12 30
> apply(m,2,sum)  # apply sum() to each column (argument 2) of m
[1]  8 16 18
```

In math, we draw matrices as rectangular arrays. For the matrix m above, for instance:

$$\begin{pmatrix} 3 & 4 & 5 \\ 5 & 12 & 13 \end{pmatrix} \tag{C.1}$$

D

PITFALL: BEWARE OF "P-HACKING"!

In recent years there has been much concern over something that has acquired the name *p-hacking*. Though such issues have always been known and discussed, things really came to a head with the publication of John Ioannidis's highly provocatively titled paper, "Why Most Published Research Findings Are False" (*PLOS Medicine*, August 30, 2005). One aspect of this controversy can be described as follows.

Say we have 250 coins, and we suspect that some are unbalanced. (Any coin is unbalanced to at least some degree, but let's put that aside.) We toss each coin 100 times, and if a coin yields fewer than 40 or more than 60 heads, we will decide that it's unbalanced. For those who know some statistics, this range was chosen so that a balanced coin would have only a 5 percent chance of straying more than 10 heads away from 50 out of 100. So, while this chance is only 5 percent for each particular coin, with 250 coins, the chances are high that at least one of them falls outside that [40,60] range, *even if none of the coins is unbalanced*. We will falsely declare some coins unbalanced. In reality, it was just a random accident that those coins look unbalanced.

Or, to give a somewhat frivolous example that still will make the point, say we are investigating whether there is any genetic component to sense of humor. Is there a humor gene? There are many, many genes to consider—many more than 250, actually. Testing each one for relation to sense of humor is like checking each coin for being unbalanced: even if there is no humor gene, eventually just by accident we'll stumble upon one that seems to be related to humor.

In a complex scientific study, the analyst is testing many genes, or many risk factors for cancer, or many exoplanets for the possibility of life, or many economic inflation factors, and so on. The term *p-hacking* means that the analyst looks at so many different factors that one is likely to emerge as "statistically significant" even if no factor has any true impact. A common joke is that the analyst "beats the data until they confess," alluding to a researcher testing so many factors that one finally comes out "significant."

Cassie Kozyrkov, head of decision intelligence at Google, said it quite well:

> What the mind does with inkblots, it also does with data. Complex datasets practically beg you to find false meaning in them.

This has major implications for ML analysis. For instance, a popular thing in the ML community is to have competitions in which many analysts try their own tweaks on ML methods to outdo each other on a certain dataset. Typically these are classification problems, and "winning" means getting the lowest rate of misclassification.

The trouble is, having 250 ML analysts attacking the same dataset is like having 250 coins in our example above. Even if the 250 methods they try are all equally effective, one of them will emerge by accident as the victor, and it will be annointed as a "technological advance."

Of course, it may well be that one of the 250 methods really is superior. But without careful statistical analysis of the 250 data points, it is not clear what's real and what's just accident. Note, too, that even if one of the 250 methods is in fact superior, there is a high probability that it won't be the winner in the competition, again due to random variation.

The problem is exacerbated by the fact that a contestant will probably not even submit his entry if it appears unlikely to set a new record. This further biases the results.

As mentioned, this concept is second nature to statisticians, but it is seldom mentioned in ML circles. An exception is the blog post "AI Competitions Don't Produce Useful Models" by Lauren Oakden-Rayner, whose excellent graphic is reproduced in Figure D-1 with Dr. Oakden-Rayner's permission.[1]

---

1. *https://laurenoakdenrayner.com/2019/09/19/ai-competitions-dont-produce-useful-models/*

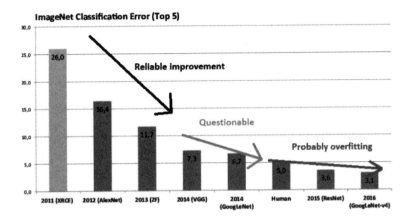

Figure D-1: AI p-hacking

Rayner uses a simple statistical power analysis to analyze ImageNet, a contest in ML image classification. He reckons that at least those "new records" starting in 2014 are overfitting, or just noise. With more sophisticated statistical tools, a more refined analysis could be done, but the principle is clear.

This also has a big implication for the setting of tuning parameters. Let's say we have four tuning parameters in an ML method, and we try 10 values of each. That's 10^4 = 10000 possible combinations, a lot more than 250! So again, what seems to be the "best" setting for the tuning parameters may be illusory.

The `regtools` function `fineTuning()` takes steps to counter the possibility of p-hacking in searches for the best tuning parameter combination.

INDEX

bike sharing dataset *(continued)*
    missing data, 26–27
    overview, 4
    polynomial models, 144–147
    predicting ridership, 4, 7–9
Bonferroni–Dunn intervals, 115–116
boosting
    AdaBoost, 101–102
    bias vs. variance, 96, 106
    call network monitoring, 103–105
    computational speed, 106
    gradient boosting, 102
    hyperparameters in, 106
    learning rate, 106–109
    overview, 7, 100
    Vertebral Column Dataset,
        105–106
bootstrap, 96–97
bounded variables, 19
Box, George, 136
Breiman, Leo, 81, 95, 97, 109
broken clock problem, 193

C

call network monitoring, 103–105
Call Test Measurements for Mobile
    Network Monitoring and
    Optimization dataset,
    103–104
CART (classification and regression
    trees), 81
categorical variables, 9–10, 17
centering, 18
channel, 203
CIs (confidence intervals), 114–115,
    133–134
classification and regression trees
    (CART), 81
classification applications. *See also*
    generalized linear models
    Area Under Curve, 46–48
    confusion matrix, 41
    error rates, 39–41
    k-NN in, 36–37
    overview, 10, 31–32
    Receiver Operating Characteristic,
        46–48
    regression function in, 32–33

Telco Customer Churn dataset,
    33–37
unbalanced data, 41–46
Vertebral Column dataset, 38–39
CNNs (convolutional neural networks),
    200–202, 207, 209. *See also*
    convolutional models
coef() function, 168
coefficients, 67, 202
combinations of factor levels, number
    of, 86
complete.cases() function, 35
computational issues in large datasets,
    61–62
computational speed in boosting, 106
conditional mean, 14
confidence intervals (CIs), 114–115,
    133–134
confusion matrix, 41, 89
consolidation, 65, 86
conv2d parameter, 202–203
conv argument, 189
convergence, 108, 183, 193
conversions, factor, 226–227
convex hulls, 174–175
convolutional models
    convolution operation,
        204–205
    dropout, 206
    image tiling, 203–204
    overview, 201–202
    pooling operation, 205–206
    recognition of locality, 201–202
    shape evolution, 206–207
    translation invariance, 208
convolutional neural networks (CNNs),
    200–202, 207, 209. *See also*
    convolutional models
Covertype dataset, 88–90
credit card fraud, 44–45
cross-validation
    in decision trees, 91
    K-fold, 55–56
    motivation, 22–23
    overview, 21, 55
    programmer and engineer data,
        56–58
    random forests, 109

general discussion, 7–9

overview, xxii–xxiii, 7

predicting bike ridership with, 7–9

kNN() function, 10, 64

Kozyrkov, Cassie, 230

krsFit() function, 187, 207

L

l_1 and L_2 regularization, 191

label, 4

LASSO, 157–159

African Soil data, 159–161

Airbnb data, 155–156

general discussion, 153–155

New York City Taxi data, 155–156

overview, xxiii

qeLASSO() function, 155

ridge regression vs., 154–155

sparseness, 161–162

leaf nodes, 82, 91–92

learning rate

convergence problems in neural
networks, 193

in gbm(), 109

general concepts, 107–109

overview, 103, 106–107

learnRate argument, 189

Least Absolute Shrinkage and Selection
Operator. *See* LASSO

least squares, 135–136, 153

linear model

baseball player data example,
124–126

bias and variance in, 142–143

blending with other methods,
148–149

dimension reduction, 130–135

holdout sets, 135

least squares, 135–136

lm() function, 126–127

modeling nonlinearity with, 145–147

NA values and impact on n, 135

overview, 123–124

qeCompare() function, 149–150

qeLin() function, 127

R^2 value(s), 137–138

residuals, 135–136

significance tests, 133–134

standard errors, 133

statistical significance, 131–132

use of multiple features, 127–130

validity of, 136–137

lines, xxiii, 170

listwise deletion, 27

lm() function, 126–127

locality, recognition of, 201–202

local minimum, 107

logistic model

bias and variance in, 142–143

Fall Detection data, 141–142

Fashion MNIST data, 200–201

Forest Cover dataset, 168

glm() and qeLogit() functions, 139

multiclass case, 140–141

overview, 138

Telco Churn data, 139–140

log-odds ratio, 138

long short-term memories (LSTMs), 211

long-term time trends, 25–26

loss functions, 21

LPH

math notation, 170–172

overview, 170, 183

separable case, 172–177

separability, lack of, 177–182

M

machine learning (ML), xix–xx

prediction and, 6–7

role of math in, xx

statistics terminology
correspondence, 223

MAPE (Mean Absolute Prediction
Error), 21–22, 25, 55–58, 74

margin of error, 15

matrices, 225–226

maxdepth argument, 92

Mean Absolute Prediction Error
(MAPE), 21–22, 25, 55–58, 74

Mean Squared Prediction Error
(MSPE), 21, 157

Million Song dataset

All Possible Subsets Method, 66

overview, 63–64

Principal Components Analysis,
66–69

minbucket argument, 92

minNodeSize hyperparameter, 99, 106

minsplit argument, 92

missing data, 27

mlb dataset

  blending linear model with other methods, 148–149

  k-NN and categorical features, 17

  linear model, 124–127

  overfitting, 53

  overview, 16–17

  scaling, 18–19

mmscale() function, 19

momentum, 193

MSPE (Mean Squared Prediction Error), 21, 157

mtry argument, 92

multiclass case, 140–141

multivariate outliers, 27

N

n (number of data points)

  overfitting, 53–54

  overview, 11

  square root of, 54

$n \times p$ data frame, 212

NA values

  in classification models, 35–36

  in large datasets, 61–62

  in linear models, 135

nCombs argument, 113, 118

nEpoch argument, 189

neural networks (NNs). *See also* image classification

  activation functions, 189–190

  bias vs. variance in, 195

  confidence intervals, 115

  convergence problems, 193

  development of, 7

  Fall Detection data, 191–192

  hyperparameters, 189

  overview, xxiii, 185–187

  polynomial regression and, 194

  regularization, 190–191

  Vertebral Column dataset, 188

  width of, 195

  working top of complex infrastructure, 187–188

neurons, 186

New York City Taxi data

  combinations of factor levels, number of, 86

  overview, 85–88

  regularization, 155–156

  tree-based analysis, 86–88

n-fold cross-validation, 55

nonlinearity, modeling with linear models, 145–147

nTree hyperparameter, 99, 106

nTst argument, 113

numeric applications, 31

nXval argument, 113, 117

O

Oakden-Rayner, Lauren, 230–231

OLS (ordinary least squares) method, 135–136

Olshen, Richard, 81

one-hot coding, 8

one-sided CIs, 114

One vs. All (OVA) method, 140–141, 168

optimizing criterion, 174–176

order() function, 8

ordinary least squares (OLS) method, 135–136

outcome variable, 4, 10

OVA (One vs. All) method, 140–141, 168

overall misclassification error (OME), 55

overfitting. *See also* dimension reduction

  best values of k and p, 54

  convolutional models, 206–207

  cross-validation, 55–58

  due to features with many categories, 37

  general discussion, 52

  in image classification, 209

  intuition regarding number of features and, 53

  overview, 51

  in random forests, 109

  relation to overall dataset size, 53–54

  retaining useless features, 35

  shrinkage, 154

  underfitting, 52

P

p (number of features), 11, 53–54. *See also* dimension reduction

parametric models, 172. *See also* linear model; logistic model; polynomial model

pars argument, 112

pef dataset, 56–57

p-hacking, 24–25, 114, 229–231

phoneme dataset, 117–119

planes, 170

plot() function, 83–85, 157

polynomial kernel, 180

polynomial model
    caution with, 149–150
    modeling nonlinearity with linear models, 145–147
    motivation, 144–145
    overview, 144
    polynomial logistic regression, 147
    programmer and engineer wages, 147–148
    qeCompare() function, 149

polynomial regression, 147, 194

pooling, 205–206

prcomp() function, 67–69

predict() function, 12–13, 69, 72

prediction. *See also* decision trees
    of bike ridership with k-NN, 7–9
    machine learning and, 6–7

pretrained networks, 209

principal component analysis (PCA), 61, 66–69, 71–72, 201

principal components (PCs)
    Bias-Variance Trade-off and, 73–74
    choosing number of, 70–71
    overview, 66
    properties of, 66–67
    qePCA() function, 71–72

print() function, 88

programmer and engineer data
    cross-validation, 56–57
    grid searching, 113–117
    polynomial models, 144, 147–148
    proxies, 65
    p-values, 90–91, 134

Q

qeAdaBoost() function, 102

qeCompare() function, 148–150

qeDT() function, 82–83, 91–92

qeFOCI() function, 75–77

qeFT() argument, 191

qeFT() function
    calling, 112–113
    overview, 112
    phoneme dataset, 117–119
    programmer and engineer data, 113–117

qeftn argument, 112

qeGBoost() function, 102–103, 105–106

qeKNN() function
    classification applications, 36–37
    direct access to regtools k-NN code, 28
    mlb dataset, 16–17
    overview, 10–13
    predicting bike ridership with, 11–13
    scaling, 18–19

qeLASSO() function, 155

qeLin() function, 127

qeLogit() function, 139, 141, 168

qeML package, xxi, 4

qeNeural() function, 187–189, 207

qePCA() function, 69, 71–72

qePolyLin() function, 146–147

qePolyLog() function, 147

qeRF() function, 97–100

qeROC() function, 47, 48

qe*-series functions
    call form, 12
    categorical features, 17
    holdout sets in, 21–22
    overview, xxii, 10
    qeDT() function, 81–82

qeSVM() function, 173–175, 182

qeText() function, 218

qeTS() function, 214

qeUMAP() function, 77

quiz data, 218–219

The fonts used in *The Art of Machine Learning* are New Baskerville, Futura, The Sans Mono Condensed, and Dogma. The book was typeset with LaTeX 2_ε package nostarch by Boris Veytsman *(2008/06/06 v1.3 Typesetting books for No Starch Press)*.

RESOURCES

Visit *https://nostarch.com/art-machine-learning* for errata and more information.

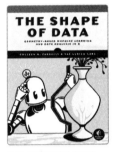

Never before has the world relied so heavily on the Internet to stay connected and informed. That makes the Electronic Frontier Foundation's mission—to ensure that technology supports freedom, justice, and innovation for all people—more urgent than ever.

For over 30 years, EFF has fought for tech users through activism, in the courts, and by developing software to overcome obstacles to your privacy, security, and free expression. This dedication empowers all of us through darkness. With your help we can navigate toward a brighter digital future.